JOURNAL OF ROMANIAN STUDIES

Vol. 2, No. 2 (2020)

JRS editors
Peter Gross and Diane Vancea

JRS review editor
Iuliu Ratiu

JRS Editorial Assistant
Claudia Lonkin

About the Society for Romanian Studies

THE SOCIETY FOR ROMANIAN STUDIES (SRS) *is an international interdisciplinary academic organization founded in 1973 and dedicated to promoting research and critical studies on all aspects of Romanian and Moldovan culture and society. The SRS is recognized as the major North American professional organization for scholars concerned with Romania, Moldova, and their diasporas.*

SRS is affiliated with the South East European Studies Association (SEESA); the Association for Slavic, East European and Eurasian Studies (ASEEES—formerly known as the American Association for the Advancement of Slavic Studies or AAASS); the American Political Science Association (APSA); the American Historical Association (AHA); and the Romanian Studies Association of America (RSAA).

SRS offers a number of programs and activities to its members, including the peer-reviewed *Journal of Romanian Studies*, a biannual newsletter, the Romanian Studies book series published in collaboration with the publishing house Polirom in Iași, a mentoring program, prizes for exceptional scholarship in two different categories, as well as an international conference organized every three years in Romania.

More information about the SRS, including current officers, the national board, and membership information, can be found on the SRS website at *https://society4romanianstudies.org*.

www.society4romanianstudies.org
The Society for Romanian Studies

Editorial Board:

PETER GROSS (pgross@utk.edu) and
DIANE VANCEA (economics@ovidius-university.net)
JRS editors

IULIU RATIU (ratiu.pfa@gmail.com)
JRS review editor

CLAUDIA LONKIN (claudia.lonkin@gmail.com)
JRS Editorial Assistant

Advisory Board:

DENNIS DELETANT (Georgetown University, USA)
JON FOX (University of Bristol, UK)
VALENTINA GLAJAR (Texas State University, USA)
PETER GROSS (University of Tennessee, USA)
BRIGID HAINES (Swansea University, UK)
IRINA LIVEZEANU (University of Pittsburgh, USA)
MIHAELA MIROIU (National School of Political Science and Public Administration, Romania)
STEVE D. ROPER (Florida Atlantic University, USA)
DOMNICA RADULESCU (Washington and Lee University, USA)
PAUL E. SUM (University of North Dakota, USA)
CRISTIAN TILEAGA (Loughborough University, UK)
VLADIMIR TISMANEANU (University of Maryland, College Park, USA)
LUCIAN TURCESCU (Concordia University, Montreal, Canada)

Bibliographic information published by the Deutsche Nationalbibliothek
The Deutsche Nationalbibliothek lists this publication in the Deutsche Nationalbibliografie; detailed bibliographic data are available on the Internet at http://dnb.dnb.de.

Bibliografische Information der Deutschen Nationalbibliothek
Die Deutsche Nationalbibliothek verzeichnet diese Publikation in der Deutschen Nationalbibliografie; detaillierte bibliografische Daten sind im Internet über http://dnb.d-nb.de abrufbar.

Journal of Romanian Studies
Vol. 2, No. 2 (2020)

Stuttgart: *ibidem*-Verlag / *ibidem* Press

Erscheinungsweise: halbjährlich / Frequency: biannual

ISBN 978-3-8382-1479-5

ISSN 2627-5325

Ordering Information:
PRINT: Subscription (two copies per year): € 58.00 / year (+ S&H: € 6.00 / year within Germany, € 10.00 / year international). The subscription can be canceled at any time.
Single copy or back issue: € 34.00 / copy (+ S&H: € 3.00 within Germany, € 4.50 international).

E-BOOK: Subscription (two copies per year): € 35.99 / year, individual copy or back issue: € 24.99 / copy. Available via ibidem.eu.
For further information please visit www.ibidem.eu/jrs.htm

© *ibidem*-Verlag / *ibidem* Press
Stuttgart, Germany 2020

Alle Rechte vorbehalten
Das Werk einschließlich aller seiner Teile ist urheberrechtlich geschützt. Jede Verwertung außerhalb der engen Grenzen des Urheberrechtsgesetzes ist ohne Zustimmung des Verlages unzulässig und strafbar. Dies gilt insbesondere für Vervielfältigungen, Übersetzungen, Mikroverfilmungen und elektronische Speicherformen sowie die Einspeicherung und Verarbeitung in elektronischen Systemen.

All rights reserved

No part of this publication may be reproduced, stored in or introduced into a retrieval system, or transmitted, in any form, or by any means (electronic, mechanical, photocopying, recording or otherwise) without the prior written permission of the publisher.
Any person who performs any unauthorized act in relation to this publication may be liable to criminal prosecution and civil claims for damages.

Printed in the EU

Special issue

Law, History and Justice in Romania

Edited by Monica Ciobanu and Mihaela Șerban

Contents

Law, History, and Justice in Romania:
New Directions in Law and Society Research
    MIHAELA ȘERBAN AND MONICA CIOBANU 9

Reversing Liberal Legality:
Romania's Path to Dictatorship, 1930–1938
    COSMIN CERCEL 23

Perceptions of Legality during the Antonescu Regime,
1940–1944
    ȘTEFAN CRISTIAN IONESCU 53

Litigating Identity in Fascist and Post-Fascist Romania,
1940–1945
    MIHAELA ȘERBAN 81

Writing History Through Trials:
The Case of the National Peasant Party
    MONICA CIOBANU 109

Restitution Reversal or "Re-nationalization"? An Analysis
of Law, Property, and History Through the Case of the
"Szekely Mikó" High School in Transylvania
    EMANUELA GRAMA 135

Institutional Memories and Transgenerational Dynamics:
The House of Terror and the Memorial of the Victims of
Communism and of the Resistance
    SIMONA LIVESCU 165

Law in Action in Romania, 2008–2018: Context, Agency,
and Innovation in the Process of Transitional Justice
    DRAGOȘ PETRESCU 195

Marian Voicu, Matrioșka Mincinoșilor: Fake News,
Manipulare, Populism.
    Review by PETER GROSS 219

Matei Călinescu, Ion Vianu, Scrisori din exil: corespondență
inedită, Cuvânt înainte de Ion Vianu, Notă asupra ediției de
Adriana Călinescu.
    Review by IULIU RAȚIU 223

Law, History, and Justice in Romania: New Directions in Law and Society Research

Mihaela Şerban and Monica Ciobanu

This special issue of the *Journal of Romanian Studies* examines law as a social institution and the ways in which it intersects with the larger social, historical, political and economic world. While the articles included here mostly explore the intersections between law, history, and justice, they consciously reject positivist and doctrinal analyses of law and an understanding of law as primarily a (repressive) instrument of the state. Instead, we focus on "living law" and the complex interactions between law and social issues, including how law is created, interpreted and implemented, and how individuals and organizations live, shape and evade it in everyday interactions within and outside of the state. We also want to situate this flourishing area of research not only within broader fields, such as transitional justice and legal history, but also in the expansive law and society tradition that has been open to interdisciplinary legal research worldwide, but is perhaps less well known in Romania.

The study of law and/in society is a relatively new, interdisciplinary field, stronger in common law countries compared to civil law ones, but growing worldwide for the past three decades.[1] Foreshadowed by the sociology of law and authors like Durkheim and Ehrlich, law and society research developed both as an intellectual and an institutional project.[2] Conceptually, the push back against legal formalism in the United States resulted in legal realists' hope that law could be an instrument of social engineering and positive social change, tackling issues from poverty to crime. Institutionally, the second part of the twentieth century saw both the infusion of resources and the creation of new institutional structures,

---

1   I will be using "law and society" and "sociolegal" interchangeably to reflect the comparable scholarly traditions focused on the interdisciplinary study of law around the world. We will also discuss it as a "field," while acknowledging the long history of debates around the nature of law and society as a field, a movement, etc., and its relations to other interdisciplinary traditions centered on law.
2   Lynn Mather, "Law and Society," in *The Oxford Handbook of Political Science*, ed. Robert R. Goodin (Oxford: Oxford University Press, 2011), 289–304; Felice Levine, "Goose Bumps and 'The Search for Signs of Intelligent Life' in Sociolegal Studies: After Twenty-Five Years," *Law & Society Review*, 24 (1990): 7–33; Bryant Garth and Joyce Sterling, "From Legal Realism to Law and Society: Reshaping Law for the Last Stages of the Social Activist State," *Law & Society Review*, 32(1998):409–71.

such as the Law and Society Association and *The Law & Society Review*, created in the mid-1960s, which channeled the emerging scholarship.

Both of these developments are less pronounced elsewhere. The British Socio-Legal Studies Association was formed only in 1990, but studies of law in action, its effects and connection to the wider social system had been ongoing for decades.[3] The French *Droit et Société* began publication in 1985, while the Oñati International Institute for Sociology of Law was established in 1988 and has since become a major hub for law and social sciences research around the world. The Asian Law & Society Association was created in 2015, the *Asian Journal of Law and Society* in 2014, and *Islamic Law & Society* began publication in 1994. Studies of law and society in Latin America have had less of an institutional base, but have thrived nonetheless within specific national contexts and also comparatively.[4] Within the American Law and Society Association, collaborative research networks and international research collaboratives have provided some institutional structure and space for collaborations.[5]

The core of the law and society approach is that law—norms, institutions, processes, etc.—must be understood in context. Law is deeply embedded in society and constituted in and through political, historical, social, and cultural interactions. Simply put, law is a political, historical, social and cultural construct, both reflecting and impacting other social systems.[6] The law and society tradition aims to understand law in action, how it functions and how it is connected to other institutions, systems, groups, etc. Law and society, in other words, are mutually constitutive.

Law and society scholarship is distinguished from other fields in the following ways: it is multidisciplinary, interdisciplinary (e.g. legal history, law and psychology) and trans-disciplinary (at its best, question-driven), drawing from cross-disciplinary methodology and theory to focus on empirical studies of "law in action" and critiques of legal positivism (the "outside point of view" on law).[7] Law and society scholarship has a normative, substantive focus on questions of justice, equality, and power (for

---

3   D. R. Harris, "The Development of Socio-Legal Studies in the United Kingdom," *Legal Studies*, 3, no.3 (1983): 315–333.
4   Rachel Sieder, Karina Ansolabehere, and Tatiana Alfonso, "Law and Society in Latin America. An Introduction," in *Routledge Handbook of Law and Society in Latin America*, eds. Rachel Sieder, Karina Ansolabehere, and Tatiana Alfonso (New York and London: Routledge, 2019), 1–21.
5   See the website of the Association, https://lawandsociety.org/crn.html, accessed January 21, 2020.
6   Mather, "Law and Society."
7   Macaulay, Stewart, Lawrence Friedman, and Elizabeth Mertz, *Law in Action: A Socio-Legal Reader* (New York: Foundation Press, 2007), 1.

example, in the critical legal studies tradition in the United States, or "law from below" in Latin America or Southeast Asia), further reflected in a commitment to advocating for progressive policy changes.[8]

Major areas of research and contributions of law and society scholarship include law and social change, such as the relationship between courts, litigation and social and political change;[9] the study of courts, disputes and disputing, including alternatives to courts and judicial behavior;[10] the study of the legal profession and other legal actors (e.g. court clerks);[11] legal ideology (meanings, ideas, beliefs, values encoded in and by law and the construction of legal meaning) and legal consciousness (how people engage with the law writ large);[12] legal pluralism (co-existence of multiple legal and regulatory regimes);[13] social control;[14] regulatory law and governance; and the intersections between law and various other systems (such as law and economics, law and development, etc.).[15]

---

8   For an influential discussion and critique, see Austin Sarat and Susan Silbey, "The Pull of the Policy Audience," *Law and Policy*, 10(1988): 97–166.
9   See Stuart Scheingold, *The Politics of Rights: Lawyers, Public Policy, and Political Change* (Ann Arbor: University of Michigan Press, 2004, 2nd ed.).
10 Classic studies include William Felstiner, Richard Abel, and Austin Sarat, "The Emergence and Transformation of Disputes: Naming, Blaming, Claiming ...," *Law & Society Review*, 15, Nos. 3-4(1980-1): 631–54; Marc Galanter, "Why the "Haves" Come out Ahead: Speculations on the Limits of Legal Change," *Law & Society Review*, 9, No. 1(1974): 95–160; Frances Kahn Zeman, "Legal Mobilization: The Neglected Role of the Law in the Political System," *American Political Science Review*, 77(1983):690–703.
11 For example, Barbara Yngvesson, "Making Law at the Doorway: The Clerk, the Court, and the Construction of Community in a New England Town," *Law & Society Review*, 22, No. 3 (1988):409–448; Carol Greenhouse, Barbara Yngvesson, and David Engel, *Law and Community in Three American Towns* (Ithaca: Cornell University Press, 1994).
12 Sally Engle Merry, *Getting Justice and Getting Even* (Chicago: University of Chicago Press, 1990); Patricia Ewick and Susan Silbey, *The Common Place of Law* (Chicago: University of Chicago Press, 1998).
13 For example, Sally Engle Merry, "Legal Pluralism," *Law & Society Review*, 22, No. 5 (1988): 869–896; Franz von Benda-Beckmann, "Who's Afraid of Legal Pluralism?," *Journal of Legal Pluralism*, 47(2002): 37–83; Brian Z. Tamanaha, "The Folly of the 'Social Scientific' Concept of Legal Pluralism," *Journal of Law and Society*, 20, No. 2 (1993): 192–217.
14 Landmark studies include Donald Black, "Crime as Social Control," *American Sociological Review*, 48, No. 1 (1983): 34–45; David Garland, *The Culture of Control: Crime and Social Order in Contemporary Society* (Oxford: Oxford University Press, 2001).
15 E.g., Guido Calabresi, "Some Thoughts on Risk Distribution and the Law of Torts," *Yale Law Journal*, 70(1961): 499–553; Ronald Coase, "The Problem of Social Cost," *Journal of Law and Economics*, 3(1960): 1–44; Richard A. Posner, *Economic Analysis of Law* (Boston: Little Brown, 1st edition, 1973); Ugo Mattei, *Comparative Law and Economics* (Ann Arbor, MI: The University of Michigan Press, 1988); Kevin E. Davis and Michael J. Trebilcock, "The Relationship between Law

There are currently 56 collaborative research networks within the Law and Society Association, covering substantive and geographical areas, theory and methodology, and newly emerging topics, such as law and emotion.[16]

While the core of the law and society approach binds sociolegal scholarship across the world, different regions inevitably have somewhat different research agendas. For fruitful comparison purposes, we will briefly discuss here Latin America. Most law and society research in Latin America has been shaped by both law and development approaches and critical reactions to a law and development agenda originating in the Global North, such as Marxist and critical legal studies ones, as well as alternative law and studies of law "from below."[17]

Latin American scholars have worked on topics most relevant to their particular contexts, such as exploring gaps between norms and practice (the gap between law in books and law in action, including non-compliance with the law), legal pluralism, clientelistic legal cultures, authoritarianism, transitional justice, socio-economic rights and social constitutionalism, inequality, violence, mobilizing international law and national constitutions to fight against discrimination, etc. They helped reconceptualize bedrock legal concepts, for example neo-constitutionalism (social constitutionalism) and specifically the extension of socio-economic rights and their justiciability, problems of implementation and structural capacity of the state, questions of excessive executive power and centralization, and brought attention to issues mostly neglected in the Global North, such as indigenous peoples' rights (claims to justice based on recognition) or the globalization of national legal fields (from practice to academia, e.g. Inter-American Court of Human Rights as a key site for regional human rights standards).[18] Latin American sociolegal scholarship has been more topic focused, less quantitative and more qualitative,[19] significantly more

---

and Development: Optimists versus Skeptics," *The American Journal of Comparative Law*, 56, No. 4 (2008): 895–946; David M. Trubek, "Toward a Social Theory of Law: An Essay on the Study of Law and Development," *The Yale Law Journal*, 82, No. 1 (1972): 1–50.

16   https://www.lawandsociety.org/crn.html; last accessed January 20, 2020.
17   Sieder, Ansolabehere, and Alfonso, "Law and Society in Latin America. An Introduction," 4.
18   Cesar Rodriguez-Garavito, "Remapping Law and Society in Latin America: Visions and Topics for a New Legal Cartography," in *Law and Society in Latin America. A New Map*, ed. Cesar Rodriguez-Garavito (New York: Routledge, 2015), 1–20.
19   Sieder, Ansolabehere, and Alfonso, "Law and Society in Latin America. An Introduction."

comparative than elsewhere in the world (facilitated by language commonalities), and theoretically creative (legal counter-mapping).[20]

Law and development and its modernization assumptions have driven Latin American sociolegal research and have left a legacy of continued focus on law and social change, one that is only partially present in Central and Eastern European (CEE) countries. The two regions do have other similarities: both belong to the civil law tradition, both are driven by a modernization paradigm that sees law primarily from an instrumentalist perspective, both have relatively weak institutional infrastructures for sociolegal research, both have strong comparative research traditions, and certain topics are important for both, such as transitional justice and corruption. However, the law and society spirit—understanding law in its context, on the ground, in action—is not as prominent in Central and Eastern European studies, and neither is the concern with the role of law in fostering progressive social change. While our own Eugen Ehrlich may have been the father of legal pluralism and living law, this is also a large missing area from contemporary CEE national or regional studies of law in society.[21]

Law and society in Central and Eastern Europe generally and Romania specifically is an even more recent field than elsewhere. While Poland and Hungary, for example, have had a longer tradition of interdisciplinary legal studies and particularly sociology of law,[22] Romania had a different historical context up to 1989. Area studies continue to be dominated by more traditional research approaches, and from a sociolegal perspective, two have been important: studies of constitutional and democratic changes in post-communism, and transitional justice studies. This is partly due to a hyper-positivist legal tradition that discourages interdisciplinary research, but also to distinctive academic traditions, contexts, and networks. Political scientists and historians have filled in some of the gaps, and some topics have received more attention than others (for example, corruption, the rule of law, governance, EU accession, property, etc.), but specifically sociolegal works of inquiry that center law in action

---

20 Rodriguez-Garavito, "Remapping Law and Society in Latin America," 5–6.
21 Of note is the continuing influence of Leon Petrażycki, the Polish sociologist of law, who was also interested in ideas of legal pluralism and living law. See Jacek Kurczewski, "Sociology of Law in Poland," *The American Sociologist*, 32, No. 2 (2001): 85–98; Roger Cotterrell, "Leon Petrazycki and Contemporary Socio-Legal Studies," *International Journal of Law in Context*, 11(2015):1–16.
22 Kurczewski, "Sociology of Law in Poland;" Grażyna Skapska, "The Sociology of Law in Poland. Problems, Polemics, Social Commitment," *Journal of Law and Society*, 14, No. 3 (1987): 353–365.

within its historical, political, social, economic, and cultural context are not as common.

Mapping law and society research in Central and Eastern Europe would have to start from the distinctive context of the region, shaped by the region's neoliberal transition from communism and the top-down process of European integration. This new law and development wave still draws from modernization assumptions, this time within a transitional paradigm (transitions to democracy, the rule of law, and market economy), with massive external funding (the World Bank, etc., later the EU). Post-communist Central and Eastern Europe focused on institutional reforms, market-oriented legal reforms, and policy-making through law.

Research followed: top areas of research and publication have come overwhelmingly from political science and economics, and broadly focused on economy, law and society, with privatization a top concern;[23] and separately transitional constitutionalism, institutional design, judicial reform, and law and politics,[24] itself with two sub-strands: transitional, and more recently law and courts/policy, with corruption and the rule of law popular subtopics.[25] European integration processes (whether

---

23 See, e.g., Roman Frydman and Andrzej Rapaczynski, *Privatization in Eastern Europe: Is the State Withering Away?* (Budapest: Central European University Press, 1994).

24 See, e.g., Andrew Arato, "Constitution and Continuity in the East European Transitions," *Tilburg Law Review*, 3, no 4(1994): 345–370; Jon Elster, "Constitutionalism in Eastern Europe: An Introduction," *The University of Chicago Law Review*, 58, no. 2 (1991): 447–482; James McAdams (ed.), *Transitional Justice and the Rule of Law in New Democracies* (Notre Dame, London: Univ. of Notre Dame Press, 1997); Gábor Halmai, "Democracy versus Constitutionalism? The Re-establishment of the Rule of Law in Hungary," *Journal of Constitutional Law in Eastern and Central Europe* 5 (1994); Claus Offe, "Designing Institutions for East European Transitions," Public Lecture no.9, delivered at Collegium Budapest 17 December 1993; Dick A.E. Howard (ed.), *Constitution Making in Eastern Europe* (Washington, DC: The Woodrow Wilson Center Press, 1993); Ruti Teitel, "Post-Communist Constitutionalism: A Transitional Perspective," *Columbia Human Rights Law Review* 26 (1994): 167.

25 See, e.g., András Sajó, "From Corruption to Extortion: Conceptualization of Post-Communist Corruption," *Crime, Law & Social Change* 40(2003): 171–194; András, Sajó, "Preferred Generations: A Paradox of Restoration Constitutions," in *Constitutionalism, Identity, Difference and Legitimacy*, Michel Rosenfeld ed. (Durham, London: Duke University Press, 1994); Herman Schwartz, *The Struggle for Constitutional Justice in Post-Communist Europe* (Chicago: The University of Chicago Press, 2000); Kim Lane Scheppele, "The Inevitable Corruption of Transition," *Connecticut Journal of International Law* 14(1999): 509; Kim Lane Scheppele, "Constitutional Negotiations: Political Contexts of Judicial Activism in Post-Soviet Europe," *International Sociology*, 18, no. 1 (2003): 219–238; Alexei Trochev, *Judging Russia: The Role of the Constitutional Court in Russian Politics 1990–2006* (Cambridge: Cambridge University Press, 2008); Marina Zaloznaya, The Politics of Bureaucratic Corruption in Post-Transitional Eastern Europe (Cambridge: Cambridge Univer-

EU or Council of Europe accessions) have spawned their own, mostly disciplinary (law and/or political science) literatures, with much of the focus on supranational courts.[26] Certain areas of research receive more attention than others, for example, crime, legal reform, and law and politics.[27] The most fruitful areas of law and society research have come from transitional justice, specifically lustration and property restitutions, particularly in the early 1990s and 2000s.[28] More recently, legal history (both in general and during socialism) and legal anthropology have made inroads.[29]

Influential voices include, among many others, Martin Krygier and Wojciech Sadurski on constitutionalism, the rule of law, and rights in the region;[30] Jiří Přibáň on the sociology of law, legal philosophy, constitutional and European comparative law, and the theory of human rights;[31]

---

sity Press, 2017; Cristina Parau, *Transnational Networking and Elite Self-Empowerment. The Making of the Judiciary in Contemporary Europe and Beyond* (Oxford: Oxford University Press, 2018).

26 See, e.g. Alexei Trochev, "All Appeals Lead to Strasbourg? Unpacking the Impact of the European Court of Human Rights on Russia," *Demokratizatsiya*, 17, no. 2 (2009): 145–178; Wojciech Sadurski, "Partnering with Strasbourg: Constitutionalisation of the European Court of Human Rights, the Accession of Central and East European States to the Council of Europe, and the Idea of Pilot Judgments," *Human Rights Law Review*, 9, no. 3(2009): 397–453.

27 See, e.g., Kathryn Hendley, "Revisiting the Emergence of the Rule of Law in Russia," *Global Crime*, 16, no. 1 (2015): 19–33; Leslie Holmes, *Rotten States?: Corruption, Post-Communism and Neoliberalism*, (Durham and London: Duke University Press, 2006); Maria Popova, *Politicized Justice in Emerging Democracies: A Study of Courts in Russia and Ukraine* (Cambridge: Cambridge University Press, 2012); Alexei Trochev, *Judging Russia: The Role of the Constitutuonal Court in Russian Politics 1990–2006* (Cambridge: Cambridge University Press, 2008).

28 See, e.g., Ruti Teitel, "Transitional Jurisprudence: The Role of Law in Political Transformation," 106 *Yale Law Journal* 106 (1997): 2009; Lavinia Stan, *Transitional Justice in Eastern Europe and the former Soviet Union* (London: Routledge, 2009); Monika Nalepa, *Skeletons in the Closet: Transitional Justice in Post-Communist Europe* (Cambridge: Cambridge University Press, 2010).

29 See, e.g., Katherine Verdery, *The Vanishing Hectare: Property and Value in Postsocialist Transylvania* (Ithaca, NY: Cornell University Press, 2003); Inga Markovits, *Justice in Lüritz: Experiencing Socialist Law in East Germany* (Princeton: Princeton University Press, 2010); Peter Solomon, *Soviet Criminal Justice under Stalin* (Cambridge: Cambridge University Press, 1996); Mihaela Șerban, *Subverting Communism in Romania: Law and Private Property 1945–1965* (Lanham, MD: Lexington Books/Rowman and Littlefield, 2019).

30 See, e.g., Adam Czarnota, Martin Krygier, and Wojciech Sadurski, *Rethinking the Rule of Law after Communism* (Budapest: Central European University Press, 2005).

31 See, e.g. Jiří Přibáň, *Dissidents of Law: On the 1989 Velvet Revolutions, Legitimations, Fictions of Legality and Contemporary Version of the Social Contract* (London: Routledge, 2019).

Wiktor Osiatyński on human rights;[32] Kim Lane Scheppele on constitutionalism;[33] and Roman David on lustration and transitional justice.[34] Anchor research centers for legal and sociolegal research have included Central European University (legal studies and human rights programs in particular), and the Max Planck Institute for Social Anthropology (legal anthropology).

Landmark sociolegal publications for the region include, among others, Inga Markovits's 2010 book *Justice in Lűritz*, Katherine Verdery's body of work on Romanian property, Lavinia Stan's body of work on transitional justice overall and in Romania separately, Kathryn Hendley's 2017 monograph *Everyday Law in Russia*,[35] and from a critical perspective, Rafal Mańko's, Cosmin Cercel's, and Liviu Damşa's works on Central Europe and Romania, respectively.[36] CEE scholars, whether based inside or outside of the region, have been reshaping more recently developed fields like memory studies,[37] and separately there is a relatively large body of research on criminal justice, both historical and contemporary.[38] Law and society research in Central and Eastern Europe and the post-Soviet space is entering a new phase, from edited volumes to special issues in various journals, some emerging out of collaborative networks based in the American Law and Society Association.[39] This special issue of law

---

32   See, e.g., Wiktor Osiatyński, *Human Rights and Their Limits* (Cambridge: Cambridge University Press, 2009).
33   See, e.g., Miklós Bánkuti, Gábor Halmai, and Kim Lane Scheppele, "Hungary's Illiberal Turn: Disabling the Constitution," *Journal of Democracy*, 23, No. 3 (2012): 138–146.
34   See, e.g. Roman David, "Lustration Laws in Action: The Motives and Evaluation of Lustration Policy in the Czech Republic and Poland (1989–2001)," *Law & Social Inquiry*, 28, No. 2 (2003): 387–439.
35   Published by Cornell University Press. While there are significant differences between the former Soviet Union and Central and Eastern European countries, this book exemplifies the best in sociolegal research in the region more broadly.
36   See, e.g., Rafał Mańko, Cosmin Sebastian Cercel and Adam Sulikowski eds., *Law and Critique in Central Europe: Questioning the Past, Resisting the Present* (Oxford: Counterpress, 2016).
37   See, e.g., Monica Ciobanu, "Criminalising the Past and Reconstructing Collective Memory: The Romanian Truth Commission," *Europe-Asia Studies*, 61, No. 2 (2009): 313–336; Monica Ciobanu, *Repression, Resistance and Collaboration in Stalinist Romania 1944–1964. Post-Communist Remembering* (London: Routledge, 2020); Uladzislau Belavusau and Aleksandra Gliszczynska-Grabias, *Law and Memory: Towards Legal Governance of History* (Cambridge: Cambridge University Press, 2017).
38   See, e.g., Lauren McCarthy, *Trafficking Justice: How Russian Police Enforce New Laws, from Crime to Courtroom* (Ithaca, NY: Cornell University Press).
39   See, e.g., William Simmons ed., *East European Faces of Law and Society: Values and Practices* (Leiden: Brill, 2014); Special Issue: A Law & Society Take on Legality in the Former Soviet Union, *Demokratizatsiya: The Journal of Post-Soviet Demo-*

and society in Romania both contributes to this broader literature and introduces it to scholars of Romanian studies.

We attempt here to undertake an innovative law and society analysis by bringing together seven seasoned scholars from several disciplines in humanities and social sciences, including anthropology (Emanuela Grama), comparative literature (Simona Livescu), history (Ștefan Cristian Ionescu), law and society (Mihaela Șerban), political science (Dragoș Petrescu), sociolegal studies (Cosmin Cercel), and sociology (Monica Ciobanu). Regardless of their academic field, the contributors engage in interdisciplinary studies of "law in action" located in various historical settings and different types of political regimes. Cercel, Ionescu, and Șerban address issues of legality during the interwar era of the authoritarian regimes of King Carol the Second (1938–1940) and Marshall Ion Antonescu's fascist wartime dictatorship (1940–1944). These authors point out that the reverse of liberal legality, which resulted in exclusionary and repressive legislation against ethnic minorities (especially the Jewish population), has to be understood within broader cultural and historical processes involving modernization, nation and state building occurring in the aftermath of the 1918 unification of the Romanian state. They emphasize that the regression of rights and liberties embodied in the 1923 Constitution that defined the interwar constitutional monarchist government was partly the result of the inherent predisposition to authoritarian practices embedded in the Versailles Treaty after the First World War.

But whether it is at the local level of the administrative courts in Timișoara where, according to Șerban, Jewish and then German claimants tried to renegotiate their ethnic identity, or within the inner circle of legal professionals under Antonescu (see Ionescu), legal institutions and legal reasoning in non-democratic regimes were not entirely shaped by decisions and practices from above. There were ongoing pressures and challenges from below that influenced the legal realm as a site for both contestation and affirmation of rights and identities. In fact, conflicts over legal rights tend to resurface after more than half a century later. Both Ciobanu and Grama examine the links, continuities, and discontinuities between the post-war transition to communist legality (1945–1947) and the post-1989 transition to democracy. Grama's article covers an even longer historical period of major legal and political transformation that

---

cratization, 28, No. 1 (2020); Peter Solomon and Kaja Gadowska eds., Special Issue: Legal Change in Post-Communist States: *Courts, Police and Public Administration, Communist and Post-Communist Studies*, 51, No. 3 (2018), reissued as *Legal Change in Post-Communist States. Progress, Reversions, Explanations* (Stuttgart: ibidem-Verlag, 2019).

spans over almost a century and a half, since the late 1800s (several decades before the formation of the Romanian state in 1918) until the post-communist transition of the early 21st century. She examines the case of property restitution involving the Miko high school built in the late 19th century as a religious institution by the Reformed Church in the exclusively (at the time) ethnically Hungarian city of Sfântu-Gheorghe in Transylvania. Whether involving legal claims over the confiscated Miko high school (Grama) or a criminal trial against the communist era prison commandant Alexandru Vișinescu (Ciobanu), local and national courts have become sites in which the meaning of family, local and ethnic communities, and even the larger national and transnational diaspora communities are negotiated and redefined.

But such struggles over issues of justice also involve the public at large through informal quasi-legal institutions. This was the case of the National Council for the Study of the Securitate Archives (CNSAS) examined by Petrescu, and the Sighet Memorial discussed by Livescu. As the two authors persuasively argue, both institutions contribute to the education and socialization of citizens in the values of human rights and justice. While CNSAS provides access to the public, in digitized form, to the files of those who collaborated with the communist secret police and impinged on the rights of their fellow citizens, the Sighet Memorial exposes its many visitors from the country and abroad to physical, visual and audio artefacts and representations of communist repression.

By combining theoretical frameworks and the methodologies of their respective disciplines with those of related areas of research, the authors bring empirical contributions to specific topics that simultaneously raise broader substantive issues and fundamental questions regarding law and society. Among the latter, the most striking relate to issues of justice, power and legitimacy, social and political change (social engineering and regime change), and the construction of meaning (as ideology or as value-systems that constitute the basis of national community or other collectivities). With respect to justice, the articles highlight that whether liberal, illiberal, authoritarian, totalitarian or democratic, every political regime rules and claims legitimacy based on a particular type of justice and corresponding sets of institutions.

Authoritarian regimes often justify their repressive measures in the name of law and order exerted on behalf of a charismatic or supreme leader. In his article, Cercel shows that Carol's return to the throne in the context of political crisis in 1930 (after his abdication five years earlier), occurred in a fashion that conflicted with the legal principles of constitutional monarchy and defined him as "an ideological and quasi-mythical figure," and not as a constitutional monarch. Similarly, Antonescu continued to subordinate and instrumentalize the judicial system in a situation of rising authoritarianism and ethno-nationalism. Both Cercel and Ionescu describe the multifaceted aspects of authoritarian legality during Carol's and Antonescu's regimes, including extrajudicial arrests, deportations and killings targeting political opponents, but mostly ethnic and religious minorities. Şerban makes a pertinent point that the 1938 constitution represented the definitive break with liberal constitutionalism that guaranteed inclusive rights and liberties to all citizens regardless of their ethnicity or religion and the establishment of ethno-constitutionalism. Both she and Ionescu provide detailed and insightful information based on archival documentation as well as firsthand autobiographical accounts of the racialist and exclusionary legal practices against members of the Jewish communities during Antonescu's regime.

The first part of Ciobanu's article examines legal developments following the August 1944 overthrow of the fascist regime during the early years of communization, the legal foundation of which was rooted in the Soviet jurisprudence of terror. By focusing on Stalinist-type show trials levelled against the leaders of the pre-war historical National Peasant Party (PNȚ), she points out that revolutionary class struggle and the claim of the Communist Party to be the sole representative of the working class constituted at the time the regime's justification for repressive action. However, following the mobilization of anti-communist civic activists and the descendants of some of the PNȚ's prominent figures after 1989, this narrative was challenged and at least partially dismantled by the legal system.

Grama also discusses how in post-communism courts become sites where ethnic and religious minorities attempt to reclaim their political, cultural and property rights. In a similar vein to the families of former political prisoners who demanded legal and moral recognition for their parents and grandparents, the Hungarian minority in Transylvania mobilized around their collective rights by invoking their own marginalization and discrimination by the communist authorities. The restitution of the confiscated community properties in 1948 in Transylvania belonging to the German and Hungarian minorities became a much politicized and legally entangled topic in post-communism. These deep-seated historical tensions and legal ambiguities are clearly illustrated by the developments following the 2012 revocation of the 2001 decision taken by the Sfântu-Gheorghe city council that gave the Reformed Church property rights over the Miko high school. The ensuing legal proceedings initiated on behalf of the rights of the Reformed Church and the Hungarians of Transylvania in local, national and international courts were paralleled by the direct involvement of the Hungarian authorities. As such, the Miko high school case reflects the ongoing contradictions between the legal system's abilities and weaknesses in defining the relationship between community and property rights. This point was also made by Șerban when analyzing the Jewish claimants' efforts to utilize legal loopholes to prove their Christian identity during the war.

Legal practices and institutions play a significant role in bringing social and political change to both non-democratic and democratic regimes. However, the degree to which political authorities utilize or subordinate the legal system varies between them. On the one hand, the creation of a purely ethnic and religiously based nation during Antonescu's dictatorship (see Cercel and Șerban), or of a classless society free of bourgeois elements ruled by a communist party (see Ciobanu) represent extreme cases of social engineering. On the other, quasi-legal mechanisms in democratic societies engage in more subtle forms of symbolic justice, which teach citizens the values of freedom, rights, and liberties. Petrescu provides a compelling argument of how after 2008, the CNSAS transformed itself from a "vetting" agency into a fact-finding institution. By providing public access, through its database, to information about individuals who collaborated with Securitate, the post-communist generations have been able to internalize important lessons in civic education. This pedagogical function is also exercised by post-communist memorial museums. Livescu's analysis of two such institutions focusing especially on repression and victimization rather than issues of collaboration and acquiescence—the Sighet Memorial in Sighet, Romania and the House of Terror in Budapest, Hungary—offers a fascinating story of how human rights museums produce a highly emotional but incomplete version of the history of communism. But as Ciobanu shows, criminal courts can also easily fall into the trap of manufacturing incomplete accounts of the past. This was the case of the Vișinescu trial that primarily represented the voices of only one segment of those victimized by the defendant and the regime, that is, the leaders of the National Peasant Party.

In fact, this uneasy relationship between legal redress and historical memory represents a common theme addressed in various ways by most of the contributors (Ciobanu, Grama, Livescu, Șerban and Petrescu). When courts, legal professionals and administrative agencies attempt to rationalize their decisions on behalf of a collective entity (our audience), legal reasoning and the ensuing application of justice become a performative act. This was the experience of Jewish defendants and their attorneys from Banat who attempted to persuade the authorities in detail of their gentile background (Șerban). The history of communism as a narrative of national victimization was dramatically re-enacted during Vișinescu's trial. Such "staged" reenactments take similarly expressive forms through practices of mis-remembering and over-remembering typical of the red and dark tourism drawn by the Sighet Memorial or advertised by the House of Terror (Livescu).

This overview of the seven contributions reveals both the strengths and the opportunities that law and society research can bring to Romanian studies. By engaging in interdisciplinary research on law, history, and justice, scholars of the social sciences and humanities can enhance current and future academic scholarship in many areas, including legal and political theory, transitional justice and memory studies, and arts and politics in post-communist societies. At the same time, some of the lessons provided by the Romanian case could constitute a source of inspiration for future studies of post-socialism in other regions of the world yet to pursue their own legal and political transitions.

Reversing Liberal Legality: Romania's Path to Dictatorship, 1930–1938

*Cosmin Cercel**

Abstract: *Romania's anti-liberal turn at the end of the interwar period is a useful case study for analysing the dissolution of the liberal nomos fostered by the Versailles arrangements against the background of the authoritarian takeover in Europe. In this article, I explore the legal and constitutional mechanisms at the core of the instauration of King's Carol II dictatorship. I propose to do so by mapping the reconstruction of the concepts of legality and authority within the political and legal processes seeking to contest, challenge and ultimately reverse the liberal features of the constitutional armature of the Romanian state. Drawing on jurisprudence, political theory, and constitutional history, I seek to unearth the ideological underpinnings of this regime of power and to reflect on the nexus between law and anti-liberal projects of state-building at the end of the interwar period.*

The current constitutional predicaments affecting the status of liberal democracies have made parallels and references to the interwar period a constant presence within public and academic discourses. The interwar years are once again read as an era apt to capture and answer contemporary concerns about the dissolution of liberal legality.

To this day, an important body of historical and jurisprudential literature has aimed to grasp the symbolic, political and jurisprudential significance of this process by focusing on the case of the Weimar Republic.[1] For either cultural, historical and jurisprudential reasons, these attacks

---

* Associate Professor University of Nottingham School of Law. I am extremely grateful to the editors of the special issue as well as to the two anonymous reviewers for their comments and suggestions. I am also indebted to Professor Manuel Guțan (Sibiu), Professor David Fraser (Nottingham), Dr Simon Lavis (Open University), Dr Rafał Mańko (Amsterdam) and Dr Przemysław Tacik (Cracow) for reading and commenting on earlier versions of this article. Research for this article was undertaken in the context of the research project entitled 'Heads of State (Princes, Kings and Presidents) and the Authoritarian Dynamic of Political Power in Romanian Constitutional History', funded by the Romanian Research Funding Agency (UEFISCDI), PN-III-P4-ID-PCE-2016-0013.

1 John P. McCormick, *Carl Schmitt's Critique of Liberalism* (Cambridge University Press, 1997); William E Scheuerman, *Carl Schmitt: The End of Law* (Rowman and Littlefield, 1999); Arthur J. Jacobson and Bernard Schlink (eds.), *Weimar—a Jurisprudence of Crisis* (Berkeley: University of California Press, 2000).

on liberal legality have become paradigmatic, offering a somewhat clear, if not entirely accurate picture of the vagaries of liberal legality in the context of the interwar era. However, this focus, while important from the standpoint of the jurisprudential debates it has sparked, offers only a limited view on the status of legality during the interwar period and obfuscates other important trends in legal thought and practice.

The fall of the Weimar Republic before the Nazi onslaught is often reduced to a number of limited constitutional events that evolve around the use of Article 48 of the Weimar Constitution,[2] and more broadly the state of exception and the suspension of the constitutional process against the background of the rise of Nazism.[3] Within the field of legal theory, it somewhat conveniently opposes Hans Kelsen's legal formalism to Carl Schmitt's defence of 'concrete order.'[4] Such analyses continue to represent the foundational epistemic lenses through which attacks on liberal legality are read to this day and form our contemporary understanding of threats to liberal democracy. I consider that there is another historical trajectory of the interwar era that needs to be analyzed, that is the gradual destitution of liberal legality within polities that have been part of the Versailles status quo, such as France, Romania, Yugoslavia or Poland, to name only a few of these states.

Shifting the focus towards an analysis of the crisis of legality in other contexts would enable the evaluation of transnational trends in the rise of emergency powers and the executive, as well as of the ambiguous reactions to competing ideologies from the left and right. Moreover, it will enable us to reflect on the reconstruction of core constitutional concepts of citizenship and belonging specific to the interwar period.

In what follows, I argue that Romania's anti-liberal turn at the end of the interwar period is a useful case study for analysing the dissolution of the liberal nomos fostered by the Versailles arrangements in the wake of the 1929 financial crisis and against the background of the rise of authoritarianism in Europe. This shift in constitutional discourse is fundamentally linked to the figure of King Carol II, who ruled Romania, first as a putatively constitutional monarch between 1930 and 1938 and later, as an overtly authoritarian King, between 1938 and 1940. The Romanian case is important for at least two central reasons. First, it captures the

---

2   Lars Vinx, *The Guardian of the Constitution: Hans Kelsen and Carl Schmitt on the Limits of Constitutional Law* (Cambridge: Cambridge University Press, 2015).
3   Augustin Simard, La loi désarmée: Carl Schmitt et la controverse légalité/légitimité sous la république de Weimar (Québec: Les Presses de l'Université de Laval, 2009).
4   Carl Schmitt, *Political Theology* (George Schwab tr.) (first published 1922, MIT Press, 1985), 45.

legal and political tensions sapping the politico-legal order within successor states following the Versailles Treaty. Second, through its unfolding during a time interval that spans over two decades, this series of crises enables one to take the measure of the gradual demise of liberal constitutionalism.

In this article I intend to explore the legal and constitutional mechanisms at the core of the instauration of King Carol II's dictatorship. More specifically, the focus is on mapping the reconstruction of the concepts of legality and authority within the political and juridical processes seeking to contest, challenge and ultimately reverse the liberal features of the constitutional armature of the Romanian state. Following this thread, I aim to examine both the symbolic place occupied by the law and its social functions within the process of the 'breakdown of democracy'[5] in interwar Romania.

Such an undertaking probes law's operation within the repressive and ideological state apparatuses set out during Carol II's rule.[6] My aim is to bring under a new light the ideological and conceptual underpinnings of this regime of power and to reflect more broadly on the nexus between law and anti-liberal projects of state-building at the end of the interwar period. Moreover, I intend to document and ground further through legal and historical analysis the insights offered by political philosopher Giorgio Agamben into the operation of the state of exception within the functioning of the law.[7] As I noted elsewhere, the concept of the state of exception, that is the possibility of suspending the law through legal means 'forces us to inscribe legality in a broader timeframe and to refine our uses of concepts that historians and political theorists borrow from the arsenal of jurisprudence.'[8] I thus aim to go beyond the visited philosophical topoi connecting the suspension of the law to the exercise of sovereign power and to explore the material and ideological conditions entailed by the dissolution of legality in a precise historical context.

---

5 Juan J. Linz, *Totalitarian and Authoritarian Regimes* (Boulder: Lynne Rienner, 2000), 137.
6 Louis Althusser, *Sur la reproduction* (Paris: Presses Universitaires de France, 1996 [1970]), 106–111.
7 Giorgio Agamben, *Homo Sacer: Sovereign Power and Bare Life*, D. Heller-Roazen transl. (Stanford: Stanford University Press, 1998 [1995]), 10–19; Giorgio Agamben, State of Exception, Kevin Attell transl. (Chicago: University of Chicago Press, 2005 [2003]), 33–39.
8 Cosmin Cercel, '"Through A Glass, Darkly": Law, History and the Frontispiece of Exception', in Cosmin Cercel, Gian-Giacomo Fusco and Simon Lavis eds., *States of Exception: Law, History, Theory* (London: Routledge, 2020), 53.

I shall analyze this transformation of legality while focusing on jurisprudence, history and political theory. My choice is determined by the fact that the conceptual apparatus of the new constitutional discourse did not emerge in a cultural or political vacuum. Key concepts founding a new understanding of legality were subjected to a long historical unfolding, which has thoroughly connected the field and practice of law to processes of modernization, state-building and nation-building since the advent of the modern Romanian state.[9] Furthermore, the law does not exist 'as such' in any historical context. It is nurtured, informed and produced by a series of discourses that are seemingly beyond its reach, such as politics, economics, or culture.[10] My reading of legal history thus tries to capture the relationship between the legal form and history with a view of documenting 'the gradual disappearance of the (...) structures on which liberal legality apparently depends.'[11] In this sense, I follow the ongoing discussion on law and authoritarian ideologies exploring the darker legacies of law in Europe and beyond.[12]

Reframing Liberal Legality

For the purposes of this investigation I understand liberal legality as a regime defined by separation of powers, equality before the law, legal certainty, and fundamental rights.[13] Under this form, and it is a matter of form rather than of a widely professed ideology, liberal legality was present in the Kingdom of Romania within the functioning of the legal apparatus at least since the proclamation of the Constitution of 1866. It therefore guided and determined the interpretive horizon of legal officials, regardless of and, at times, in opposition to, their personal political, and ideological creeds. However, these constitutional arrangements were effectively constrained by a series of legislative provisions, by judicial practice

---

9   Manuel Guțan, 'The Challenges of the Romanian Constitutional Tradition, I. Between Ideological Transplant and Institutional Metamorphoses', (2013) 25 *Giornale di Storia Constituzionale* 223.
10 Pierre Legrand, 'Comparative Legal Studies and the Matter of Authenticity', (2006) 1 *Journal of Comparative Law* 365.
11 David Fraser, 'Afterword. Through the Looking Glass: Thinking About and Working Through Fascist Criminal Law', in Stephen Skinner ed., *Fascism and Criminal Law: History, Theory, Continuity* (Oxford: Hart, 2015), 203.
12 Christian Joerges and Navraj Singh Ghaleigh eds., *Darker Legacies of Law in Europe* (Oxford: Hart, 2003).
13 Hans Kelsen, *The Essence and Value of Democracy*, Brian Graf trans. (Lanham: Rowman and Littlefield, 2013 [1929]); Hans Kelsen, 'Foundations of Democracy', (1955) 66 *Ethics* 1.

as well as by political informal agreements undoing the normative core of constitutional promises.

These limits found their legal embodiment in the discrimination of subjects who had limited access to citizen status,[14] of the primacy of the executive in its relation to the legislative power,[15] as well as—since the beginning of the First World War—of the recurrent use of the state of siege.[16] These ur-type ambiguities setting the ground for the politico-legal drama of the interwar period affect thus the evolution of constitutional discourse on three interconnected levels. First, we can find the conceptualization of nation as a subject that is not yet defined in purely political and legal terms, as a community created by the law, but, owing to the Romantic tradition, in cultural and linguistic forms. This is quite obviously at odds with the universal promises of formal equality present within the same constitutional structure. Second, the primacy of the executive in political life encroaches on the abstract and impersonal character of legality, let alone its predictability and certainty, thus marking a tension between the liberal imperative of limiting the potentially arbitrary power of the monarch and the factual need for achieving consensus. Third, the recourse to exceptional measures, effectively suspending the constitutional process, recreates within the liberal framework the possibility of an unregulated exercise of power specific to the absolute rule of the *ancien règime*.

To fully understand the ways in which this institutional path, and the inherent ambiguities of this constitutional model have been transformed in order to give way to the very different project of royal dictatorship, a number of further historical clarifications seem to be needed. The first is to map the constitutional changes brought about by the Versailles Treaty and Romania's participation in the Great War and its aftermath.

Romania's participation in the Great War on the side of the Entente was eventually crowned by a victory on the diplomatic front, the country being awarded most of the territorial claims stated at the beginning of

---

14 Such was the case of the Jewish inhabitants who gained naturalisation under the draconian conditions of the Statute Revising the Constitution of 12 October 1879, *M.Of.*, No. 323, 13 October 1879. See also, Ștefan Cristian Ionescu, *Jewish Resistance to 'Romanianization', 1940–1944* (Basingstoke: Palgrave Macmillan, 2015), 4–13.
15 Keith *Hitchins, Rumania, 1866–1947* (Oxford, Oxford University Press, 1994); Daniel Barbu, Republica absentă (Bucharest: Nemira, 1999), 173.
16 Constantin Dissesco, 'L'évolution du droit public roumain', in *Les transformations du droit dans les principaux pays depuis cinquante ans: livre du cinquantenaire de la Société de législation comparée* (Paris: L.G.D.J, 1922), 301; Cosmin Cercel, 'The « Right » Side of the Law. State of Siege and the Rise of Fascism in Interwar Romania', (2013) 2 *Fascism* 205.

hostilities. While these territorial gains were indeed remarkable, especially having in mind Romania's rather limited military success in the initial campaign of 1916–1917 and the separate peace with the Central Powers signed in Bucharest in March 1918,[17] they came tied with a series of guarantees imposed by the Entente that were regarded with suspicion, if not utter discontent by the Romanian statesmen involved in the negotiations, as well as by the public opinion.[18] The Treaty signed in Paris on the 9th of December 1919 was key both in fuelling local discontent and in effectively tackling one of the central limitations of Romanian liberal legality, namely the status of minorities.[19] By the provisions of the Treaty, adopted half-heartedly by Romanian diplomats and ratified by the Parliament in 1920,[20] the Romanian state bound itself to extend citizenship to its inhabitants and to guarantee equal protection under the law to all its citizens. The Treaty provided that the principles enshrined in its core articles were to be recognized as fundamental laws, and that no law or internal regulation would prevail over them and contradict their content.[21]

The provisions of the Treaty were included in the Constitution of 1923, thus creating a direct link between the international obligations of the Romanian state and its internal structures.[22] This strengthened the material and conceptual relation between the liberal pledges of the Romanian state in its foreign and local policies, to which the law and the particular liberal understanding of legality were key.

Post-war another limit of the initial liberal path embedded in the constitutional discourse was addressed, namely the electoral basis. Universal male suffrage was secured as early as 1918 through a Decree Law.[23] The provisions of the Decree were also enshrined in the Constitution of

---

17 GE Torrey, 'Romania in the First World War: The Years of Engagement, 1916–1918', (1992) 14 The International History Review 462–79.
18 Charles Upson Clark, *United Romania* (New York, Dodd, Mead and Co, 1932), 240–248.
19 'Treaty between the Principal Allied and Associated Powers and Roumania', 9 December 1919, *League of Nations Treaty Series* (1921) 5: 335–50.
20 Clark, *United Romania* 221–50; Erwin Lowenfeld, 'The Protection of Private Property under the Minorities Protection Treaties' (1930) 16 *Transactions of Hugo Grotius Society* 41, 47–50.
21 Treaty between the Principal Allied and Associated Powers and Roumania', 9 December 1919.
22 Article 5 and Article 7, Constitution of Romania of 28 March 1923, *M. Of.*, No. 282, 29 March 1923.
23 Decree Law of 15 November 1918 on the Elections for the Representative Assembly and the Senate, *M.Of.*, No. 191, 19 November 1918.

1923, which restated the classical inventory of political freedoms and fundamental rights existing in the previous Constitution.[24]

However important this reconfiguration of the body politic, the actual organization of constituted powers did not change significantly, thus continuing to counterbalance the liberal form. Under the new Constitution, the King continued to play a significant role in the articulation of power as well as in political praxis. Symptomatically, he shared with the National Assembly legislative powers, thus having a right to refuse the sanction of a statute.[25]

For its part, the practice of appointing the government with a view to organizing elections continued. To curb the authoritarian tendencies intrinsic to these arrangements, the Constitution also provided for the control of constitutionality of laws, exercised by the Court of Cassation.[26]

Beyond the Kelsenian thrusts of the politico-legal theory infusing Romanian constitutional life after the Great War lurked a more Hobbesian reality.[27] It took the form of an increasing militarization of political life and constant recourse to the state of siege and expedite administrative measures. If there is little doubt about how the participation in the Great War has shaped Romanian constitutionalism of the early 1920s, there is an equally central, if less explored, trajectory that has come to mark significantly the politico-legal landscape of the period, namely the October Revolution and the series of local revolutions, uprising and regional conflicts following the fall of the Winter Palace. The Romanian project of liberal legality is thus a reaction to the state of civil war looming at the borders of the country on the ruins of the fallen empires.[28]

The constitutional and international legal commitments of the polity thoroughly placed the country within the orbit of the Versailles status-quo, whose staunch defender was France.[29] At the same time, the state defined itself through these commitments as part of the *cordon sanitaire* aimed at containing Soviet influence and, more broadly, revolutionary

---

24 Article 64 and Article 67, Constitution of Romania of 28 March 1923.
25 Art. 88, Ibid.
26 Article 103 of the Constitution of Romania of 28 March 1923.
27 Hans Kelsen, 'La garantie juridictionnelle de la Constitution', (1928) 45 *Revue du droit public et de la science politique en France et à l'étranger* 197.
28 Enzo Traverso, *Fire and Blood: The European Civil War 1914–1945* David Fernbach trasn. (London: Verso, 2017 [2007]), 48.
29 J. W. Wheeler-Bennet, 'The European Status Quo. 1919–1930', (1930) 7 *Bulletin of International News* 3, at 7–8; Francis Deák, 'Can Europe Unite?' (1931) 46 *Political Science Quarterly* 424.

communism.[30] What is revealed in these arrangements is a very split within the functioning of the liberal normative core, which was forced to err between a logic of security and militarism and a normative and procedural protection of its fundamental tenets. This structural ambivalence manifests itself as a series of political and institutional hesitations between policies aimed at containing dissent and a formalist approach asserting the supremacy of the constitutional values. This apparent antinomy shall make the substance of public law developments before the assertion of the royal dictatorship.

What is important to note at this stage is the specific structural and authorless dimension of this process, distinguishable from political actors' tendencies and decisions. To put it simply, constitutional provisions regarding the separation of powers or ministerial responsibility were related to the personal and political abilities of the King and those exercising offices, and relative to their commitment in upholding the normative foundations of the state. However, the rise of militarization and its subsequent consequences, such as the provisional suspension of the same constitutional values the law was defending, was dependent on both geopolitical considerations and on a deep ideological inscription of the polity as a state opposing "world revolution." Furthermore, the connection between liberal pledges and security concerns should not be overlooked. As Mark Neocleous noted, '(f)ar from disputing the priority of security, classical liberalism gave it a fundamental place in regimes supposedly founded on consent.'[31]

This position transpires quite clearly during the interwar period. Security concerns were explicitly present in both the text of the Constitution and in politico-legal praxis. In this historical context, such considerations were perhaps largely correct in appraising the potential threats to the established constitutional order until the late 1920s, and before Carol II's arrival in 1930. On the one hand, the eastern border with Soviet Russia was not internationally recognized and was only subject to factual arrangements between the two states.[32] The signing of the Litvinov Protocols in 1929 and the overall turn in Soviet foreign policy since Rapallo had

---

30   Wheeler-Bennet, 'The European Status Quo. 1919–1930', 4; Michael T. Florinsky, 'World Revolution and Soviet Foreign Policy', (1932) 47 *Political Science Quarterly* 204.
31   Mark Neocleous, *Critique of Security* (Edinburgh University Press, 2008), 24.
32   Rebecca Haynes, *Romanian Policy towards Germany, 1936–1940* (Basingstoke, Palgrave Macmillan, 2000), 4.

left the issue of Bessarabia unscathed.[33] Indeed, the acquisition of Bessarabia was regarded as a matter of foreign policy by the Soviet State, as an expression of the imperialist tendencies of Romania.

Border tensions sometime amounted to open armed conflict, such as in the case of the Tatar Bunar uprising of 1924, when the local and foreign communist insurgents were allegedly supported by the Red Army in their contestation of state sovereignty.[34] As a result of these tensions, Bessarabia as a whole or regions on the border with the USSR had found themselves under martial law since joining Romania until the early years of the Carol II's regime.[35]

On the other hand, relations with the neighbour in the West, Hungary, were, perhaps unsurprisingly, tensed. Not only Romania was exercising sovereignty over important parts of the former Hungarian Crown, but between 1919 and 1920 it was in open military conflict with the short-lived Hungarian Soviet Republic, playing a central role in quelling the Bolshevik Revolution.[36] The main aim of Romanian foreign policy in the region within the framework of the Little Entente was to oppose, alongside Yugoslavia and Czechoslovakia, any form of revisionism supported by Hungary and Austria.[37] During the decades following the Great War this was not a mere theoretical matter, as tensions related to transport of ammunitions, military manoeuvres on the border lines, or attempts of restoration of the Habsburg Monarchy in Hungary and Austria alike caused serious concerns within the three countries party to the Treaty.[38] Consequently, the border regions with Hungary would find themselves often under temporary suspensions of constitutional provisions under the state of siege.[39]

These particular military and international concerns manifested themselves within the institution of the state of siege, which effectively limited the scope of the constitutional inventory of fundamental rights

---

33 Florinsky, 'World Revolution and Soviet Foreign Policy', 230; S.A.H, 'A Security Pact in Eastern Europe', (1934) 11 *Bulletin of International News* 3, at 4.
34 Charles Upson Clark, *Bessarabia, Russia and Roumania on the Black Sea* (New York, Dodd, Mead and Co, 1927) 223-31; William Brustein and Amy Ronnkvist, 'The Roots of anti-Semitism: Romania before the Holocaust', (2002) 4 *Journal of Genocide Research* 211 at 226.
35 Clark, *United Romania*, 173.
36 Alfred D. Low, 'The Soviet Hungarian Republic and the Paris Peace Conference', (1963) 53 *Transactions of the American Philosophical Society* 10, at 62-86.
37 Wheeler-Bennet, 'The European Status Quo. 1919-1930', (1930) 7 *Bulletin of International News* 3, at 6-7.
38 Piotr Wandycz, 'The Little Entente: Sixty Years Later' (1981) 59 *Slavonic and East European Review* 548.
39 Cercel, '"Right" Side of the Law', 225.

and freedoms and opened the way for the direct interference of military logic within the sphere of the law.

It is against this background, marked by a conflation between the classical categories of liberal legalism, remnants of pre-modern monarchical authority, and military and administrative expediency, that the political developments in Romania appear in a new light. If indeed, in contradistinction to the years following Carol II's rise to power, this period tends to be read through the lenses of either reconstruction or nation-building, embodying the transition to the rise of authoritarianism, what continues to be overlooked is the inherent antinomy of the liberal legal infrastructure informing these projects and the strained European interwar context marked by political violence and social division that was witnessing the vagaries of the Ruhr occupation, the Beer Hall putsch, and the rise to power of Fascism in Italy.[40]

The Path to Dictatorship

The sphere of parliamentary politics, for its part, was undoubtedly marked by the effects of the arduous process of incorporating new territories into the state, the introduction of universal male suffrage and the agrarian reform.[41] These changes led to the disappearance of the now obsolete Conservative Party, the main political force representing the landed aristocracy before the war. New parties and movements such as the National Peasant's Party (NPP) were taking on the political stage. A result of a union between the social progressive Peasant's Party based in the Old Kingdom and the National Romanian Party, a former promoter of Romanian communities' interests in the Austro-Hungarian Empire, the NPP was initially supporting a rather progressive agenda in defending what it perceived to be the interests of the peasantry.[42] Its dual constituency and the internal ideological contradictions opposing a rather confusing non-Marxist conception of class struggle reminiscent of the late 19th century Narodnik movement and the nationalist creeds of 19th century

---

40   Payne, *A History of Fascism: 1914–45*, 79; Konrad Heiden, *A History of National Socialism*, Vol. II (London: Routledge, 2010) 104–106.
41   Statute concerning the Land Reform in Oltenia, Muntenia, Moldova and Dobrogea, 14 July 1921, *M.Of.*, No. 82, 17 July 1921 and Statute for the Land Reform in Transylvania, Crișana and Maramureș, 30 July 1921, *M. Of.*, No. 93, 30 July 1921; O. Gorni, 'Les réformes foncières en Europe orientale et centrale leurs causes économiques et sociales' (1931) 3 *Annales d'histoire économique et sociale* 207 at 218–223.
42   Hitchins, *Rumania 1866–1947*, 391.

were however limiting the scope of the reforms proposed.[43] Indeed, the NPP was explicitly arguing that 'on the ruins of capitalism a new form of State shall be built in the image and according to the likeness of the Romanian worker, who is the peasant,'[44] while its commitment in terms of economic policy was that of a staunch supporter of free trade.[45]

The main opponent of the NPP was the National Liberal Party (NLP), who found itself at the helm of Romanian politics with only some minor interruptions since the end of the war. While the 'liberal' stance of this party is perhaps a misnomer,[46] the party's politics was one of defending the existing status-quo and primarily its position within the political arrangements. The NLP relied on strong support within the ranks of the local industrialists and promoted a protectionist policy that affected Romania's financial standing by antagonizing foreign lenders.[47] According to foreign commentators, it was exercising a quasi-authoritarian control, as 'the country lived under virtual martial law.'[48]

Drawing on King Ferdinand's support, the leader of the party, Ion I. C. Brătianu, was held to be the founder of modern Romania while at the same time being considered by the opposition as 'practically the dictator of his country.'[49] In order to respond to the political fragmentation already at work under the new regime, and to secure their prominence in the renewed Parliament (representing a significantly larger electorate), the 1926 electoral statute instituted a majority bonus.[50] Accordingly, any party obtaining more than 40 per cent of the votes in the elections automatically obtained a bonus in representation of over half of the seats in Parliament. As Barbu observed, 'the parties and only them gained the monopoly over national sovereignty.'[51]

Faced with an ageing King, the liberals also supported Prince Carol's renunciation of the throne due to his estrangement from his wife, Princess Helen of Greece, and to what was euphemistically described by the press as a disdain for monarchical conventions.[52] Consequently, legislation con-

---

43 Michael Kitch, 'Constantin Stere and Romanian Populism' (1975) 53 *Slavonic and Eastern European Review* 248–71.
44 Ioan Scurtu, *Istoria României între anii 1918–1944* (Bucharest, Editura didactică și pedagogică,1994) 7.
45 Joseph S. Roucek, 'Social Background of Roumanian Politics' (1932) 10 *Social Forces* 419 at 424.
46 Hitchins, *Rumania 1866–1947* 390.
47 Roucek, 'Social Background of Roumanian Politics', 423.
48 Ibid.
49 Ibid., 422.
50 Statute of 27 March 1926, *M.Of.*, No. 71, 27 March 1926.
51 Barbu, *Republica absentă*, 173.
52 'The Succession and the Political Situation', *Adevărul*, No. 12901, 5 January 1926, 1.

cerning the succession to the throne designated Prince Michael, Carol's son, as the heir.[53]

The death of King Ferdinand, followed by that of the leader of the National Liberals, Ion I.C. Brătianu, left the country, and especially the informal network of political informal arrangements, in disarray.[54] The situation was rendered even more challenging by the looming financial crisis,[55] as well as by the dire economic situation in which Romania found itself. This was the consequence of the fall of the prices of agricultural products on the world market and of the tarrif barriers levelled by the liberal governments in order to protect national initiative.[56] With a slump in production and a fluctuating currency, securing a foreign loan was anything but an easy prospect.[57] Faced with an economic and political debacle as well as threats of NPP-fueled uprising, the liberal Prime Minister Vintilă Brătianu resigned in November 1928, and the Regency appointed Iuliu Maniu, the leader of the NPP, as the new head of government.[58] The elections organized in December were won by an NPP-led coalition. The expectations for this government were indeed high, and while in economic terms it managed to stabilize the fall of the national currency and secure a credit, politically it became entangled in the constitutional conundrum of the return of Carol and his claim to the throne.[59] At that time, Carol was a simple citizen living under the name of Carol Caraiman in London and Paris and did not have the right to enter the territory, nor any valid legal claim to the throne.

The return of the former Crown Prince took the form of a *coup d'état*: Carol arrived clandestinely in a rented plane which landed in Băneasa with the assent of the military authorities and entered Bucharest while having previously obtained the support of the garrison of the city.[60]

---

53 Statute Recognising HRE Prince Michael as heir to the throne of Romania of 4 January 1926, *M.Of.*, No. 4., 5 January 1926. 'The National Assembly and the legal regulation of the renunciation to the throne: a legal controversy with political consequences', Adevărul, No. 12901, 5 January 1926, 3.
54 Roucek, 'Social Background of Roumanian Politics', 424.
55 Hamilton Fish Armstrong, 'Danubia: Relief or Ruin', (1932) 10 *Foreign Affairs* 600 at 606.
56 Nicholas Roosevelt, 'Salvaging the Debts of Eastern Europe' (1933) 12 *Foreign Affairs* 134 at 136–37.
57 Ibid.
58 Joseph S Roucek, 'The Political Evolution of Roumania' (1932) 10 *Slavonic and East European Review* 602–15, 614.
59 Ibid., 614–15.
60 Clark, *United Romania*, 324–26; 'Le prince Carol proclamé roi', Ministère des Affaires Etrangères, *Bulletin périodique de la presse roumaine: du 26 mai au 25 juin 1930*, No. 92, 3 July 1930, 4.

As the French Foreign Ministry's reports on the press in Romania over this event note, all the involved parties executing the plan 'knew themselves to be assured by high approvals.'[61] Indeed, even if Prince Carol considered himself to have been the author of the entire manoeuvre,[62] he had both the support of his brother, Prince Nicolae, who was a member of the Regency Council, as well as the conditional support of the NPP Prime Minister Iuliu Maniu.[63]

Prime Minister Maniu presented his formal resignation insofar as he was legally bound by the oath of allegiance to the young King Michael.[64] On June 8th, the Parliament repealed the Statutes concerning the order of succession of 1926 and took act that the rightful heir to the throne was Prince Carol.[65] On the same occasion, the National Assembly proclaimed Prince Carol as the King of Romania.

The return of Carol was ostensibly unconstitutional despite all the precautions taken by himself and his political allies insofar as the renunciation to the throne was not revocable. What stays as a matter of law and historical significance is that the formal legal status quo was disregarded by the highest dignitaries of the state and the status of the monarchy was questioned beyond the true, putative or simulated respect for the person of the prince and of the future King.

Regardless of the motivations guiding the numerous actors of this constitutional drama, there was an official explicit acknowledgement that the country could be united only under the figure of the King.[66] Such a stance was at odds with the constitutional dimension of the monarchical Institution and it is precisely at this interface between law and politics that the essential crisis of Romanian politics becomes apparent: Carol's return with disregard to the rule of law is not a return as a constitutional monarch, but as an ideological quasi-mythical figure that is not captured or contained by modern models of legality.

The first official addresses of the King were directed to the military in a High Order of the Day published in the Official Journal before the publication of the actual proceeding of his proclamation as the King.[67] The choice of addressing the Army as the first official act as a King is telling about the sources of legitimacy of the King and the importance placed by

---

61 'Le prince Carol proclamé roi', 4.
62 Ibid.
63 Clark, *United Romania*, 324.
64 'Le prince Carol proclamé roi', 4
65 Ibid.
66 Livezeanu, *Cultural Politics in Greater Romania* 24.
67 High Order of the Day, *M.Of.*, No. 126, 11 June 1930.

Carol on this state apparatus. For its part, the country was addressed in a subsequent message that underlined two important topoi that were to constitute themselves in recurring ideological tropes over the following years: on the one hand, there was the need for unity and hard labour, while on the other hand, the imminence of danger.[68] The message was conveyed 'during the hard moments that the country faces,'[69] while its form was that of a call for all 'to unite as a bundle around the Throne.'[70]

Dismantling Liberal Legality

The King's assessment of the situation was not inexact. Romania was facing in 1929 a deficit of no less than 4 billion lei,[71] while continuing to borrow money on the international market just in order to repay the existing debts accumulated largely as a result of supporting military expenditure and some timid projects of local industrialization.[72] Moreover, a level of uncertainty reigned in international relations. Internally, new forces were fermenting opposition to parliamentary politics.

The Legion of the Archangel Michael, the main ultranationalist organization of a fascist type, was already gaining momentum.[73] Initially a paramilitary movement involved in strike-breaking activities during the first years after the Great War under the name of the Guard of National Awareness, the Legion's history is enmeshed in the politico-juridical thread explored so far.[74] First, its emergence is historically connected to the practice of the state of siege in the years following the war during Marshal Averescu's government,[75] while its growth is closely connected to the evolution of forms of state repression, either criminal law or of a military nature. Moreover, its organization dates back to the waves of anti-Semitism engulfing Romania before the enactment of the 1923 Constitution.[76]

With firm roots in the ultranationalist and antisemitic milieu originating in *fin de siècle* cultural and political associations,[77] the Legion grew

---

68   Report on the ceremony of the Proclamation of H.R.E Prince Carol as King of Romania, 2.
69   Ibid., 3.
70   Ibid.
71   Roosevelt, 'Salvaging the Debts of Eastern Europe', 136.
72   Armstrong, 'Danubia: Relief or Ruin', 606.
73   Clark, *Holy Legionary Youth*, 63–86.
74   Rebecca Haynes, 'Corneliu Zelea Codreanu: The Romanian "New Man"' in *In the Shadow of Hitler: Personalities of the Right in Central and Eastern Europe*, Rebecca Haynes and Martyn Rady (London: Tauris, 2011), 170–71.
75   Cercel, 'The « Right » Side of the Law', 230.
76   Clark, *Holy Legionary Youth*, 28–49
77   Ibid., 20–26.

as a student organization under the leadership of Corneliu Zelea Codreanu, a law student at the University of Iași with former military education,[78] who distinguished himself as an antisemitic agitator during the early years of the interwar period. The Legion acted first within the ranks of the anti-Semitic League of National Christian Defense, and later as a distinct and competing organization. During the 1920s it became a staunch oponent of the established legal order and politics, and launched a first wave of political assassinations that were sistematically acquitted by the courts, while drawing further public support. However, either by conviction or as a matter of political realism, the Legion was not contesting monarchical authority as such, and until 1935 found itself on Carol's side. As a matter of fact, the Legion was one of the first mass-movements 'to show open support on his return.'[79] The initial rapprochement between the Legion and the King testifies to a weakening of the liberal *nomos*, insofar as the rights enshrined in the Constitution of 1923, as well as its rather careful attempts at balancing state powers were deemed by the Legionaries as nothing short of being foreign imports going back to the un-Romanian legacies of the turbulent liberal ideals of 1848.[80] The King, for his part, was very much determined to rule the country as 'a business,' with very little respect to the limitations of his power.

By the time the rupture between the King and the Legion became an important element in configuring Romanian politics, both interested parties had come a long way in sapping even further the foundations of the liberal political order. The NPP government, while succeeding in negotiating with foreign lenders a repayment strategy,[81] had to face the decision of implementing the highly unpopular budgetary cuts known as the 'sacrifice curves' affecting primarily the personnel servicing state-owned companies, such as the railway services, refineries and mines.[82] Strikes followed, first in the extractive sectors, and then in the railways.[83] In response, the government declared the state of siege and called in the Army to quell the revolts. The outcome of the repression was seven deaths and

---

78 Constantin Iordachi, 'God's Chosen Warriors: Romantic Palingenesis' in Constantin Iordachi (ed.), *Comparative Fascist Studies: New Perspectives* (London: Routledge, 2010), 339.
79 Rebecca Haynes, 'Reluctant Allies?', 110.
80 Ornea, *The Romanian Extreme Right*, 25–31.
81 League of Nations, Agreement establishing an advisory technical cooperation in Romania, 28 January 1933.
82 'La situation économique et financière' in Ministère des Affaires Etrangères, *Bulletin périodique de la presse roumaine: du 2 février au 18 mars 1933*, No. 111, 25 March 1933, 5–7.
83 Ibid., 4.

tens of wounded on the side of the strikers,[84] and marked a clear line of continuity in the executive's response to the social crisis, despite the assurances made by the NPP of ruling within the confines of the Constitution. What makes the February repression the watershed in the series of measures signaling a clear inscription of the state apparatus within an authoritarian trajectory, is not only the level of violence, but the very perception that the institution of the state of siege was grounded fundamentally on political concerns, rather than actual threats.[85]

The parliamentary debates over the authorization of the state of siege for a period of 6 months indicate a shared sense of disarray within the ranks of the democratic opposition and a keen awareness of the gravity of the situation.[86] The debates paint a vivid image of a polity facing the economic and social maelstrom of the interwar period. The central place occupied by both the dire financial situation and the exercise of sovereign power bring to the fore the main divisions within the construction of legality and democracy and open the Romanian context to a transnational analysis. It is indeed worth noting that the debate in the Romanian Parliament took place just weeks before the Reichstag fire decree in Germany, and was echoing the politico-legal intricacies of the use of the infamous Article 48 of the Weimar Constitution, constantly reported in Romanian newspapers.[87]

Once the left-wing agitation was quelled and the leaders of the communist movement were brought before martial courts in a trial counting no less than one hundred defendants,[88] the state directed its efforts towards combating the fascist threat. At first, this was done still reluctantly as the King was hoping for a rapprochement with the fascist movement in order to increase his power base. Thus, in April 1933 the NPP government led by Alexandru Vaida Voevod instructed the police to curb ultranationalist propaganda with the intention to limit the fascists' exposure during the campaign for the elections in December.[89]

---

84 Sandra Halperin, *War and Social Change in Modern Europe* (Cambridge: Cambridge University Press, 2004), 196.
85 Corneliu Pintilescu, 'Dezbateri publice privind decretarea stării de asediu', (2018) 57 *Anuarul Institutului de Istorie «George Barițiu» din Cluj-Napoca* 303 at 315–18.
86 Chamber of Representatives, Plenary Meeting of 3 February 1933, *M. Of.*, Part III, No. 32, 9 February 1933.
87 'Mr Hitler asks the Reichstag for exceptional measures', *Adevărul*, No. 2 February 1933, 5.
88 Elis Neagoe-Pleșa, 'Gheorghe Gheorghiu-Dej și "procesul ceferiștilor" (1933–1934)' in Adrian Cioroianu (ed.), *Comuniștii înainte de comunism* (Bucharest: Editura Universității București, 2019) 169–256.
89 Clark, *Holy Legionary Youth*, 99.

The Legion, now operating under the name The Iron Guard, responded by terror and overt attacks on state authorities.[90] The caretaker government appointed by the King in November 1933, under the leadership of the National Liberal Ioan Gheorghe Duca, attempted a further move against the fascist Iron Guard by dissolving it on December 9th in order to prevent its participation in the elections.[91] In retaliation, the Guardists assassinated the prime minister on December 29th.

This acceleration of historical and social tensions towards an even further presence of military and security concerns in the administration of justice, while certainly legitimate in reaction to the terror campaign unleashed by the Iron Guard, nonetheless left its traces on the deeper constitutional framework. Let us recall here the fact that the trial of Duca's assassins was entrusted to a military tribunal as a result of the declaration of the state of siege, even though the decree to this effect was enacted *after* the prime minister's death.[92] The obvious retrospective application of the rules of procedure with regard to the jurisdiction *ratione temporis* is indicative of the symbolic intricacies of the recourse to extraordinary measures insofar as for the new uses of legality, neither time, nor space can act as symbolic limits to state repression.

To be sure, neither the state of siege, nor political violence were specific Romanian features of the interwar experience. From the Brest trials in Poland, to the Reichstag fire in Berlin, or the assassination of King Alexander of Yugoslavia, the early 1930s were already witnessing a first wave of political unrest. What is of particular interest in this dynamic is the minute accumulation of political tension and the drift of legality towards new uses of an authoritarian kind. While the state reaction was determined by the brutal actions of the fascist movement, it was nonetheless disrupting the already shaky constitutional foundations of the state. In its search to reassert sovereignty, the shaky and limited liberal consensus was dissolving.

For instance, as part of the government's attempt to curb fascist violence, the state of siege was once again instituted in 1934,[93] and a Statute for the defense of order within the state was passed in April that year.[94] But the position of state authorities and political actors continued to be

---

90   Ibid., 100–103.
91   Ibid., 103.
92   Pantelimonescu, *Starea de asediu*, 50–54.
93   Statute concerning the State of Siege of 16 March 1934, *M.Of.* No. 63, 17 March 1934.
94   Statute for the defense of order within the State of 6 April 1934, *M.Of.*, No. 82, 7 April 1934.

ambivalent towards the Iron Guard. The newly appointed liberal government under the maverick Gheorghe Tătărescu was taking a rather appeasing stand, authorizing the Legion to congregate in Târgu Mureș and rebrand itself as a new party under the name All for the Country.

The King himself was still a contributor to the 'Friends of the Legion,' a charity supporting the Iron Guard movement,[95] and did not even attend the funeral of I.G. Duca.[96] It is only in 1935 that a clear rift between King Carol II and the fascist Iron Guard intervened, allegedly as a result of the attacks of the movement against the King's entourage.[97]

Towards a New Legality

At this stage it is important to note the general tendency in the historiography of the Romanian interwar period to put forward psychological or biographical details as explanations for central events of this period. Not only is Carol II depicted as a power-thirsty monarch,[98] with an eccentric life-style and an obvious attraction towards corruption,[99] but these traits serve as explanations for major political shifts as well as for constitutional trends. For instance, Carol's relation with various political forces, from the NPP to the Iron Guard, is depicted in terms of exploitation and manipulation.[100]

Yet, such frames of reading Carol's regime and his rise to power as a dictator simply act as stop-gaps for a deeper understanding of the processes through which the state's liberal legal and constitutional armature was reversed and ultimately transformed. While for the Legionary movement the monarchy had continuously occupied an important ideological trope that was central to their strategy of legitimation, from this moment on the figure of the King would become secondary. This position was amplified by a starker denouncement of the state's authority, which was now challenged not only in its exercise, but as a matter of principle as well.

As a result of this conflict, the Legionary movement affirmed its claim to sovereignty, which was reactionary and contained an anti-systemic core. For his part, Carol's opposition to the fascist movement,

---

95 Rebecca Haynes, 'Germany and the Establishment of the Romanian National Legionary State, September1940', (1999) 77 *Slavonic and East European Review* 700, 705–706.
96 Clark, *Holy Legionary Youth*, 105.
97 Haynes, 'Reluctant Allies?', 111.
98 Payne, *A History of Fascism*, 71.
99 Paul D. Quinlan, *The Playboy King*: *Carol II of Romania* (Westwood: Greenwood Press, 1995).
100 Haynes, 'Reluctant Allies?', 109; Hitchins, *Rumania, 1866–1947*, 416–17.

opportunistic as it might have been, is indicative of a deeper ideological tension with the anti-systemic core of the movement. This does not take the form of an unequivocal refusal of the anti-Semitism engrained in the Legion's ideology and project, and Carol's flirting with fascism should say enough about his commitment to the liberal universalism protected by the 1923 Constitution. As Constantin Iordachi suggests, within this struggle is a conflict between two forms of legitimation, 'caesarism' on the side of the monarch and 'charismatic fascism' on that of the Legionaries.[101]

It is worth noting that within the Romanian Parliament of 1935, there were a number of avowed anti-Semitic parties, with an explicit goal of devising policies directed against citizens of Jewish origins. Such was the case of the National-Christian Defence League (LANC), as well as of the National Agrarian Party (PNA).[102] These parties were acting under the cover of legality, which indicates the extent to which the political system was accommodating such a position. Carol's opposition to the Legion was related to an ideological emphasis on law and order and the rejection of the anti-establishment features supported by the Legionary ideology.

The trope of national unity under the law should be read as an element of organic ideology disregarding class opposition and aimed at rallying the people around the King. Its emergence as a feature of the official ideology started well before the enactment of the Constitution of 1938. The Sentinel of the Motherland, an organization purporting to offer youth the necessary frames for a disciplined education within the values of the country, was founded in 1935.[103]

The adoption of the new Criminal Code in 1936 is not mere marginal to the regime of power set out by the King. As a matter of law, the Code was officially entitled the 'Code Carol II.'[104] Such an imprint connected directly the person of the King to the legislative framework set out for grounding state repression and for defining the meaning of legality, as well as for drawing the limits of permissibility within the boundaries of the state and beyond. The new Code integrated as a matter of principle the changes brought by the repressive legislation passed in 1924 and 1933, primarily directed against left-wing movements. Along these lines,

---

101 Constantin Iordachi, 'A Continuum of Dictatorships: Hybrid Totalitarian Experiments' in A Costa Pinto and A Kallis (eds), *Rethinking Fascism and Dictatorship in Europe* (Basingstoke, Palgrave Macmillan, 2014), 248.
102 PA Shapiro, 'Prelude to Dictatorship in Romania: the National Christian Party in Power, December 1937–February 1938', (1974) 8 *Canadian-American Slavic Studies* 45–88.
103 Iordachi, 'A Continuum of Dictatorships', 252.
104 Statute on naming the Codes for unifying legislation of 26 March 1936, *M. Of.*, 27 March 1936.

it challenged classical concepts of legal certainty by criminalizing preparatory acts before any attempt at commission. Significantly, it set both the constitutional and social order at the core of its structure and function.

But while this grounding of power in and through the mechanisms of the law was taking place with important symbolic and social consequences, there were other factors accelerating the dissolution of the status quo. The growing dependency of Romanian trade on Germany,[105] as well as the increasing worldwide tension brought about by the Italian aggression of Ethiopia and the German remilitarization of the Rheinland raised new challenges to the institutional arrangements that supported the existent constitutional framework. The year 1936 witnessed a significant shift in Romania's foreign politics of conciliation towards Moscow and a visible retreat from the traditional politics of the Little Entente.[106] While still following the British and French position as a matter of principle,[107] Romania refused the possibility of a non-aggression pact with the Soviet Union as part of the French-Soviet Treaty of Mutual Assistance. Faced with Germany's rising claims to becoming a major power again, the King and the Romanian ruling elite fell captive to an ideological framework that placed the threat of Bolshevism as a quasi-existential threat to the sovereignty of the polity. This position pervaded the state's actions at national and international levels and fuelled the judgment that right-wing extremism was ultimately something that could have been accommodated, or at least less of a menace.

This stand was to some extent consistent with the ideological postulates described above: whereas Soviet Russia was unwilling to recognise Romania's rights over Bessarabia, and subsequently rendered the Eastern border uncertain, Germany had no direct claims over any Romanian territories.[108] Therefore, the new direction guiding foreign policy was to secure a rapprochement towards Germany within the framework of the existing treaties, based primarily on commercial cooperation.

It is against this background that the 1937 elections debacle should be read. The final act of whatever was left of Romanian liberal legality was played within a relatively calm atmosphere. Reorganised as a new party, but holding to the same ideological creeds, the Legionary movement embraced a legalistic strategy.[109] Posturing a law-abiding attitude and a

---

105 Rebecca Haynes, *Romanian Policy towards Germany, 1936–1940* (Basingstoke, Palgrave Macmillan, 2000), 21.
106 Ibid., 6.
107 Ibid., 20.
108 Ibid., 22.
109 Clark, Holy Legionary Youth, 211.

provisional return to its initial veneer of respectability, it entered a pact with the main parliamentary parties, the NPP and the National Liberals.[110]

For their part, the established politicians did not find any impediment in negotiating with a reactionary, anti-Semitic and antidemocratic movement that even contemplated a revolutionary seizure of power, if necessary.[111] To their discredit, neither did the radical left led by the illegal Communist Party, which emphasized the threat to the working class raised by the King. The pact was nothing more than an agreement aiming to put an end to violence during the electoral campaign and assure that the elections take place free of undue interference.

The election ended up in a stand-still, with the Iron Guard in third place, following the NLP and NPP.[112] Given the electoral bonus system introduced in 1926, with no party able to pass the required threshold for claiming the redistribution of seats, there was no winner and no government to be formed as a result of the elections. In an attempt to break this deadlock, the King, making use of his powers granted by a lax interpretation of Article 93 of the Constitution, named Octavian Goga as Prime Minister and entrusted him with the task of forming a caretaker government in preparation for the snap elections planned for March 1938.[113] The Romanian nationalist poet, formed as a politician in the tense atmosphere of the last years of the Austro-Hungarian Empire, guilty of anti-Semitism and xenophobia,[114] was a telling choice for the King's political positioning.

Even if Goga's faction, the National Christian Party was ranked only the fourth in the elections, its anti-Semitic and pro-German stand made it a likely competitor to the fascist All for the Country. The NCP was the result of a merger between Goga's National Agrarian Party, originally a minor pro-monarchist conservative movement that veered more on the path of anti-Semitism, and the League of National and Christian Defence (LNCD), one of the oldest ultranationalist movements in Romania, under the leadership of A.C. Cuza. To be sure, Carol II was not supporting wholeheartedly this government, however it deemed it fit to rule the country and to curb the rise of the fascist Iron Guard. There was an undeniable symbolic dimension pertaining to the new government's outlook and membership. The pro-German position shared by both the Prime Minister and the minister of foreign affairs, Istrate Micescu, was a clear signal that

---

110 Haynes, 'Reluctant Allies?', 115–17; Clark, *Holy Legionary Youth*, 214.
111 Haynes, 'Reluctant Allies?', 116.
112 Hitchins, *Rumania 1866–1947*, 420.
113 Shapiro, 'Prelude to Dictatorship', 70–71.
114 Ibid., 49.

Romania wanted to move even further away from its traditional policy of supporting the international status-quo.

Following this path, the legislation passed in January 1938 seeking to revise the citizenship of Romanians of Jewish origins appears as an important moment within the series of attacks against the 1923 liberal constitutional framework. Under the guise of clarifying citizenship, the decree-law issued by the King at the proposal of the Prime-Minister targeted Jews who had acquired citizenship after 1918.[115]

The procedure instituted by this legislation was nothing short of a *probatio diabolica*. It required Romanian citizens of Jewish origin to prove once again their citizenship in relation to an outdated legislation. Beyond the technicalities of this legislation was a clear attack on the core principle of the Constitution securing equality before the law and prohibiting discrimination on religious grounds.

The decree law closed an arch through time, as Article 7 had been a matter of contestation and discord from the time of its drafting. At that time, no other than A.C. Cuza, Goga's close collaborator, was organizing the dissent to this constitutional provision.[116] Furthermore, the indirect attack on this constitutional protection under the guise of a mere clarification of status is indicative of the uncertain legal protections offered to Romanian citizens of Jewish origin, as well as of the tensions between constitutional guarantees and the legal and administrative levels supporting the exercise of these rights. It is important to note that Jews were singled out explicitly by this procedure, and they had to prove a status that they had already been granted according to the law. While local administrative authorities were entrusted to devise territorial lists with Jews struck by these provisions, the judiciary was given the final say.[117]

Both the application of the law and its echoes were a fiasco. Internally, the law faced the staunch resistance of the Jewish community, who 'boycotted work and withdrew their money from the banks.'[118] For its part, France threatened to consider itself relieved of any guarantees towards Romania if the policy was pursued. Both Britain and the United States stressed their dissatisfaction with Romanian non-compliance with the Minorities Protection Treaty.[119] Faced with these reactions, the

---

115 Royal Decree concerning the revision of citizenship of 21 January 1938, *M. Of.*, 22 January 1938.
116 Clark, *Holy Legionary Youth*, 29–31.
117 Article 13–Article 19, Royal Decree concerning the revision of citizenship of 21 January 1938.
118 Haynes, *Romanian Policy towards Germany*, 46.
119 Shapiro, 'Prelude to Dictatorship', 74.

government decided to step back. While this prologue to the racial policies of the Romanian state ended up in failure, it already underlined the willingness of state officials to break with the deeper layers supporting the constitutional order and certainly emphasized that liberal legality was no longer part of the consensus. Rather, owing to the new ideological turn, a new consensus was emerging.

In a final attempt to muster support for the snap-elections that he was hoping to win, Goga entered an agreement with Codreanu. After all, as both anti-Semites and pro-Germans, there was room for a united front against the last remnants of liberalism. Consequently, the Iron Guard decided to abstain from participating in the electoral campaign.[120]

However, the agreement antagonized the King. Rumours of Soviet troops being massed across the Eastern border,[121] as well as an increasingly strained relation with the USSR, pressured Carol to act. First, he asked Goga to cancel the elections, which the latter refused. The King then asked and accepted his resignation. On February 10th, the Goga government resigned. This opened the path for the King to start his own 'royal revolution.'[122]

Beyond Liberal Legality

The change of regime took the form of communications addressed by the King to the country followed by a series of decrees that opened the way to the proclamation of the new constitution.

The new chief of government was Patriarch Miron Cristea, the Head of the Romanian Orthodox Church. Symbolically, the state was retreating to a pre-modern polity in which the distinction between temporal political power and pastoral religious vocation was effectively blurred.[123] In his Proclamation to the Country, the King presented his task as a rescue mission: 'Romania needs to be saved and I am decided to do it.'[124] The 'spiritual trouble' befalling the country was due to the 'constituted political organizations,' which through their electoral politics brought a 'ceaseless perturbation (...) both in the life and the soul of [the] people.'[125] The King's

---

120 Ibid., 83–84.
121 Ibid., 85.
122 'Le premier ministère Miron Cristea', Ministère des Affaires Etrangères, *Bulletin périodique de la presse roumaine: du 9 février au 28 avril 1938*, No. 92, 17 May 1938, 8.
123 Iordachi, 'A Continuum of Dictatorships', 244.
124 'Le premier ministère Miron Cristea', 8.
125 Ibid., 7.

pledge was to put an end to 'this dangerous state of affairs.'[126] The task of the new government was to 'de-politicize the administrative and economic life of the state.'[127] The proclamation ended emphatically with the promise to lay down the supreme law, which was 'the salvation of the country.'[128]

Echoing the proclamation, the following day the state of siege was declared on the whole territory of the country, instituting once again the jurisdiction of military authorities in matters related to public order, state security and political crimes.[129] A minor, albeit significant, feature distinguished this decree from prior ones, as it did not provide a time limit for the exercise of these extraordinary powers. Article VI stated: 'the state of siege prescribed by this decree shall end when it will be considered appropriate.'[130]

It is under these conditions that on February 20th the new Constitution was issued and later submitted to a plebiscite. According to the Proclamation, the Constitution was deemed to establish 'decidedly the primacy of the Romanian Nation which through its sacrifices and faith has created [the] national State.'[131] The Constitution also aimed to assure 'a fairer representation of the (...) productive factors' by recourse to a corporatist model, devised to keep away 'the dangerous outcomes of political troubles.'[132] Lastly, the new Constitution aimed to 'assure an equal justice to all the people of another race which were present for centuries on the soil of the united Romania.'[133] The Constitution was presented as a document 'that answered the legitimate exigencies of national necessities.'[134] It asserted in a decisive manner the supremacy of the executive over the legislative, while granting the King a central role within the functioning of the state.

The King was identified as the Head of the State, which was reminiscent of the formulation used in the 1866 Constitution. However, as constitutionalists noted, the use of this formula was not a mere restatement, but 'signifies that the King is not only a symbol, and that he also has a role in governing, of providing indications that have to be established under

---

126 Ibid., 8.
127 Ibid.
128 Ibid.
129 Royal Decree No. 856, *M.Of.*, No. 34, 11 February 1938.
130 Ibid.
131 Proclamation, *M.Of.*, No. 42, 20 February 1938.
132 Ibid.
133 Ibid.
134 Aurelién Ionasco, 'La nouvelle constitution roumaine', (1939) 68 *Bulletin de la Société de Legislation Comparée* 345 at 345

the form of binding norms.'[135] Furthermore, Article 31, with its ambiguous formulation 'the legislative power is exercised by the King through the National Representation,' served as a basis for an interpretation of the King's powers as 'an unique legislative organ.'[136]

Under the rules of the new Constitution, the monarch was able to legislate both in his own right and through the mediation of the chambers. Interpreting the powers of the King in this context, a contemporary author noted that 'by his participation in all the powers of the state he reunites in his hand (...) all these powers. He represents their link and is the symbol of the organic unity of the state.'[137] Moving away from the position defended by the former Constitution, the new fundamental law took away the obligation of the Assemblies to reunite and function on a fixed day. The King had thus 'an absolute right' to convoke the legislative bodies. The only limitation to the exercise of this right consisted in the duty to issue such a convocation once every year.

Article 45 of the Constitution also instituted the King's right to dissolve both the Senate and the Chamber of Deputies. This right was balanced only by a condition setting out the duty to convoke new elections, but without setting any temporal limits to this end. In fact, the Constitution granted the King the power to dissolve the representative bodies at his own leisure. The primacy of the King over the national assemblies was furthered by the provisions of Article 31, which asserted the King's power of legislative initiative, while limiting the latter's power to matters related to the 'public interest of the state.'[138] In addition to this, the King retained an exclusive right to initiate a revision of the Constitution, which was limited only by a duty to consult the representative bodies on the provisions that were to be subjected to change.

The King had unsurprisingly retained all the traditional constitutional prerogatives specific to the executive power, such as naming and revoking ministers, exercising grace and punishment reduction, and being the Head of the Army. However, he was also granted the right to declare war and conclude peace, as well as to conclude international agreements. It was only on commercial and non-military matters that the King's decisions were to be brought under the scrutiny and approval of the Representative Assembly.

---

135 A Tilman-Timon, *Les actes constitutionnels en Roumanie de 1938 à 1944* (Bucharest, Imprimerie Cugetarea, 1947); A Rădulescu, *Noua Constituție* 2nd ed. (Bucharest, Cuvântul Românesc, 1939), 12, 39.
136 Paul Negulescu, *Principiile fundamentale ale constituției din 27 februarie 1938* (Bucharest, Atelierele Zanet Corlățeanu, 1939), 90.
137 Rădulescu, *Noua constituție*, 39.
138 Art. 31, The Constitution of Romania of 1938.

In exercising his executive prerogatives, the King was also issuing decrees, which had force of law, subject to ratification by the Parliament. Moreover, given the specific historic conditions of the adoption of the Constitution in the absence of a Parliament, the King was granted the power to issue decrees with force of law, obviously not subjected to ratification.[139]

In order to conclude the analysis of the monarchical institution, it is important to note the suppression of the provisions present in the former constitutional text stating that all King's powers were grounded in the Constitution.[140] Such a disappearance was not a mere omission. Through it, the very nature of the new constitutional regime is revealed, as the King can also exercise powers which are not explicitly attributed by the Constitution and can therefore escape any form of constitutional scrutiny.

There is little doubt that the 1938 Constitution instituted a formal authoritarian regime. Its core provisions, related to the powers of the King, were articulating legally and symbolically the pre-eminence of the King as a sovereign constitutional subject at the expense of the reduced electoral body. For their part, representative authorities were simply limited both legally and practically to being a subsidiary legislative, merely complementing the unique legislative power granted to the King. While the Constitution continued to attest formally that 'all the powers of the state emanate from the Romanian Nation,'[141] this provision should be read in relation to the fact that it was now the King, not the National Assemblies, who symbolized the unity of the Romanian nation.[142]

It is significant that the Constitution starts by introducing the duties of Romanian citizens towards the country. These duties were considered to precede their rights, at least symbolically and within the economy of the constitutional framework. The Nation itself is less of a political community based on citizens endowed with fundamental rights, and more of a cultural if not yet ethnic community organized around the Fatherland. As the article opening the Constitution states: 'all Romanians regardless of their ethnic origin and religious faith, have the duty to consider the Fatherland as the most important ground of their being.'[143] The citizens are no longer individuals exercising rights attested by the Constitution, but subjects of the State,

---

139 Rădulescu, *Noua constituție*, 43.
140 The Constitution of Romania of the 28 March 1923 art. 91; Ionasco, 'La nouvelle constitution roumaine' 359.
141 Art. 21, The Constitution of Romania of 20 February 1938.
142 Rădulescu, *Noua constituție*, 39–40.
143 Art. 4, The Constitution of Romania of 20 February 1938.

which owe duties to the 'organic Nation.' As subjects, they cannot preach, let alone engage in 'the distribution of wealth of others (...) or class struggle.'[144]

These duties are compensated by the traditional list of fundamental rights and freedoms, such as the freedom of thought, freedom of press and assembly, as well as rights to privacy. Moreover, electoral rights are granted to women for the first time in Romanian constitutional history,[145] yet one should keep in mind that political parties were dissolved. Even traditional rights were limited by the uncertainty reigning over the subjects bearing them. For instance, the clause introducing the list of rights, that is 'regardless of ethnic origin and religious faith,' had been supressed.[146] Consequently, equality before the law was construed within the new regime only as a matter of duties, rather than rights.

This position becomes legible against the background of the former anti-Semitic legislation devised under the Goga government, and opened the possibility to create a fracture within the political community. As subjects of the state, the link with the public institutions is created through duties, while the full exercise of rights became the privilege of an uncertain category of citizens. In this reversion of classical constitutional concepts, we witness both the emergence of novel forms of articulating the polity, specific to the authoritarian wave of the interwar period, as well as echoes from the previous century.

The core attributions of the King as Head of State and Head of Army, doubled by its legislative and executive attributions, erase the classical separation of powers and blur distinctions between administration and legislation. Moreover, they reveal a deeper historical homonymy between these activities that liberal legality struggled to overcome in Romania during the second half of the 19th century. It is not by mistake that the Constitution of 1938 was compared by historians with the Organic Regulations—the early constitution instituted by Russia as a Protecting Power in the 1830s.[147]

Conclusion

In its content and substance, the Constitution of 1938 represents a regression to a legal state that is resolutely anti-liberal, if not entirely anti-modern. Through it, a return to the traditional constituents of power—military, political and administrative—which were features of pre-modern

---

144 Art. 7, Ibid.
145 Art. 61, Ibid.
146 Tilman-Timon, *Les actes constitutionnels en Roumanie de 1938 à 1944*, 28.
147 Vlad Georgescu, *Romanians: A History* (A Bley-Vorman trans) (Columbus: Ohio State University Press, 1991) 207.

monarchs, was reinstituted. However, this regression took place in a very different political, cultural and social context than that of the early 19th century. It is thus a reconstruction of the already modern texture of legality and attempts to overcome it. In this sense, it is an attempt at going beyond the liberal horizon by restating the unlimited power of the sovereign and by organizing the country around corporatist principles.

Carol's regime found its end in September 1940, in the wake of a series of territorial cessions to the Soviet Union and Hungary. The fascist movement pressured for his abdication and the King abdicated the throne once again, granting full powers to the military dictator Marshal Ion Antonescu. In the months before his abdication, the royal dictatorship was transformed through a decree in a totalitarian state. A further decree bearing on the Status of the Jews was passed, depriving the Jewish population of their rights. The full reversal of liberal legality was thus achieved. As this historical analysis tried to underline, the main jurisprudential conundrum at the core of the path towards dictatorship is whether a transformation took place, or Carol's regime simply realized the authoritarian potential already at work in the existing legal arrangements. Given the inherent limitations of liberal legality and the contingent political choices affecting its existence, the second seems to be the more appropriate answer.

Indeed, to put it in Althusser's jargon, the ideological state apparatuses supporting the liberal project of universal rights, in their tension with the military repressive and ideological apparatus, were not able to transform the core of the constitutional discourse. Rather, the liberal understanding of the polity was constantly shadowed by the representation of the country as an object of security, military and economic concern that had to be saved from internal and external enemies. Under the strain of the Great Depression and changes in international politics, this deeply seated construction of the nation prevailed.

What seems important to note as a provisional conclusion of this historical excursus is that the authoritarian ideological tropes were not external to the legal discourse, rather they were central to its legitimation and acted from within as a positive antinomy to the liberal and emancipatory potential of the law. The general dissolution of the Versailles consensus and the turn towards a new geopolitical order, which became stark in the wake of the Munich Agreement, determined further levels of tension within the constitutional apparatus that could no longer be contained. Such a trajectory could perhaps serve as a reminder of the nefarious consequences of an under-analysis of the legal discourse as a foundational structure of liberal democracy. Furthermore, in light of the current populist turn and the manifold reactions to the global pandemic that have entailed a resurgence of exceptional measures and explicit uses of the state of emergency, the example of law under Carol II is useful to highlight the areas of constitutional law, of legal praxis and legal education, as well as public uses of legal tropes that expose fault lines within the rule of law.

Perceptions of Legality during the Antonescu Regime, 1940–1944*

Ștefan Cristian Ionescu

Abstract: *This article examines how legality was perceived by the highest officials of Romania's pro-Nazi Ion Antonescu regime and by a group of intellectuals (mostly jurists) closely connected with the judiciary. For Antonescu, legality meant a new type of authoritarian understanding of the role of the law in a state and its subordination to the will of the ruler; for him, legality mainly had an instrumental role. He understood his power to be discretionary and, usually, not bound by the extant law, even though he sometimes referred to the idea of constitutional order (a convenient source of legitimacy). Intellectuals, including jurists, harbored a diversity of opinions regarding legality. Some jurists supported the regime's authoritarian legalism, or at least accepted it, while others, especially those with a more democratic mindset or belonging to minorities, perceived legality differently than Antonescu, and favored a liberal democratic version of legality involving the rule of law.*

Introduction

During World War II (henceforth, WWII) Romanian dictator General Ion Antonescu headed a regime that pursued its own genocidal program by targeting various groups of "enemies" (especially Jews) and producing the largest number of Holocaust victims after its Axis partner, Nazi Germany. At the same time, Antonescu claimed that he respected legality and constitutional rights and, sometimes, permitted an autonomous judiciary to rule in favor of the Jews and other persecuted individuals and groups. This paradoxical status of legality in Antonescu's Romania and the citizens' perceptions of it remain an under-researched and controversial

---

* The research for this article was supported by a grant of the Romanian National Authority for Scientific Research, UEFISCDI, grant PN-III-P1-1.1-TE-2016-0091, no. 5/2018, Transcultural Networks in Narratives about the Holocaust in Eastern Europe. Theodore Zev and Alice R. Weiss-Holocaust Educational Foundation Visiting Associate Professor in Holocaust Studies at Northwestern University. I am very grateful to the editors of this special issue, Mihaela Serban and Monica Ciobanu, the journal editor, Peter Gross, and the anonymous peer reviewers for their helpful comments and suggestions.

topic in the history of WWII dictatorships.[1] The examination of how legality was seen by Antonescu's highest officials and by a group of intellectuals (mostly jurists)[2] closely connected with the judiciary is doubly significant. On the one hand, such a study would deepen our historical understanding of how this dictatorship functioned in its specific time. On the other hand, it might offer broader insights on how *authoritarian legality*—the concept popularized by scholars such as Anthony W. Pereira and Jose Toharia—is envisioned and constructed by dictators during a period of crisis and how intellectuals/jurists perceive such actions and how they might respond to authoritarianism.[3] My understanding of legality relies on lawfulness as a set of rules that require a state's legal provisions to be clear, public, and non-retroactive. It simultaneously implies that the decision makers resolve the conflicts affecting their society by implementing the existing legal rules while refraining from the use of discretionary power to influence the laws and the result of such conflicts, and accepting some form of accountability. As Mihaela Șerban has recently argued in her book on property in communist Romania, for most types of repressive regimes legality provides not only a useful tool of governance that separates law from morality and allows repression, but also provides political legitimacy, while simultaneously allowing citizens a "space for resistance" and

---

1   There are numerous studies on legality in Nazi Germany, but only a few scholars have briefly explored some aspects of legality in WWII Romania. On Nazi Germany, see Alan E. Steinweis and Robert D. Rachlin (eds.), *The Law in Nazi Germany: Ideology, Opportunism, and the Perversion of Justice* (New York: Berghahn Books, 2013), Ingo Muller, *The Courts of the Thirds Reich* (Cambridge: Harvard University Press, 1992), Michael Stolleis, *The Law Under the Swastika: Studies of Legal History in Nazi Germany* (Chicago: University of Chicago Press, 1998); On Romania, see Dennis Deletant, *Hitler's Forgotten Ally: Ion Antonescu and His Regime, Romania, 1940-1944* (London: Palgrave Macmillan, 2006); Stefan Cristian Ionescu, *Jewish Resistance to 'Romanianization,' 1940-44* (Basingstoke: Palgrave Macmillan, 2015); Mihaela Serban, *Subverting Communism in Romania: Law and Private Property, 1945-1965* (Latham: Lexington Books, 2019).

2   Due to space limitation, from all the potential groups of citizens I chose to explore only the perceptions of legality among intellectuals/jurists at the side of examining the highest regime officials' perspective. The intellectuals recorded personal documents—diaries and memoirs (which, of course, have their own subjectivity)—about the WWII judiciary and frequently interacted with the system. Thus, they were able to have better insights on how legality functioned in Antonescu's Romania and due to their education and professional habits they were more inclined to write about their careers and lives.

3   See Anthony W. Pereira, *Authoritarianism and the Rule of Law in Brazil, Chile, and Argentina* (Pittsburg: University of Pittsburg Press, 2005); Jose Toharia, "Judicial Independence in an Authoritarian Regime: The Case of Contemporary Spain," *Law & Society Review*, Vol. 9. No. 3 (1975): 475-496.

for negotiating their rights.[4] Legality played almost similar roles in Antonescu's Romania.

During and after the war years, some intellectuals (mostly jurists) recorded in their diaries and memoirs their perceptions of legality during the Antonescu regime and their responses—active or passive, public or private—to the regime's avalanche of problematic laws and judicial practices. Based on ego-documents as well as official and archival documents, my article examines the Antonescu regime decision makers' views on legality (as usually reflected in the minutes of the government meetings) and the perceptions of gentile Romanian intellectuals—many of whom were legally trained—(as reflected in their diaries and memoirs) in respect to the status of legality between 1940 and 1944. In order to capture these eye-witnesses' views on legality, I chose from all its numerous aspects—impossible to be exhaustively covered here—to consider several of its crucial features. These are: the independence of courts and judges; the laws; the status of minority rights and particularly property rights (focusing on the largest and most discussed minority, the Jews); extra-judicial punishments.

First, I will explore the historical context of the Antonescu regime, followed by a discussion of the independence of courts and judges. Then, I will examine the perception of the laws and of the minority (Jewish) property rights. Lastly, I will scrutinize the perceptions of extra-judicial punishments.

Historical Background

The decline of the liberal legal framework—already fragile—started in the late 1920s and continued in the following decades aggravated by the traditions of anti-Semitism and ethno-nationalism and by the political and social turmoil plaguing interwar and WWII Romania. This was done mainly by establishing a state of exception, which meant a suspension of the rule of law and of the normal function of institutions in the name of national sovereignty and public good, and occurred during a period of time when the state faced real or imagined external and domestic crises and threats, which allowed various governments to restrict their citizens' rights and freedoms.[5] Recent scholarship illustrates this development. For

---

4   Șerban, *Subverting Communism*, 32.
5   On the state of exception "as a paradigm of government," used by governments or authoritarian leaders to increase their power, eliminate political opposition, suspend the rule of law, and limit, suspend, or revoke citizens' rights, see Giorgio Agamben, *State of Exception* (Chicago: University of Chicago Press, 2005).

example, Cosmin Sebastian Cercel has connected the emergence of violent ultra-nationalist groups—such as the Legion of the Archangel Michael (henceforth, the Legion) that later joined Antonescu during his first four months in power (September 1940–January 1941)—to the "confused legal situation created by the enactment of the state of exception."[6] Scholars such as Maria Bucur, Armin Heinen, Carol Iancu, Constantin Iordachi, Irina Livezeanu, Marius Turda, and Leon Volovici have shown how the problems of interwar Romania—among which one counts political violence, the spread of radical ideologies (xenophobia, anti-Semitism, fascism, racism, and eugenics), corruption, flawed modernization, the rise of non-democratic parties (such as the Legion and National Christian Party) and regimes (King Carol II's dictatorship)—chipped away the fragile liberal democracy.[7]

Coming to power in 1930, Carol II pursued a policy aiming to modernize the state and consolidate his personal power. To achieve the latter goal, he weakened the traditional parties and dismantled the country's rule of law system (especially between 1938 and 1940). During that time, Carol II proclaimed himself a fascist-style dictator, banned all parties except his own National Renaissance Front (later on Party of the Nation), adopted a new authoritarian Constitution (1938), engaged in extrajudicial torture and killing of his Legionary adversaries (who challenged his regime mainly through violence), and a series of protectionist and discriminatory laws targeting foreigners and minorities, especially the Jews.[8]

Agamben's book is a response to Carl Schmitt's conceptualization of the state of exception. See Carl Schmitt, *Political Theology: Four Chapters on the Concept of l Sovereignty* (Chicago: University of Chicago Press, 2006).

6   Cosmin Sebastian Cercel, "The 'Right' Side of the Law. State of Siege and the Rise of Fascism in Interwar Romania," *Fascism: Journal of Comparative Fascist Studies*, 2 (2013): 227.

7   Maria Bucur, *Eugenics and Modernization in Interwar Romania* (Pittsburgh: University of Pittsburgh Press, 2001; Armin Heinen, *Legiunea 'Archanghelui Mihail'* (București: Humanitas, 1999); Carol Iancu, *Evreii din Romania: De la Emancipare la marginalizare, 1919–1938* (București: Hasefer, 2000); Constantin Iordachi, *Charisma, Politics, and Violence: The Legion of the "Archangel Michael" in Inter-war Romania* (Trondheim: Trondheim Studies on East European Cultures and Societies, 2004); Irina Livezeanu, *Cultural Politics in Greater Romania: Regionalism, Nation Building, and Ethnic Struggle: 1918–1930* (Ithaca and London: Cornell University Press, 1995); Marius Turda, *Eugenism și antropologie rasială în România, 1874–1944* (București: Cuvântul, 2008); Leon Volovici, *Nationalist Ideology and Antisemitism: The Case of Romanian Intellectuals in the 1930s* (Oxford: Pergamon Press, 1991).

8   On King Carol II's reign and his non-democratic and, especially, (inconsistent and ambivalent) antisemitic policy, see Jean Ancel, *The History of the Holocaust in Romania* (Lincoln: University of Nebraska Press, 2012), 25–50; Iancu, *Evreii din Romania*; Deletant, *Hitler's Forgotten Ally*, 8–36.

The rising ethno-nationalism and authoritarianism during the 1930s also affected the judiciary, including the courts and Bar associations, the majority of whose members embraced ethno-nationalism, anti-minority (especially anti-Semitic), and fascist ideas.[9] This trend was illustrated by the fact that many jurists—especially law school students and lawyers—supported the discrimination of the Jews and their exclusion from Bar associations and judicial courts, participated in the elaboration of anti-Semitic and authoritarian legislation and administrative measures (or at least accepted them), and joined fascist violence or showed leniency to fascist perpetrators.[10] Anti-Semitism became state policy from 1937 on, when Carol II appointed governments such as those led by Octavian Goga–A.C. Cuza and Ion Gigurtu, who adopted explicit anti-Semitic laws, including the Law for the Revision of Romanian Citizenship (1938) and the Decree Law for the Legal Status of Jewish Inhabitants (1940). In this context, the majority of judges were rather conservative and endorsed law and order and did not directly participate in physical violence, and a minority of them actively opposed it. Nevertheless, the relentless nationalist and fascist propaganda (that promised to resolve all the problems of the national community) and violence and the conservative organizational culture of the judiciary created an atmosphere of anti-Semitic and ethno-nationalist mobilization and a willingness to support, or at least to accept—in spite of their socialization under interwar democratic governments—radical "solutions" targeting the Jews and other enemies, especially during the Antonescu regime.[11]

When Carol II abdicated in favor of his son, Mihai, in September 1940, he suspended the 1938 Constitution and granted General Ion

---

9   Tuvia Friling, Radu Ioanid, and Mihail Ionescu (eds.), *Final Report* (Iasi: Polirom, 2004), 19–55.
10 On the participation of law students, lawyers and other jurists in fascist activism, see Mariana Conovici et al (eds.), *Tara, Legiunea, Capitanul: Miscarea legionara in documente de istorie orala* (Bucuresti: Humanitas, 2008); Alexandru Paleologu, *Sfidarea memoriei: Convorbiri cu Stelian Tanase* (Cluj-Napoca: Dacia, 2002); Nae Tudorica, *Marturisiri in duhul adevarului* 4 vols. (Bacau: Plumb, 1993); Nistor Chioreanu, *Morminte vii* (Iasi: Institutul European, 1992); on the lawyers' antisemitic violence in and outside the courtrooms and the judges' acceptance or indifference towards this violence, see Arnold Schwefelberg, *Amintirile unui intellectual evreu din România* (Bucuresti: Hasefer, 2000), 106–117; Wilhelm Filderman, *Memoirs and Diaries*, 2 vols. (Jerusalem: Yad Vashem, 2004, 2015); Friling et al. (eds.), *Final Report*, 19–55.
11 This evolution of Romanian judiciary somehow resembles the case of Chilean judiciary. As Lisa Hilbink has shown, the judges trained and appointed under democratic regimes significantly supported Pinochet's repressive military dictatorship. Lisa Hilbink, *Judges Beyond Politics in Democracy and Dictatorship: Lessons from Chile* (Cambridge: Cambridge University Press, 2007).

Antonescu full powers to rule the state. King Mihai I confirmed Antonescu as prime minister—through High Decree no. 30-72 of 7 September 1940—a document that increased Antonescu's powers and diminished the prerogatives of the Monarchy. Due to these changes, the constitutional basis of the Antonescu regime was ambiguous and controversial—"difficult to define" according to legal scholar Eleodor Focseneanu.[12] Overall, Antonescu continued the non-democratic tradition inaugurated by Carol II that curtailed local liberal democracy based on the state of exception and concentrated power in the hands of one dictator (leader).[13] Moreover, Antonescu went a step further from his (royal) authoritarian predecessor. While Carol II replaced the 1923 democratic Constitution with his own version of an authoritarian Constitution (from 1938, drafted by anti-Semitic lawyers such as Istrate Micescu)[14] and preserved the Parliament (yet one based on the one party system), Antonescu refrained from adopting a new Constitution and dismissed the Parliament and all political parties (except the Legion of the Archangel Michael, which quickly vanished after the failure of its January 1941 Rebellion against Antonescu). In what seems to be a legal approach inspired from legal theories of Nazi jurist Carl Schmitt, Antonescu ruled the country based on an authoritarian type of legality enforced through decree laws. Even though the 1938 Constitution was no longer operational, sometimes Antonescu invoked the Constitution and its principles to gain legitimacy and referred to the citizens' rights and the Constitution he planned to adopt.[15] While he came to power aiming to end the extrajudicial violence targeting political adversaries, the corruption and other abuses perpetrated by his authoritarian predecessor (Carol II), Antonescu himself employed (even more extensive) extrajudicial punishments, such as camp internment and execution, especially targeting Jews, Roma, and communists.

A few scholars have noticed this paradox of a dictatorship lacking a fundamental law in which the dictator sometimes invoked the Constitution and liberal democratic rights, while he was simultaneously conducting deportations, sending citizens to concentration camps and ghettos

---

12 Eleodor Focșeneanu, *Istoria Constituțională a României, 1859–1991* (București: Humanitas, 1998), chapter 6.
13 On the use of the state of exception in interwar Romania, see Cercel, "The Right Side of the Law."
14 Ioan Muraru, Gheorghe Iancu, *Constituțiile României* (București: Actami, 2000).
15 See, for instance, Marcel Dumitru-Ciucă et al. eds., *Stenogramele ședințelor Consiliului de Miniștri: Guvernarea Ion Antonescu*, vol. II (București: Arhivele Naționale, 1998), 380.

based on administrative decisions, and engaging in mass executions.[16] As legal scholar Barbu B. Berceanu has argued, in addition to a generic—in fact suspended—"Constitution," Antonescu also invoked legality and justice, including specific constitutional principles such as non-retroactivity of laws, guarantee of private property, maintaining the judicial control of the constitutionality of laws, and the non-interference of the executive into the judiciary.[17] However, significant parts of this legalistic rhetoric need to be regarded with suspicion because in practice the regime broke its much-publicized legal principles. As I will show later in my article, the idea of non-interference into the judiciary affairs, for instance, was not at all an absolute policy: the regime fired and moved judges, just as it attempted to influence the (sensitive) decisions of ordinary courts while controlling the military courts that dealt with most of the political cases, and it sent people to camps without (or against) a court decision or executed them *en masse*. Overall, rather than copying a typical fascist regime, such as Mussolini's Italy or Hitler's Germany, the status of legality in Antonescu's Romania resembled more the authoritarian legalism in the military conservative dictatorships of Spain, Chile, and Argentina as examined in the studies of Toharia and Pereira.[18] These similarities show that the typology of military dictatorship and its authoritarian legality transcends a narrow historical time and place and could function similarly in completely different societies such as WWII Romania and 1970s Spain and Latin America.

Perceptions of the Independence of Courts and Judges

Antonescu permitted the existence of relatively independent (autonomous) ordinary courts—as opposed to military courts—whose judges sometimes ruled against his government in cases that mostly lacked political implications, and often boasted publicly that he held honesty and legality in the highest esteem. He seemed to believe in law and order (as long as administering them conformed to his ideas about these concepts) and promised a just treatment for honest and loyal citizens, including loyal Jews (of the Old Kingdom) and minorities. Antonescu's view on the role of laws and the judiciary was one of the main reasons explaining the autonomy of the courts and the partial success of Jewish (and gentile)

---

16 Barbu B. Berceanu, *Istoria constituțională a României in Context Internațional* (București: Rosetti, 2003), 380–383, 402–403; Deletant, *Hitler's Forgotten Ally*.
17 Berceanu, *Istoria*, 383.
18 See Pereira, *Political Injustice*; Toharia, "Judicial Independence"; Deletant, *Hitler's Forgotten Ally*, 69–75.

court litigation and administrative petitioning against the regime's oppressive measures.[19] In spite of his public rhetoric, Antonescu did not have much respect for courts and judges and sometimes, especially at the beginning of his regime, fired unreliable judges and those suspected of supporting Carol II's controversial policies.[20]

The minutes of government meetings during his tenure in power offer useful insight into Antonescu's peculiar view of authoritarian legality, which emphasized, among other things, an autonomous but obedient ordinary court system and strict enforcement of severe and exemplary criminal punishments (especially by the military courts), the marginalization and discrimination of the Jews and other minorities, and extrajudicial punishments. During those meetings, Antonescu repeatedly complained about judges—especially from ordinary (civilian) courts—and their decisions that allegedly interfered with his ethno-nationalist policies. At the same time, he urged his Ministers and other officials to respect the laws and the courts' independence, but only to a certain extent. For example, on April 4, 1941, during a discussion with Constantin Stoicescu, the Minister of Justice, Antonescu emphasized his view of the separation between the judiciary and politics and supported the independence of the judiciary during the investigation of a bureaucrat suspected of corruption: "I do not interfere with the judiciary. You should decide as you like. This has no political implication."[21] This incident suggests that Antonescu viewed the much-invoked judiciary's independence in the sense that he should get involved in the judiciary's affairs only when political implications were at stake, and that his approach to legality resembled the one adopted by other military-conservative dictators, such as Franco and Pinochet.

Antonescu continued to muse on the issues of observing legality and the judiciary's independence. On December 16, 1941, Antonescu instructed the governors of Bukovina (Gen. Corneliu Calotescu), Bessarabia (Gen. Constantin G. Voiculescu), and Transnistria (Gheorghe Alexianu) to respect the independence of local judges to a certain extent during their administration of those provinces: "Naturally, you will not interfere in the

---

19   While the Jews of Nazi Germany, occupied countries, and Axis partners also tried to use petitions as a method to defend their rights, it seems that this type of non-armed resistance did not reach the same extent as in Romania. See Wolf Gruener and Thomas Peggelow Kaplan (eds.), *Resisting Persecution: Jews and Their Petitions during the Holocaust* (New York: Berghahn Books, 2020).
20   For example, Antonescu and his Legionary partners fired (in fall 1940) Andrei Rădulescu, the head of Romania's Supreme Court. Andrei Rădulescu, *Amintiri* (București: Editura Academiei Române, 1995).
21   Ciuca (ed.), *Stenogramele*, vol. 3, p. 74.

judges' decisions ... You don't have the right to appoint or remove a magistrate. If a magistrate opposes any of your decisions that aim to restore progress in those provinces ... then punish him and report him ... But if that man respects the technical instructions received from the center and fulfills his obligations, you cannot interfere."[22]

Sometimes Antonescu expressed his frustration with legal formalities that slowed down the ordinary court system and urged judges to speed up the procedures, as some jurists noted in their diaries. This was the case of Constantin Argetoianu, a former Prime Minister with a background in law and medicine, who recorded in his diary (on May 27, 1942) his conversation with a journalist who accompanied Antonescu on an inspection in Southern Bukovina. During a meeting with a local judge, Antonescu urged the judge "to resolve cases quickly and not to get caught in formalities."[23] This incident shows that Antonescu's publicized respect for judges' independence was not that genuine. In other instances, the regime pressured, fired, or moved judges.[24] This was the case in Timișoara, where the dean of the local bar association complained to the Prime Minister's Chancellery about the removal of "good magistrates."[25] Additionally, Antonescu often changed his mind, opinions, and decisions, and this affected the judiciary. In time, Antonescu started to believe that he allowed judges too much independence, which they allegedly abused by being too lenient with law offenders.[26]

Mihai Antonescu, the Deputy Prime Minister, the Minister of Foreign Affairs, and a professor of international law, was even more blunt about the government's initiatives to control the judiciary and boasted with his

---

22 See the minute of the 16 December 1941 government meeting, in Ciuca et. al (eds.), *Stenogramele*, vol. V, pp. 444–446.
23 Argetoianu, *Însemnări zilnice*, vol. X, 356.
24 According to historian Florin Muller, who consulted only the official publication *Monitorul Oficial*, Antonescu reorganized the court system and public prosecution offices in spring 1941 in order to establish an obedient body of magistrates. As a result, 53 magistrates were fired. Florin Muller, *Metamorfoze ale politicului românesc, 1938–1944* (București: Editura Universității din București, 2005), 327–328; see also the case recorded in the minute of the government meeting of September 4, 1943, Ciuca et. al (eds.), *Stenogramele*, vol. IX, p. 412.
25 In its response, the Ministry of Justice argued that only the incompetent and corrupt judges had been dismissed. Arhivele Naționale ale României (ANR), Președinția Consiliului de Miniștri (PCM)-Serviciul Special de Informații (SSI) 121/1939, pp. 229–230, 233–237.
26 See the case discussed during the May 13, 1943 government meeting, when Antonescu criticized judges for acquitting a corrupted bureaucrat and thus, abusing the independence he granted them. Ciuca and Ignat (eds.), *Stenogramele*, vol. IX, 225–226.

authoritarian approach to legality.[27] This was illustrated by his measures of dismantling the tenure of judges and purging the judiciary—by firing a third of all magistrates—allegedly to strengthen the judges' position, as he told his colleagues during a 1941 government meeting:

> For Magistrates the situation was more difficult because they had constitutional tenure, which transformed every magistrate into a public servant invested with a thick armor of rights ... I dismantled their tenure through the suspension of the Constitution ... And then the magistrates became just like other ordinary civil servants who, based on the Statute of Public Servants, are relying on the principle of stability—that is the right of the bureaucrat not to be removed from his office except after a disciplinary procedure ... By a previous law I suspended their stability ... today, from a legal point of view, all public servants are subordinated to the will of the government to decide their fate ... and I made the most radical purge of the Magistrature ... I asked all the supervisors and judiciary inspectors to evaluate each magistrate. Then we established a central commission of judges to assess ... My goal, after finishing this revision of the body of magistrates, was to strengthen the position of judges and give the reform a prestigious meaning ... I can assure you that due to the harshness I implemented at the MJ concerning the quality of magistrates—I reduced the number of judges by one third.[28]

Paradoxically, in time, Ion Antonescu, the military dictator and non-jurist, grew more flexible concerning the issue of the stability of judges and more understanding towards their private life circumstances, as he explained to his ministers in fall 1941: "Ion Antonescu: What should we do with the tenure of judges? Should we still keep them in uncertainty? C. Stoicescu: Yes, because we have not decided yet the number of judges that we will send to the liberated provinces ... Antonescu: We have to end with this threat that looms over the head of all civil servants. Each of them has a family, hardships ... I suspended this tenure of judges ... only temporarily."[29] Indeed, in October 1941, Antonescu reestablished the judges' tenure.[30] However, this did not mean the end of the regime's interference into the judiciary.

Antonescu's and the Legionaries' measure of abolishing the judges' tenure system in 1940, aiming to remove undesirable judges, created

---

27 Mihai Antonescu taught international law at the Commercial Academy, the University of Bucharest Law School, and the Gendarmes' Officer School. He played a crucial role in the regime's legislative policy, especially in the promotion of Romanianization, which was the local equivalent of Nazi Aryanization and envisioned the transfer of Jewish wealth to ethnic Romanians, in other words it was a form of economic nationalism on the domestic front.
See the May 9, 1941 government meeting minutes, in Ciuca (ed.), *Stenogramele*, vol. III, pp. 356, 374.
28 Ciuca (ed.), *Stenogramele*, vol. III, pp. 382–4.
29 Ciuca (ed.), *Stenogramele*, vol. IV, p. 666.
30 See Law no. 947 of October 25, 1941.

uncertainty among those who stayed in the profession. For a while—before tenure was re-established in October 1941—these changes allowed Antonescu and his collaborators to radically influence judges and their decisions, and many worried legal professionals noted these non-democratic attempts to suppress the independence of the judiciary. For example, Supreme Court judge Constantin I. Navarlie recorded in his diary the authorities' initiatives of controlling the judiciary by limiting the independence of magistrates especially through the suspension of tenure. An experienced magistrate with more than three decades of professional activity, Navarlie confided in his diary (in fall 1944) that every non-democratic regime that ruled Romania after 1938 suspended the judges' tenure. He noted how that had happened three times over the previous six years:

> So far, the tenure had been suspended for three times in several years—even though it is a constitutional principle—to the extent that we can say that it does not exist anymore. Carol II suspended it for the first time; then, the legionaries [and Antonescu] did the same when they tried to replace the magistrates whom they suspected of working against them ... As we can see, every new regime in our country suspends the tenure of magistrates, [which is] the cornerstone of a fair justice, [and] which we acquired after so much struggle.[31]

In spite of the regime's pressure, some judges ruled against the Antonescu regime in politically sensitive trials, even if they risked losing their jobs. This was the case involving Pro-Transilvania Association—an organization established (in October 1940) by ethnic Romanian refugees from Northern Transilvania—which protested to the German legation against the Second Vienna Arbitrage and denounced the persecution of ethnic Romanians unleashed by the new Hungarian administration. Bothered by such protests, the German diplomats demanded that Antonescu should dismantle Pro-Transilvania and the government complied with this request in November 1940. Undeterred, Pro-Transilvania hired several prominent lawyers and asked the Bucharest Court of Appeals to cancel the government's decision. The Antonescus pressured the Court of Appeals judges—such as Gheorghe A. Petrescu—to reject Pro-Transilvania's claim due to the political requirements of the Axis partnership. However, Petrescu convinced two (out of four) of his co-panelist judges to rule in favor of Pro-Transilvania, thus cancelling the government's initial decision. As Vasile Netea, a prominent PNT and Pro-Transilvania member who attended the trial remembered in his postwar memoirs, this ruling

---

31 Constantin I. Navarlie, *România între abandon și crucificare: România, 1944–1946* (Craiova: Editura de Sud, 2000), vol. 1, pp. 30, 54.

triggered Antonescu's anger—he anyway banned the activity of Pro-Transilvania—and retaliation against those magistrates by firing them and sending Petrescu to the frontline.[32]

Perceptions of the Laws

The perception of the laws was another crucial aspect of citizens' understanding of legality during the Antonescu regime. The sense of the ambiguous legal basis of the Antonescu regime was illustrated by official discourses and policies. For example, complaining about the abuses perpetrated by his legionary partners, Antonescu invoked the Constitution in October 1940 to reject the fascist squads' violation of citizens' rights: "I will not admit any violation of residences, because the inviolability of residences is guaranteed by the Constitution."[33] Antonescu continued to emphasize the necessity of full commitment to legality among his subordinates. On April 1, 1941, Antonescu urged his ministers to abide by the laws during their field inspections and when taking measures against domestic enemies, such as legionary agitators and corrupt bureaucrats: "I recommend that you observe the legal framework. We do not represent a certain political party or a caste, we represent our country."[34]

Acquiring legislative power, the Antonescu government issued a string of decrees whose elaboration apparently followed ordinary legal procedure: drafted by various ministers, the decrees were subjected to the examination of the Legislative Council, then signed by the appropriate ministers, and published in *Monitorul Oficial* to enter into force. However, Antonescu's legislative system was neither efficient, nor democratic. Some intellectuals and bureaucrats disagreed with the new process of elaborating laws and with its results. Gheorghe Ionescu-Sisești, the head of the Agricultural Institute and a professor at the Agronomy University, was one of them. He recorded in his diary (on November 23, 1943) his frustration with the Antonescu regime's legislative process, which he regarded as dysfunctional and inferior to the traditional domestic process involving parliamentary procedures: "I went to the Prime Minister Chancellery [PCM] and we discussed the amendments to the draft law ... I sadly

---

32   Vasile Netea, *Memorii* (Târgu-Mureș: Editura Nico, 2010), 144–6; Gheorghe A. Petrescu, "Un episod istoric din lupta poporului român contra Dictatului de la Viena din 30 august 1940," in *Revista de Istorie*, no. 9 (September 1980): 1765–1779.
33   Berceanu, *Istoria*, 402.
34   See the minutes of the April 1, 1941 government meeting, in Ciuca (ed.), *Stenogramele*, vol. 3, 29–30.

reflected about the way laws are being made nowadays. It is absolutely necessary to have a deliberating body, no matter how tiny."[35]

Various jurists as well as foreign diplomats who were keen observers of the era noted that the legislative policy of the Antonescu regime was characterized by an inflation of laws—sometimes contradictory—that constantly kept changing.[36] Other sources show Romania's dictatorships' tendency to over-legislate. A report produced by the judicial authorities of the era illustrates this dramatic increase in the number of legal provisions during the regimes of both Carol II and Antonescu exactly at the time of the rise of political authoritarianism. While between 1926 and 1936, the average number of yearly new laws was between 105 and 272, in 1937 the government adopted 364 laws. During the next year, their number grew to 798, only to reach 1,110 in 1941.[37] Ion Antonescu himself acknowledged this trend of legislative inflation (and its negative consequences such as citizens' and jurists' difficulty to keep pace with the laws, which resulted, among other things, in contradictory court decisions) during the first years of his rule and pledged to curb it. He informed his ministers about this intention during the September 9, 1941 government meeting: "We are drowning in laws. The exceptional circumstances have forced even us to increase the number of laws even further compared to one year ago. We must simplify this legislation, because we are suffocated by it. A court decides in one way and another court decides in a different way."[38]

To produce such an avalanche of legislation, some of the Antonescu officials tried to speed up the process of adopting laws, complaining that its slowness affected the efficiency of governance. Mihai Antonescu, who directed the regime's legislative policy, was one of the officials who tried to speed up the process. For example, he complained to the other

---

35 Gheorghe Ionescu-Sisești, *Jurnal* (București: Editura Academiei Române, 2013), vol. II, p. 150.
36 Barbu Berceanu, *Probleme de românizare: Nominalizarea acțiunilor la purtător* (București: Atelierele Grafice Socec&Co., no year), 3–5; for the observations of foreign diplomats on Antonescu's laws, see Dumitru Hâncu (ed.), *Confidențial: București Berna—Rapoartele diplomatice ale lui Rene de Weck 1940–1944*. București: Hasefer, 2002); Ottomar Trașcă and Dennis Deletant (eds.), *Al III-lea Reich și Holocaustul din România: 1940–1944. Documente din arhivele germane* (București: Editura INSHR-EW, 2007); Carol Iancu (ed.), *Shoah în România: Evreii în timpul regimului Antonescu 1940–1944: Documente diplomatice franceze inedite* (Iași: Polirom, 2001).
37 Iosif Schnapp, "Fisierul legislatiei romane," *in Pandectele Romane*, XXIII (1944), Partea a III-a, p. 58; for the concern of some of Antonescu's officials about the legislative inflation, see Ionescu-Sisești, *Jurnal*, vol. II, p. 172.
38 Ciuca (ed.), *Stenogramele*, vol. IV, p. 666.

ministers (September 1941) that the experts from the MJ and the Legislative Council took too much time to draft the decree for the expropriation of Jewish rural houses: "This decree will never be finished. What happened with it? Gen, Zwiedeneck: The Legislative Council is studying it. M. Antonescu: I ordered so many days ago that this decree should be completed ... There are laws that are made in two hours and this one—for which I gave the guiding principles—takes years? This is unacceptable! Tell them that ... in five days they should show me the decree."[39]

The avalanche of anti-Semitic and other repressive laws and the subsequent court cases attracted the attention of numerous jurists of the era, who researched, lectured, and published on these topics and, thus, promoted their professional expertise, reputation, and material interests. Lawyers and judges were among the most active scholars publicizing Romanianization laws and their implications among their fellow citizens by commenting in their books and articles on the legal provisions of various laws and jurisprudence, or by suggesting improvements to specific Romanianization provisions.[40]

Resembling the position of Ion Antonescu, Mihai Antonescu also seemed to harbor an authoritarian, as well as ambiguous, approach to legality. While he seconded Ion Antonescu in promoting laws and mass violence against the Jews and other enemies, he sometimes invoked legality and complained about bureaucrats who did not respect the law and the rights of citizens. For example, during the government meeting of May 6, 1941, he complained to his fellow ministers that some bureaucrats, especially from the Ministry of Labor, acted unprofessionally and disregarded the rights of coal miners who went on strike demanding improvements in labor conditions, and that the authorities too easily dismissed those social demands, which they blamed on communist and legionary instigators: "[The authorities] broke the legal order ... There are some prestigious principles ingrained in the idea of the state as an institution which the State should never abandon ... In the current circumstances, a labor conflict should be solved by using social and persuasive educational measures, calmness and understanding, while never abandoning the principle of the legality of [public] authority. There are several laws

---

39 Ciuca (ed.), *Stenogramele*, vol. IV, 697.
40 See Berceanu, *Probleme de Românizare*; Titus Dragoș (ed.). *Românizarea— Înfăptuiri: 6 Decembrie 1941–6 Decembrie 1942* (București: Curierul Judiciar, 1942); Nicolae Ghimpa et al. (eds.), *Codul de Românizare* (București: Editura Ziarului Universul, 1942); L. Sorin, *Exproprierea Urbană a Bunurilor Evereiești: Repertoriu de Jurisprudență* (București: Biblioteca Evreiască, 1942); see also the legal journal *Pandectele Romanizării*, edited by lawyer Vasile Christodorescu.

concerning the legal regime of the strikes ... I want that the law and the legal regime be respected."[41]

The anti-Semitic laws adopted by the Carol II and Antonescu regimes and the subsequent litigation faced a variety of reactions from Romania's gentile public. While some endorsed the legal persecutions of Jews, others disagreed with those unjust measures, but mostly in private. In an era obsessed with theories of ethnicity and race, various politicians, bureaucrats, and intellectuals debated the meaning and the scope of Romanian ethnicity and the question of belonging to the national community. Jurists were usually aware of the difficulty to grasp the concept of ethnicity from a legal perspective. However, only a few actually dared to criticize publicly the repressive laws and the injustices they created.[42]

One of the few examples of courageous jurists who challenged some aspects of Antonescu's racial laws and the obedient judges who implemented them uncritically was the Armenian refugee and lawyer Hurmuz Aznavorian.[43] Aznavorian published (in 1943) two articles in the legal journal *Pandectele Românizării*, in which he criticized some aspects of the laws that excluded Jews and other minorities from the local economy, and disparaged parts of the court decisions that applied those laws. In his articles, Aznavorian argued that the term "ethnic origin" used in Carol II's and Antonescu's legislation and in judicial practice was a vague, imprecise, and illegal concept that some judges recklessly used to motivate their decisions on cases related to minorities and transfer of property. Aznavorian considered that ethnic origin was a political concept disconnected from the positive laws and the judiciary—whose proper functioning required precise legal terminology—and that the judges' use of "ethnic origin" caused serious legal conflicts.[44] According to Aznavorian, those

---

41   See the minutes of the 6 May 1941 government meeting in Ciuca (ed.), *Stenogramele*, vol. III, pp. 264–5, 271.
42   While some of the jurists who worked for the Antonescu regime, such as the Minister of Justice Constantin Stoicescu, criticized the concept of ethnicity in a diplomatic manner, they usually did so behind the closed doors of official and private meetings. See the 16 December 1941 government meeting in Ciuca et al. (eds.), *Stenogramele*, vol. V, pp. 464–465.
43   Born in Trebizonda (Trabzon), Aznavorian fled as a child together with his family from the Hamidian massacres in the late 19th century Ottoman Empire and became a Romanian citizen after WWI. Rodica Sfințescu, *Oile mele* (București: Albatros, 1999).
44   Hurmuz Aznavorian, *Excelența legii* (București: Editura Semne, 2007); see also H. Aznavorian, "Observațiuni în jurul noțiunei "originea etnică," in *Pandectele Românizării*, year III, no. 1–4 (1943): 13–24; H. Aznavorian, "Rolul Curții de Casație față de noțiunile legale nedefinite nici de drept nici de lege," in *Pandectele Românizării*, year III, no. 13–16 (1943): 300–303.

judges made a mistake by stretching the law, as he wrote in his article "Observations about the Concept of Ethnic Origin" published in 1943 in *Pandectele Românizării*:

> Romania has adopted several laws stipulating ... a concept that, despite being completely new and lacking a legal definition, is used together with the notorious principles of the Romanian law, and causes uncertainty and confusion concerning the interpretation of the laws as well as serious consequences on people's legal status. Thus, some court decisions have introduced in their motivations the concept of "ETHNIC ORIGIN," which has no legal definition, and is not defined in other social sciences ... This notion could have been harmless if some judges would have not based their decisions—recklessly, in our opinion—on this concept without any legal criteria and positivist texts, thus causing painful moral and financial consequences for the families that were legally entitled to consider themselves Romanian, until the emergence of these strange and incomprehensible judicial documents. In order to clarify and to stop the uncontrolled evolution of these errors, I have written this article to be used by those empowered to issue decisions that would eliminate arbitrarily—without any legal text and general discriminatory norms—so many Romanian families from the Romanian community. Based on what right? So far, I haven't seen any valid legal justification for these decisions.[45]

Aznavorian argued that the existing domestic and international legislation allowed Romania to subject only foreign citizens and some categories of Jews to a different (harsher) legal treatment but not Christian minorities (probably he had in mind the Armenians) holding Romanian citizenship. He equally held that local judges could not extend the discriminations to other groups of people through (a creative) interpretation of the laws, as in countries following common law principles, because it would contradict the laws that stipulated such an exceptional (restrictive) legal regime only for the Jews.[46] In his article, Aznavorian especially emphasized the negative consequences for individual citizens and for the country—including foreign policy problems deriving from breaching Romania's international obligations—in case of employing the concept of ethnic origin in court decisions. He therefore urged judicial authorities to stop using it:

> It is possible that the process of discrimination BASED ON ETHNIC ORIGIN [sic] will affect areas not envisioned by the authors ... and will lead to ... the revision of all titles and positions, thus contesting ... the legitimacy of the established situations of people ... Because these are anti-Semitic laws, exceptions [from the rule, and thus must be interpreted strictly], they cannot resolve the problems concerning the origin of the Romanian bourgeoisie, whose history does not allow any discrimination; on the contrary, it endangers the fundamental laws of the Romanian state, which assumed international obligations to treat Christian national minorities equally, regardless of their ethnicity. See the treaty on minorities from 9 December

---

45 Aznavorian, "Observațiuni,"13–24.
46 Aznavorian, "Observațiuni," 15–16.

1919. This idea of political and legal unity [equality] is a cornerstone of the Romanian state and no law had challenged it so far.⁴⁷

Perhaps trying to avoid antagonizing the authorities too much by appearing philo-Semitic, Aznavorian failed to mention that the 1919 minority treaties protected not only Christian minorities, but also the Jews. A few months later, Aznavorian continued his criticism of Antonescu's laws and their problematic terminology in another article published in *Pandectele Românizării,* in which he urged the Supreme Court to take action and limit the abuses caused by the judges' use of various non-legal terms and to guide Romania's lower court judges on "the path of legality," and thus, to avoid major damages to legal order and the economy.⁴⁸

Aznavorian's criticism went beyond the narrow audience of the legal journals. In another courageous article—"The Interpretation of the Laws," published on March 27, 1942 in the popular newspaper *Curentul* (apparently without the knowledge of the chief editor)—Aznavorian noted the widespread opportunism of many bureaucrats and jurists, who accepted Carol II's and Antonescu's turn to authoritarianism and adapted to their repressive policies. He accused the opportunistic jurists of "arrogant intent" for elaborating discriminatory legal provisions by ignoring the country's traditional legal principles: "Sooner or later in the legal system, all the results obtained by raping the Law and its principles will take revenge and an entire social and political system will collapse if [the authorities] will persist [to act] against the eternal legal principles."⁴⁹ Aznavorian emphasized the crucial role of judges, the real interpreters of the laws in courts, and urged them to moderate the radical content of some laws by adapting them to the existing legal system and removing their "excesses and passions" in order to prevent chaos in society triggered by the collapse of the legal peace and order. Even though the article was written at an abstract level and avoided naming specific laws, politicians, and judges, it was probably clear for the public opinion that Aznavorian criticized Carol II's and Antonescu's discriminatory legislation. Following the publication of this article, the regime temporarily suspended *Curentul.*⁵⁰ Aznavorian's criticism of the ethnicization of Romania's legal system was quite remarkable during a dictatorship obsessed with identity politics, ethnicity, and race, which tried to classify its citizens based on blood—using "certificates of ethnic origin"—and shaped most

---

47 Aznavorian, "Observațiuni," 14.
48 Aznavorian, "Rolul Curții de Casație," 300–303.
49 Aznavorian, *Excelența legilor,* 63–64.
50 Aznavorian, *Excelența legilor,* 95.

of its policies according to the degree to which they belonged to the imagined ethno-national community.[51]

During the Economic Council meeting from February 27, 1941, Nicolae Dragomir, the Minister of Economic Coordination, complained about the reluctance of ordinary courts to sentence offenders of economic speculation because the law stipulated too severe punishments. Dragomir argued that the Romanian society needed an adjustment period to such severe laws. Dragomir's suggestion outraged Antonescu, who criticized the judiciary for its leniency and pledged to restructure the justice system, to punish non-compliant magistrates, and to adopt even more severe criminal laws, following Nazi Germany's model of discipline, law and order, and his paternalistic view of society:

> No! On the contrary! We need more severe laws! And the judiciary should be punished for not doing its job! ... A German soldier defected in Făgăraș and within one hour he was tried and after 5 minutes he was shot ... Only thus can we create discipline in a State. Only thus can we have order and peace ... After I will build the judiciary the way it has to be, whoever will not do his duty will answer for his deeds ... I won't interfere with the justice system because I am consistent with my principles and I gave my word to the judiciary. Judges are sovereign. But if they won't fulfill their duties, I will interfere. We will judge the judiciary! ... We will not diminish the criminal punishments! ... We need to set some examples! ... Instead what have we done? We have not enforced the law, because we were satisfied with the indulgence... It is better to punish someone seriously once in order to set an example for the others. In this way, all [citizens] will comply... The time will come when we will strictly enforce the laws; when we will make justice; when we will organize the judiciary.[52]

Perceptions of Minority (Especially Jewish) Rights, Particularly Property Rights

The persecution of minorities, especially Jews, was one of Antonescu's main repressive policies, even though sometimes he claimed the opposite. For example, during a government meeting from February 18, 1941 discussing the fate of the Jewish property Romanianized by legionaries, Antonescu emphasized that the authorities should investigate the transactions: he expected that some of the assets acquired through violence be returned to their former owners while others should be nationalized, and

---

51 For more details on Antonescu's ethnicization of domestic politics and the citizens' negotiation of their ethnic identity, including through petitioning to courts, see Mihaela Serban, "Litigating Identity in Fascist and Post-Fascist Romania, 1940–1945," in this issue of the *Journal of Romanian Studies* (2020).
52 See the 27 February 1941 minutes of the Economic Council meeting, in Ciuca et. al. (eds.), *Stenogramele*, vol. II, p. 402.

that the state would pay partial compensation to Jewish owners. In order to uphold legality, Antonescu declared that he would not confiscate Jewish property because he publicly guaranteed the private property of all citizens.[53] In another government meeting (November 16, 1943), Antonescu declared that he would respect minorities who defended their rights through legal means: "If a man defends his nationality within the [state's] legal framework, only then will that person receive my consideration; I will shake his hand because he proved to be a man of character, a determined man, who manifested his personality and nationality, and this is not a condemnable thing."[54]

Sometimes, worried by the international consequences of the regime's tendency to adopt harsh discriminatory and public laws, some civil servants, especially jurists, pleaded for a more cautious and discrete legislative policy regulating sensitive issues related to minorities—such as the dispossession of the Jews, redistribution of their property to Romanians and Germans, and other controversial laws—advising the government to replace the repressive public laws with secret administrative orders. For example, advising Antonescu how to better oppose the local ethnic Germans' attempts to acquire real estate from Jews and other foreigners in the borderland area of Banat, government jurists suggested (in 1943) that "it is not good to adopt a specific law for this...because we might face objections from the German Ethnic Group (henceforth, GEG) based on the Vienna Arbitrage which recognized their equal rights with ethnic Romanians. However, if we adopt this measure as a secret directive, GEG cannot raise any objection, because the authorities' refusal to authorize a purchase does not have to be justified [to potential buyers] as it would be based on military reasons."[55] In the second part of the war, Antonescu became concerned with the necessity not to leave a paper trail of some of his radical policies, which could have triggered negative consequences for him and Romania at the end of the war. As a result, on February 19, 1943, Ion Antonescu refused to sign the draft laws allowing the "transfer" of assets from Transnistria to Romania because he did not want the law to be published in the official bulletin of his government and, thus, to be used by the Soviets as a legal basis for compensations at the end of

---

53 Ciuca (ed.), *Stenogramele*, vol. II, p. 308.
54 Ciuca et. al. (eds.), *Stenogramele*, vol. IX, p. 545.
55 ANR, Ministerul Justiției (MJ)-Direcția Judiciară (DJ) 129/1942, pp. 73–80; see also M. Antonescu's suggestion to use legal technicalities to prevent Germans from buying real estate in Romania's borderlands, in Ciuca et al. (eds.), *Stenogramele*, vol. IV, pp. 403–404, 764.

the war.⁵⁶ Other prominent bureaucrats also warned the government to avoid publicizing specific (anti-Semitic) laws due to potential negative foreign policy consequences: they could damage Romania's relations with the Allies and burden its case at the future peace talks. This was the case of the well-known diplomat Raul Bossy, at that time the Romanian ambassador in Berlin and then in Bern, who considered that Antonescu should not have published the anti-Semitic laws.⁵⁷

The anti-Semitic regimes of Carol II and Antonescu considered that legal professionals—a key sector of any society—were a priority for the regime's nationalist project. The major anti-Semitic law adopted by Carol II on August 9, 1940 (Decree Law 2650 for the Legal Status of Jews), which classified Jews into three groups, with each group allowed different degrees of rights, paved the way for the exclusion of the Jews classified into the first (Jews who came to Romania after 30 December 1918) and third (the Jews who were not part of the first and second group) categories from the judiciary and bar associations. Due to military merits (fighting in Romanian army in previous wars or being wounded, crippled, or decorated), and the early date of obtaining Romanian citizenship (becoming citizens before 1918), those Jews and their heirs were part of the second category Jews, which benefited from more rights and were able to keep a private legal practice.⁵⁸ The joint Antonescu-Legionary government continued to enforce and escalate Carol II's anti-Semitic policies and many jurists and bureaucrats supported the exclusion of Jews from the legal profession. For instance, in October 1940, the Under Secretary of Colonization and Refugees, C. Georgescu, advocated for replacing Jewish lawyers with ethnic Romanian refugees, and complained to Antonescu that while 1,400 "Yid lawyers" had been already excluded from the bar, 800 of them kept their positions and took over all the cases of their excluded coreligionists.⁵⁹ Georgescu also suggested that "all Yids should be excluded from bar associations."⁶⁰ Antonescu generally agreed with Georgescu, but

---

56   Lya Benjamin et. al. (eds), *Evreii din România. 1943–1944: Bilanțul tragediei, renașterea speranței*, vol. IV (București: Hasefer, 1998), pp. 223–224; Antonescu showed the same concerns about a local anti-Semitic ordinance displayed in public in the city of Galați that required Jewish inhabitants to pay more for bread. Benjamin (ed.), *Evreii din România*, doc. no 174.
57   See the diary of General Radu R. Rosetti. Radu R. Rosetti, *Pagini de jurnal* (București: Adevărul, 1993), 196.
58   For more details on the August 1940 Decree Law for the Legal Status of the Jews, see Mihaela Serban, "Litigating Identity in Fascist and Post-Fascists Romania, 1940–1945," in the current issue of the *Journal of Romanian Studies*.
59   See the 1 October 1940 minute of the government meeting, in Ciuca et. al (ed.), *Stenogramele*, vol. I, pp. 128–129.
60   *Ibid*, 128–129.

argued that the Jewish lawyers should lose their right to practice law except in the cases when they were hired by other Jews.[61]

The Antonescu regime faced significant pressure from below—from various legal professionals—to Romanianize the country's legal institutions by excluding the Jews. In January 1941, a rooky lawyer from Iași wrote to Antonescu, asking him to nationalize the Bar associations and to purge them of their Jewish or (philo-Semitic) gentile undeserving members. To support his claim, the lawyer emphasized that the Bar autonomy had become a problem and the law profession had degraded because of the corrupting influence of "the Yids."[62]

Even though Mihai Antonescu authored the Romanianization laws that expropriated Jewish rural and urban assets, he sometimes seemed to regret his involvement in this process due to the problems it created and the impact on his reputation. During a government meeting from June 1941, M. Antonescu told his colleagues that "Romanianization is a drama that tortures me especially because I was the author of the expropriation laws and I realize that people might think that I've done a superficial thing, with which I aimed to hide other intentions... or that I do not have the capacity to see the realities of Romania and of understanding what an effective Romanianization means."[63] This incident suggests that, confronted with the legal complications created by the Romanianization laws and the criticism from many citizens, Mihai Antonescu posed as a misunderstood legal genius in front of his colleagues.

While Romanianization created many problems that plagued the local society, such as uncertainty of property rights, increased litigation, corruption, and criticism, it also benefited many ethnic Romanians, especially numerous legal professionals, who participated in the transactions, administration, and litigation of the nationalized Jewish property. For instance, Miron Butariu, a young lawyer from Arad remembered in his memoirs how the Romanianization of a Jewish business by one of his former clients, a wealthy aristocratic entrepreneur, brought him a permanent job as a legal counsellor of the newly enlarged company, a substantial income, and accommodation in a nationalized Jewish palace.[64] While in his memoir, Butariu criticized especially Legionaries' laws and measures, including Romanianization, as abusive, at the same time he benefited from some of their discriminatory legislation and policies. Even though he was a convinced follower of liberal democracy, Butariu

---

61   *Ibid*, 129.
62   ANR, MJ-DJ 20/1941, p. 82.
63   Ciuca (ed.), *Stenogramele*, vol. III, p. 606.
64   Miron Butariu, *O viață de om: Note autobiografice* (Los Angeles: ARAS, 1991), 62.

accepted (and adapted to) Antonescu's authoritarian legality: he claimed that things did not change much in the judiciary and that the courts functioned as usual, except that many lawyers and judges were drafted in the army, but as a disabled man who stayed at home he took over the cases of his Bar colleagues.[65]

Other jurists of the era complained privately about the legal and practical implications of Antonescu's authoritarian legality and repressive policies that targeted especially the Jews. The young lawyer Boris Deșliu complained in his diary that Antonescu's "nefarious and illegitimate war" against the USSR negatively impacted his small legal practice because many of his clients were drafted into the army while others liquidated their businesses, which led to a smaller number of commercial-civil lawsuits. Deșliu also defended Jews indicted by the military courts for breaching the forced labor law, but after a while even these cases ceased.[66] In addition to these problems, Deșliu also noted in his diary the depressing atmosphere in WWII courts and Antonescu's draconian legislation, which he depicted as military orders disguised under a superficial legal cover. In particular, Deșliu criticized the law against economic sabotage and the Romanianization legislation, which he considered as one that "denied justice."[67]

Even though some jurists agreed with the discrimination of most of the Jews, they disagreed with the persecution of Christian minorities. In his article "Observations on the Concept of Ethnic Origin," Aznavorian argued that the law expropriating urban Jewish property (from March 27, 1941) clearly stipulated in its introduction that it aimed to protect the "Romanian Christian bourgeoisie," regardless of their ethnicity, thus using religious criteria and not biological-racial criteria. Additionally, he noted that the law for the expropriation of Jewish urban houses did not stipulate that the assets should pass into the hands of "ethnic Romanians," unlike the law for the expropriation of Jewish rural estate, because it aimed to protect "Christian property." According to Aznavorian, this approach followed the historical tradition of the Romanian principalities and the modern Romanian state who saw its bourgeoisies in religious terms and accepted and integrated Christians of different ethnicities.[68]

---

65 Butariu, *O viață de om*, 74.
66 Boris Deșliu, *Jurnal de avocat* (București: Vremea, 2002), 27, 37–39.
67 Deșliu, *Jurnal*, 36.
68 Aznavorian, "Observațiuni," 17–21.

Perceptions of Extra-Judicial Punishments

In spite of the much-publicized independence of the courts, sometimes Antonescu disregarded (and by-passed) the ordinary courts' decisions and ordered extrajudicial punishments—such as camp internment or firing—for law offenders that deserved, according to him, an exemplary and swift punishment. For instance, after he was informed, in May 1943, about a case of corruption and nepotism involving a former Romanianization bureaucrat, Antonescu ordered his arrest and camp imprisonment in spite of the judges' decision to exonerate him:

> When the judiciary complained that they could not serve justice because of the interferences of [pre 1940] politicians, I gave them full independence ... Well, exactly under this regime who abstains, I think, one hundred percent, from intervening with the judicial system, well, exactly right now, the judiciary releases all thieves, stating that there is no evidence against them ... I ordered that those liberated by the judiciary be immediately arrested and a communiqué published saying that this person was sent to camp by order of Marshal Antonescu. I will shame the judiciary [in this way].[69]

This incident suggests that Antonescu considered himself to be the final arbiter of justice and legality, situated above the judiciary, which he saw in instrumental terms as a useful tool of governance and legitimization. At the same time, he displayed a paternalistic attitude towards judges who needed to be taught a public "lesson" when they proved too lenient in politically sensitive cases.

Sometimes Antonescu fired judges indicted for various crimes despite the fact that courts found them not guilty, thus triggering controversy in the government. This was the case with several judges suspected of participating in the 1941 Legionary Rebellion. Afterwards, Antonescu signed the decrees to fire those judges based on information that they had joined the fascist rebels, even though military courts acquitted them of such accusations. Following his formalist view of legality, the Minister of Finance Gen. Nicolae Stoenescu complained against the order to fire those judges, emphasizing the need for positive law: "Gen I. Antonescu: You have to take this measure, which we usually adopt in the army ... Gen. N. Stoenescu: But I do not have any legal basis, except your order."[70] While Antonescu saw the government and the judiciary as an army unit in which his subordinates—ministers, judges, and prosecutors—should have

---

69 See the May 13, 1943 government meeting minutes, in Ciuca et al. (eds.), *Stenogramele*, vol. IX, pp. 225–226.
70 See the April 4, 1941 minutes of the government meeting in Ciuca (ed.), *Stenogramele*, vol. III, 87–8.

obeyed the orders and the chain of command just like disciplined militaries, Stoenescu, a career officer, had doubts about adopting such a radical measure (of firing judges) without a legal basis and contradicting a court decision. He seemed to have not realized that the will of the dictator was the ultimate source of law and trumped all other sources of positivist legality and that the dictator was willing to adopt extrajudicial measures when even his favorite military courts ruled against his will in politically sensitive cases.[71]

Ironically, the Minister of Justice, C. Stoicescu, proved more flexible about legality and suggested a legal loophole to Stoenescu to fire those judges: "Stoicescu: You have to use the law. Once the tenure of the public employee is suspended, they cannot sue in administrative courts against the measure to fire them. Gen. N. Stoenescu: ... I need a legal basis ... Stoicescu: There is such legal basis. Before, when we had the tenure of public employees, you had to send the guilty bureaucrats in front of the discipline commission. These commissions have been replaced with the ministers' assessment. For magistrates, who have tenure, the law allows me to make an assessment and fire those guilty."[72]

The problematic legitimacy of the regime and the authoritarian way it envisioned legality—adopting extrajudicial measures such as interning people in camps without a court decision—drew the attention of jurists and other intellectuals who harbored different views of legality. While for some intellectuals and jurists the Antonescu regime meant business as usual as long as their interests were not directly affected by his policies—such as in the case of Butariu—for others the legal practices of the Antonescu regime seemed abusive. This was illustrated by an argument between Ionescu-Sisești, the head of the Agricultural Institute, and Ovidiu Vlădescu, the Secretary General of the government and a law professor at the Commercial Academy. The discussion was recorded in the former's diary entry from March 18, 1942. Ionescu-Sisești was outraged that Ion Antonescu ordered the camp internment of three honest and hard-working employees of the Agricultural Institute based on a report (accusing them of corruption) by an inexperienced controller from the Prime Minister's Chancellery. Antonescu's order was issued without waiting for a

---

71 Antonescu's decision in this case suggests a more draconic type of authoritarian legalism that resembles the cases of political repressions adopted by military dictatorships in Chile and, perhaps even in Argentina, depicted by Pereira in his study on authoritarianism and the rule of law in Latin America. Pereira, *Political Injustice*.
72 See the April 4, 1941 minutes of the government meeting in Ciucă (ed.), *Stenogramele*, vol. III, 87–8.

court investigation, prompting Ionescu-Sisești to intervene in favor of his subordinates with the government. As it transpired from their dialogue, the two university professors had a very different understanding of legality and governance. Vlădescu supported Antonescu's view of a speedy revolutionary and authoritarian legality, while Ionescu-Sisești rather supported a democratic governance based on the rule of law:

> [Ionescu-Sisești]: I told Vlădescu some hard truths concerning the art of governing and the errors made by the regime ... You cannot rely only on investigations made by incompetent people, like army generals transformed [overnight] into state controllers, you cannot rely on investigations made behind closed doors without asking clarifications from people who know the case ... You cannot adopt [penal] sentences concerning the freedom and honor of people without giving them the right to defend themselves. You cannot anticipate the result of pending judiciary investigations through such orders [camp internment]. It is not acceptable that people be sentenced without trial and outside courts. ... We have to restore legal guarantees at least where it is possible ...
> [Vlădescu]: Do not forget that we are in the middle of a revolution, Vlădescu argued.
> [Ionescu-Sisești]: Yes, we are in the middle of a revolution, with all its negative consequences. We do not need to aggravate the consequences of this revolutionary era through measures we can avoid. People ... live in panic and uncertainty about the future ... Only in an atmosphere of calm and safety life could be normalized and the state could fulfill its functions ...
> [Vlădescu]: The justice system works too slow. It is better to fire a suspected clerk and send him to a camp. Then he will struggle for his court case to end sooner.
> [Ionescu-Sisești]: So, I am thinking, if the government cannot speed up the court proceeding, the accused person will succeed. To such an unusual theory, I reply to Vlădescu: What about the honor and the reputation of the person you fired and sent to camp? What if one of them cannot stand the injustice and commits suicide?[73]

The meeting between Ionescu-Sisești and Vlădescu ended unsuccessfully for the former. A disappointed Ionescu-Sisești reflected in his diary on the Antonescu officials' problematic approach to legality and governance: "I left sad and worried. We are not governed well. The Marshal does not have good advisors."[74] Apparently, at that time Ionescu-Sisești still believed in the myth of the well-intended ruler misinformed by evil or incompetent counsellors. He failed to consider that, perhaps, Vlădescu's authoritarian view of governance and legality reflected Antonescu's worldview and approach to legality. Another incident shows that Vlădescu at least accepted Antonescu's view of authoritarian legality that rejected liberal democratic methods of defending individual and

---

73   Ionescu-Sisești, *Jurnal*, vol. II, pp. 38–39.
74   Ionescu-Sisești, *Jurnal*, vol. II, p. 39.

collective rights—such as petitioning—and dismissed the Jews' petitioning efforts as lawyerly tricks and a "typical case of Jewish pettifogging."[75]

In his memoir, lawyer Deșliu further remembered the problematic law against economic speculation (sabotage) that filled criminal courts with a lot of small business owners he defended. Deșliu complained that after a while, the regime changed its approach and many of these "offenders" were "interned in concentration camps without having ever been tried in court."[76]

Conclusion

Legality was a major topic of discussion during the Antonescu regime, both for the highest officials and for intellectuals, especially jurists. A controversial notion at that time, legality was perceived differently within the official circles of the Antonescu regime and among the intellectuals/jurists, who harbored various authoritarian or liberal democratic worldviews. For Ion and Mihai Antonescu, as well as for many influential bureaucrats, legality meant a new type of authoritarian understanding of the role of the law in a state and its subordination to the will of the ruler (the *Führerprinzip*); for them legality mainly had an instrumental role. Their approach was revolutionary at a discursive level in its early period but proved to be conservative in practice. In their view, the regime drew its legitimacy from the ruler, legality, and the legalistic rhetoric and involved various uses and abuses of the law, such as governing by decree laws, legal confiscation of Jewish property, restrictions of minority rights, firing judges, speeding up legal procedures, and ordering extrajudicial punishments (camp internment and executions). As such, Antonescu's view of legality violated some aspects of the principle of (traditional) legality because he understood his power to be discretionary and, usually, not bound by the law. Nor did he always apply the law, but sometimes kept sensitive laws and administrative measures secret and used military courts for political repression. This resembled a severe form of authoritarianism and political repression discussed by Pereira in his study on authoritarianism and the rule of law in Latin America, particularly the type of *authoritarian legalism* adopted by the Chilean military dictatorship in the 1970s.

---

75 See Vladescu's letter (November 3, 1941) to Filderman. Filderman, *Memoirs and Diaries*, vol. 2, pp. 242–244.
76 Deșliu, *Jurnal*, 36.

Even though the Constitution was suspended, Antonescu did not reject the idea of constitutional order—which was instrumental for the legitimacy of his regime—and claimed to pursue the goal of reforming (improving) the local national community. Practically, his view of legality meant that Antonescu ruled by law and used and abused the existing legal tools to achieve his radical goals of nation and state building by purifying Romania of minorities, especially the Jews, and communists and by promoting economic nationalism (Romanianization). Antonescu permitted the ordinary judiciary—such as the courts handling civil and commercial cases, including separate Romanianization panels—to maintain a relative independence (autonomy), which enabled them to rule against the government and its agencies from time to time. This allowed the members of the persecuted groups, especially the Jews, to carve up a legal space for their rights. At the same time, unhappy with ordinary courts' judges—suspected of being too lenient and taking too much time to resolve their cases—Antonescu sometimes fired them or overruled their decisions by ordering extrajudicial punishments. Additionally, he kept a tight surveillance on political criminal cases, usually tried in military courts, which resembles the status of the Spanish judiciary during the Franco regime and the Chilean military courts under Pinochet. According to Antonescu's worldview, the judiciary, just like other state institutions, should have functioned as a military obeying the order of the leader, who selectively relied on law. Thus, for the Romanian dictator legality had an instrumental role because it provided a cover for his abuses (such as extrajudicial punishments, restriction of minority rights, and confiscation of property from Jews) by legalizing such acts as well as providing legitimacy, stability, and order.

Intellectuals, including jurists, harbored a diversity of opinions regarding Antonescu's legality. Some jurists, especially those who joined the regime or sympathized with fascism, anti-Semitism, and ethno-nationalism, supported the regime's authoritarian (and ethnic) legalism or at least accepted it, either because they shared the same worldview, benefited from it, were indifferent, or because they wanted to avoid problems. Other jurists, especially those with a more democratic mindset or belonging to minorities and other persecuted groups, perceived legality differently than Antonescu and supporters of authoritarianism, and seemed to favor a liberal democratic version of legality involving the rule of law. Nevertheless, in spite of their disproval of Antonescu's legality, many of these critical intellectuals/jurists tried to adapt to the regimes' authoritarian legalism, problematic policies and judicial practices in order to defend and negotiate their (or others') rights in and outside the ordinary court system.

After WWII, the Allies regarded the Antonescu regime as a fascist dictatorship that enforced a non-democratic and authoritarian legality, breached the rights of many citizens, and ordered extrajudicial punishments, which resulted in numerous war crimes perpetrated against Romanian and Soviet citizens, especially the Jews. Therefore, the Allies requested the postwar Romanian governments—through the September 1944 Armistice Agreement—to indict Antonescu and his collaborators, including jurists such as Mihai Antonescu and Gheorghe Alexianu, for war crimes and for the disaster of the country brought by the alliance with Nazi Germany. The pro-communist Petru Groza government implemented this requirement and the newly established People's Tribunal found (in 1946) Ion Antonescu, Mihai Antonescu, Gheorghe Alexianu, and other high-ranking collaborators guilty of war crimes and sentenced them to death.

Litigating Identity in Fascist and Post-Fascist Romania, 1940–1945

*Mihaela Şerban**

Abstract: *This paper examines legal mobilization and resistance to efforts through law to delineate ethnic identities during World War Two in Romania. Anti-Semitic legislation adopted under the fascist regime attempted to create and classify Jewish identity, while the end of war legislation formally reversed all discriminatory statutes and decrees and more broadly banned all inquiries into the ethnicity of Romanian citizens.[1] Under both legal regimes, one's identity, whether* de jure *or* de facto, *was decisive for repressive state policies that targeted Romanian citizens based on their ethnic identity. The concept and content of ethnic identity, however, were far from a clear matter. I explore in this paper how the local administrative court in the city of Timişoara (both first instance and appeal) constructed ethnic identity based on the wartime racial legislation, and how the court continued to apply this judge-made identity to the newly disfavored groups, primarily Germans, at the end of the war.*

What does it mean to be Romanian, and what does a Romanian nation-state look like? Post-1918, the significantly enlarged Romanian state was obsessively focused on the second question, while somewhat taking for granted the answer to the first. Romanian state-building defined the interwar period and became particularly heated in the 1930s. Key philosophical and ideological debates pitted nationalist purists—focused on Romanian-ness as a spiritual/mystical, traditional, rural, religious (Orthodox), blood and national destiny discourse, against pragmatic ration-

---

* Associate Professor of Law and Society, Ramapo College of New Jersey. I am grateful to my co-editor for this special issue, Monica Ciobanu, and to Marina Zaloznaya, Marley Weiss, Alma Begicevic, Ole Hammerslev, Anna Dolidze, Andrea Carteny, Gergely Romsics, Ioan Marius Eppel, Tamás Révész, Adrian Cioflâncă, and the anonymous reviewers for their feedback and comments on various versions of this article.
1 While Antonescu's regime is often described as a military dictatorship, rather than a fascist regime in the strict sense after January 1941, I use the term in this article in a broad sense because the legislation discussed traverses the Iron Guard and Antonescu periods.

alist progressives more concerned with state building (economic and social progress).[2] Education was a front runner in the subjectification and identity building project,[3] solidifying what it meant to be Romanian and who counted as Romanian.[4] Yet law was also an obvious space, both from instrumentalist and meaning-making perspectives.

Law is never just a spectator in state and nation-building, or simply a reflection of broader political, social, or cultural trends. Most modern legalities, whether in democratic or authoritarian regimes, can be understood on at least four dimensions: providing justice (whether formal, substantive, equality, fairness, class-based, as in communism, or race-based, as in fascism, etc.), order (which includes basic dispute resolution, regulatory functions, and social control), social change (social engineering), and constructing meaning (values, community, culture, or, in Clifford Geertz' phrasing, "a distinctive manner of imagining the real").[5]

Like other types of authoritarian legalities (such as communist), late interwar Romanian legality was characterized by duality, the co-existence of the law of repression (specifically racialized) and that of ordinary life,[6] an instrument of the state, and a space for identity and community-building, drawing from traditionalism and nationalism as normative and discursive sources within the highly positivist civil law tradition.[7] This very co-existence constructs authoritarian legality as simultaneously, albeit

---

2   Erwin Kessler, "Ideas and Ideology in Interwar Romania," *Plural Magazine: Culture and Civilization*, 29, no. 1 (2007), https://www.icr.ro/pagini/ideas-and-ideology-in-interwar-romania/en, accessed April 9, 2017.
3   Irina Livezeanu, *Cultural Politics in Greater Romania: Regionalism, Nation Building, and Ethnic Struggle, 1918–1930* (Ithaca: Cornell University Press, 1995 & 2000).
4   Lucian Boia, *Cum s-a românizat România* (București: Humanitas, 2015 & 2018).
5   Clifford Geertz, *Local Knowledge: Further Essays in Interpretive Anthropology* (New York: Basic Books, 1983).
6   This conceptualization originates in analyses of communist law, see Inga Markovits, "The Death of Socialist Law?" *The Annual Review of Law and Social Science*, 3 (2007):233–253; John Hazard, *Communists and Their Law* (Chicago: University of Chicago Press, 1970). Exploring various types of authoritarian legality has recently flourished, for example, Mary Gallagher, *Authoritarian Legality in China* (Cambridge: Cambridge University Press, 2017); Jothi Rajah, *Authoritarian Rule of Law: Legislation, Discourse and Legitimacy in Singapore* (Cambridge: Cambridge University Press, 2012); Michael Livingston, *The Fascists and the Jews of Italy* (Cambridge: Cambridge University Press, 2014).
7   A recent study of interwar legality in Romania is Cosmin S. Cercel, "The Enemy Within: Criminal Law and Ideology in Interwar Romania," in *Fascism and Criminal Law. History, Theory, Continuity*, ed. Stephen Skinner (Oxford: Hart Publishing, 2015), 101–26. A study of early communist legality is Mihaela Șerban, *Subverting Communism in Romania: Law and Private Property, 1945–1965* (Lanham, MD: Lexington Books/Rowman and Littlefield, 2019).

unequally, an instrument of power and a space of (some) resistance.[8] The exercise of power usually provides openings for resistance, and their co-dependence means that not only power is "everywhere" (Foucault), but so is resistance. Law—norms, practices, ideology, meaning-making, belongs to this liminal space between power and resistance.

The focus of this article is the infrapolitics of resistance[9] through legal mobilization (the process by which individuals claim their rights and pursue those claims in court),[10] specifically resistance to efforts through law to fix, delineate ethnic identities and implicitly determine the meaning of Romanian-ness and otherness in the context of nation-state building. I focus on two moments here: the first is litigation on the basis of Decree 2650/1940, a Nuremberg-inspired piece of anti-Semitic legislation concerning the judicial status of Jewish inhabitants of Romania. The Decree classified the Jewish population into three categories (based on religion and birth) and imposed political, economic, social and educational restrictions on all three categories. Jewish claimants mobilized and asked administrative courts to decide on their legal status (either as Christian or as Jewish category II, the most favorable of the three). The second moment came at the end of the war with the adoption of measures that imposed punishments such as forced labor and expropriations on the basis of social and political affiliation, and ethnicity, specifically German and Hungarian. Once again, the same administrative courts were swamped by claimants asking them to decide upon their ethnic status under the law. Most of these claims requested the classification of petitioners and their families as Czech, French, Hungarian or Slovak.

I explore in this paper how the local administrative court in the city of Timișoara (both first instance and appeal) constructed ethnic identity based on the wartime racial legislation, and how the court continued to

---

8   See Steve Pile, "Opposition, Political Identities and Spaces of Resistance," in *Geographies of Resistance*, eds. Steve Pile and Michael Keith (London: Routledge, 1997), 1–32; Michel Foucault, *Power* Vol. 3, ed. James D. Faubion (New York: The New Press, 2000); James H. Mittelman and Christine B.N. Chin, "Conceptualizing Resistance to Globalization," in *The Global Resistance Reader*, ed. Louise Amoore (London: Routledge, 2005), 17–27; James C. Scott, *Weapons of the Weak: Everyday Forms of Peasant Resistance* (New Haven and London: Yale University Press, 1985); Steven Lukes, *Power: A Radical View* (New York: Palgrave MacMillan, 2nd ed., 2005).

9   Acts, gestures, etc. that are not overtly political yet collectively amount to, or are recognizable as political action. James C. Scott, *Domination and the Arts of Resistance: Hidden Transcripts* (New Haven and London: Yale University Press, 1990).

10 Charles Epp, *The Rights Revolution* (Chicago: The University of Chicago Press, 1998).

apply this judge-made identity to the newly disfavored groups, primarily Germans, at the end of the war. While under fascism and throughout Antonescu's regime judges used original intent and literalism to further the racist ideology embedded in legislation, during the transitional period to communism that immediately followed they deployed a legal instrumentalist, realist approach driven by policy-making priorities. On a case by case basis, building on prior cases (although not strictly precedent), the court constructed an essentialist concept of ethnicity tied to the redistribution of power and resources in a region historically dominated by fluid, mixed identities. The consequences for the two groups—Jewish and German/French/Czech—were distinct: the vast majority of Jewish claimants lost, while the majority of the non-Jewish claimants won.

This historical episode informs at least three different areas of research: first, a better understanding of the role of courts during authoritarianism, in particular lower level courts in everyday life, and a more nuanced understanding of how the type of authoritarianism matters; second, the extent to which citizens mobilize the law even under very repressive conditions; and third, how authoritarian regimes skillfully use law to construct identity, community, history and memory.

History and Identity in Banat and Interwar Romania

Decree-Law 2650/1940 concerning the legal status of the Jewish inhabitants of Romania was adopted on August 8, 1940 and remained one of the keystone pieces of racial legislation in the country during the Second World War. The Decree defined and categorized the Jewish population of Romania based on "blood" and religion, and imposed restrictions based on these classifications. However, it was not consistent with other pieces of legislation, some of which stressed parentage, others religion (anti-Semitic legislation started in 1938 with numerous statutes, decrees, and other lower order acts).[11]

This statutory incoherence is not surprising given that there was little concept of what it meant to be Romanian, or German, or anything else (Law 724/1924 that regulated Romanian citizenship conflated citizenship and nationality). While much of the anti-Semitic legislation reflected

---

11 For example, Decree-Law 3347 from October 4, 1940 considered Jewish all those with at least a Jewish parent, regardless of religion, while Decree-Law 3438 from October 14, 1940 similarly forbade access to schools to those born from Jewish parents, again regardless of religion. Federația Comunităților Evreiești din România (henceforth FCER), *Evreii din România între anii 1940–1944*, Vol. I (București: Hasefer, 1993), XXVIII–XXIX.

the scientific racism broadly popular at the time, which emphasized race as a biological, immutable attribute, its implementation turned out to be a different matter altogether in a region defined by complex ethnic and religious mixes and "slippery" identities.[12] How the administrative court approached the identity cases that came before it was shaped not just by the formalist, legal positivist civil law tradition, but also by the recent concerted state-led efforts to construct the Romanian nation state, and separately (but related), the autochthonous anti-Semitism that impacted Banat in specific ways.

Timișoara and the historical Banat region were pluralistic from an ethnic, linguistic, and religious perspective (more than either Hungary or Austria, or Wallachia and Moldavia).[13] The region's main groups included Serbs, Hungarians, Romanians, Germans, Bulgarians, and Jews. In 1930, Timișoara had 91,866 inhabitants, was the seventh largest city in Romania, and had 26 percent Romanians, 30 percent Hungarians, 30 percent Germans and 8 percent Jewish population.[14] In the entire Banat region, Romanians were barely over 50 percent, with Germans the next group, almost a quarter of the population. There were 11,248 Jewish inhabitants in Banat, representing 1.2 percent of the population of the region. Over 80 percent of them were urban, and languages spoken were primarily German, Hungarian, and Yiddish. By comparison, of the total Jewish population of Romania (a little over 700,000, and representing 4.2 percent of the total population of the country), 68 percent were urban, and 32 percent rural.[15] By 1942, primarily due to the 1940 Hitler-Stalin pact, that number grew to 14,009, as Jewish refugees fled to the south of the new border.[16] The 1930 census does not quite capture the diversity of the Jewish communities based on region,[17] but the conception of ethnicity at the

---

12 In Margaret MacMillan's words, this was an area "where the whole notion of national identity was as slippery as the Danube eels." Margaret MacMillan, *Paris 1919* (New York: Random House, 2002), 132.
13 Victor Neumann, "Timișoara Between "Fictive Ethnicity" and "Ideal Nation." The Identity Profile During the Interwar Period," *Balcanica*, 44 (2013):391–412; Rudolf Gräf, "Germanii din Banat sau istoria între două emigrări. Cercul care s-a închis," in *Germanii din Banat prin povestirile lor*, ed. Smaranda Vultur (București: POLIROM, 2018), 28.
14 Ioan Munteanu and Rodica Munteanu, *Timișoara. Monografie* (Timișoara: Mirton, 2002), 150.
15 FCER, *Evreii din România între anii 1940–1944 Vol.II*, 68–72, 74–76, 83, 92–94.
16 Ibid., 90.
17 For an overview, see Raul Cârstocea, "Anti-Semitism in Romania: Historical Legacies, Contemporary Challenges," European Center for Minority Studies, Working Paper #81 (2014).

heart of the census was subjective—the state recorded identities as chosen by individuals, did not create them. Unlike prior censuses, the 1930 census recorded ethnicity/nationality, religion, and languages.

Post-1918 Romania struggled with democratization, economic development, and perhaps more than anything, incorporating the new minorities, who were overall more urban, educated, and modern than ethnic Romanians, while also belonging to different religious traditions. The project of building a unitary Romanian nation state centered "the peasant" as the symbol of the new nation (even as the focus increasingly shifted to Romanianizing the cities), imposed uniformity and homogenization (basically Romanianization), deployed education and culture as key instruments of state building, and was defined by struggles between urban and rural, Romanian and foreigner, new and old elites.[18] This also included efforts to clarify and redefine ethnic boundaries, such as only partially successful attempts to re-Romanianize the Romanians from Transylvania or Banat who had been part of Austro-Hungary, especially those who belonged to the "wrong" Greek Catholic Church (as Orthodoxy was increasingly seen as central to Romanian identity), but also "encouraging" Magyarized Germans to re-Germanize by banning them from Hungarian schools. Jews who were Magyarized (spoke Hungarian) were not allowed in Hungarian language schools (sent to Romanian schools), and German-speaking Jews were similarly redirected to Romanian schools.[19]

The 1938 legislation and later the 1940 Decree were outgrowths of nationalism (such as the extreme nationalism among university students that gave rise to the Iron Guard), anti-urbanism, anti-Semitism and general xenophobia.[20] Equal rights for minorities had been seen as "illegitimate, alien grafts",[21] specifically vis-à-vis the Jewish community, for some time.[22] The 1923 Constitution finally established equal rights for all Romanian citizens, but also described Romania as a "national state, unitary and indivisible" (Article 1), and banned "foreign colonization" (Article 3).[23] Despite formal equal rights, widespread anti-Semitism across the po-

---

18 Livezeanu, *Cultural Politics in Greater Romania*, 7–25, 135.
19 Boia, *Cum s-a românizat România*, 70–71.
20 Livezeanu, *Cultural Politics in Greater Romania*; Roland Clark, *Holy Legionary Youth. Fascist Activism in Interwar Romania* (Ithaca: Cornell University Press, 2015).
21 Livezeanu, *Cultural Politics in Greater Romania*, 7–8.
22 E.L. Woodward, *The Congress of Berlin 1878* (London: HM Stationery Office, 1920); Livezeanu, *Cultural Politics in Greater Romania*; MacMillan, *Paris 1919*.
23 See Constantin Iordachi, *Liberal, Constitutional Nationalism, and Minorities: The Making of Romanian Citizenship, 1750–1918* (Brill, 2019) on the exclusion of Jews from citizenship and their political emancipation prior to 1918.

litical, ideological, and cultural spectrum was the rule, rather than the exception, in interwar Romania. While Romania's anti-Semitic legislation was of German inspiration, its anti-Semitism is indigenous to a very large extent, merely taking advantage of the Nazi era developments to flourish.[24] The internal contradictions of the far right, in particular the fights between the Iron Guard and General Antonescu, merely signal different approaches towards Romania's "Jewish question."[25] By the end of the war, more than half of Romania's Jews had been murdered in the Holocaust.[26]

Throughout this period, however, the imprecision and ambiguity plaguing key concepts such as ethnic Romanian/Romanian by blood, Jewish or German did not really disappear. Different branches of the government understood it differently, and there were diverse public perceptions and subjective definitions. Unlike the Nazis, the Antonescu regime did not rely primarily on scientific racism during the Romanianization process.[27] In December 1941, the Ministry of Foreign Affairs published a consular textbook for diplomatic offices, "Who is Jewish According to the Romanian Judicial System." In a government meeting also in December 1941, however, the Minister of Justice Constantin Stoicescu admitted the difficulty of establishing ethnic origins.[28] In practice, the most commonly used proxy for identity was last names, for example in order to deny or allow a child to enroll in a particular school (German or Hungarian; ethnic Germans were often suspected of being Jewish).[29] When needed, bureaucrats also relied on proxies such as certificates of nationality and baptism certificates,[30] although these were also open to forgery.[31]

---

24 See Jean Ancel, *Contribuții la istoria României: Problema evreiască* (București: Hasefer, 2001); Victor Neumann, *Istoria Evreilor din România* (Timișoara: Amarcord, 1996).
25 See FCER, *Evreii din România între anii 1940–1944* Vol. II.
26 Yad Vashem, "Murder of the Jews of Romania," https://www.yadvashem.org/holocaust/about/final-solution-beginning/romania.html, accessed December 3, 2019.
27 Ștefan Cristian Ionescu, *Jewish Resistance to 'Romanianization', 1940–44* (Basingstoke: Palgrave Macmillan, 2015), 45. An exception was the case of the Csangos, a Hungarian and Romanian speaking minority from Moldova, see Chris R. Davis, *Hungarian Religion, Romanian Blood. A Minority's Struggle for National Belonging, 1920–1945* (Madison, WI: The University of Wisconsin Press, 2018).
28 Ionescu, *Jewish Resistance*, 46.
29 Boia, *Cum s-a românizat România*, 71.
30 Ionescu, *Jewish Resistance*, 46–7.
31 There is evidence of criminal cases against forgers. National Archives of Romania Timișoara (henceforth ANR), Fond Curtea de Apel Timișoara, Inv. 1708 (1938).

Identity and Racialized Injustice

The 1938 Constitution, Decree-Law 2650/1940 and its explanatory report, which was central to the judges' interpretation of the statute, crystallize the ascendance of primordialist, essentialist conceptions of ethnicity and race, respectively, which see identity as a biological, immutable attribute, as well as a rather static one. Social constructivist approaches, by contrast, see identity in flux, as contingent historically, socially, culturally, etc. Unlike ethnicity, less plagued by power distinctions, processes of racialization are intertwined with systematic power imbalances based on conceptions of inferiority and superiority, implying not only differential status, value, and privilege, but also justifying stigmatization and vilification, inside and outside of the law.[32]

The 1938 Constitution laid the foundations for dictatorship and for the shift from liberal constitutionalism towards ethnic constitutionalism (although racial constitutionalism seems the more appropriate description, and for purposes of this article, I use them interchangeably). Classical liberal constitutionalism is organized around the concept of citizenship with equal rights and duties, with no distinctions between members of different minority groups. By contrast, ethnic/racial constitutionalism has the distinctions as foundational. In its most problematic variations, the constitution entrenches the hegemony of one ethnic group above all others, and the legal system becomes one instrument in maintaining this hegemony.[33] The 1938 Constitution declared Romania a unitary, national, and indivisible state (Article 1), forbade "foreign populations" from settling on Romania's territory (Article 3), declared the Romanian Orthodox Church as the national church (Article 19), and imposed various restrictions on non-citizens "taking into account the majoritarian, state-creating function of the Romanian nation" (Article 27).

This constitutional framework shaped how the Decree regulated the spiritual, political, and economic status of Romania's Jewish population. While formally preserving freedom of thought, religion, religious education, and association, the Decree aimed to insure the separation of the

---

32 See Henry E. Hale, "Explaining Ethnicity," *Comparative Political Studies*, 37, no.4 (2004): 458–485; Philip Q. Yang, *Ethnic Studies: Issues and Approaches* (Albany: SUNY Press, 2000); Hazel Rose Markus, "Pride, Prejudice, and Ambivalence: Toward a Unified Theory of Race and Ethnicity," *American Psychologist*, 63 (2008): 651–670; Stephen Cornell and Douglas Hartmann, *Ethnicity and Race: Making Identities in a Changing World* (Thousand Oaks, CA: Pine Forge Press, 1998), 42.

33 Yash Ghai, "The Implementation of the Fiji Islands Constitution," in *Confronting Fiji Futures*, ed. A. Haroon Akram-Lodhi (Canberra: The Australian National University, 2016).

Jewish community from the Romanian majority. Its explanatory report also reinterpreted concepts of equality before the law and the right to work, and stressed the priority of duties over rights (all Romanian citizens were equal before the law in terms of their duties, but not rights). Article 2 of the Decree used religion and descendance to define who counted as "legally Jewish," a category that included persons belonging to Judaism, their children (even if baptized, but parents had not converted, as well as children from mixed marriages with a Jewish father, and illegitimate children with a Jewish mother), and atheist Jews. Baptized women married to Christians were exempt, but only if they converted before June 22, 1939.

Article 3 of the Decree divided the Jewish population into three categories, with the third the default and therefore the largest, and the second with the least restrictions. Category I included Jews who entered Romania after December 30, 1918. Category II (Article 5) included, among others, those who had obtained citizenship on an individual basis before December 30, 1918, as well as those who had "actively fought for Romania, in Romania's wars, with the exception of those taken prisoner/captured, missing, or deserters." Restrictions for all categories included a ban on owning rural properties, possible loss of custody for baptized children, and a ban on obtaining Romanian names (Article 14). What counted as a Romanian name was not defined. Bans for individuals belonging to categories I and III were extensive. Among others, they could not be civil servants, lawyers, experts, notaries public, in the military, or book or newspaper editors (Articles 7,8). Military duties were explicitly transformed into financial obligations, or labor duty (Article 10). By contrast, individuals belonging to category II were only subject to the general bans. However, even for this less-discriminated against category, it was forbidden to pursue a military career, or to become a civil servant if not already one.

Decree 2650 and its explanatory report (the author was the Minister of Justice Ion Gruia, a constitutional law professor at the University of Bucharest Law School) placed Romanian anti-Semitism within the framework of racialized constitutionalism, and redefined citizenship and Romanian-ness. The basis of the state was the Romanian nation, defined as a legal and political community, as well as "a spiritual and organic community based on blood, which gives rise to a hierarchy of political rights."[34] Gruia argued that the 1938 constitution-maker distinguished between Romanian citizens—a formal legal category, and Romanian citizens by blood, with the latter the truly significant category, and that a key goal of

---

34   FCER, *Evreii din România între anii 1940–1944* Vol. I, 39.

Decree 2650 was to regulate "the rights of the Jews without taking away their citizenship, which is unimportant at the moment."[35] As it turned out, the goal was to redefine citizenship itself, as the Decree created a three-tiered, unequal citizenship system: a somewhat favored category of Jews, the rest of the Jewish inhabitants of Romania, and everyone else. Since "Romanians by blood" were not defined, they appeared to include all other ethnic and religious minorities at the time: the 1930 census found that 28 percent of Romania's population identified themselves as belonging to eighteen different ethnic groups (Hungarians, Germans, Bulgarians, Serbs, Czech, Tatars, Albanians, Armenians, etc.).[36]

The only indication about what being "Romanian by blood" might mean came only at the end—"our nation is a nation of peasants"—and is reflected in the interdiction for Jews to acquire rural properties. Only 30 percent of the Jewish population of Romania lived in rural areas, and in regions like Banat that percentage was smaller (20 percent), so the interdiction must be understood less from an economic and more from a symbolic perspective. It was not linked to numbers (or other ethnicities, since not all peasants were ethnic Romanians), but to the hypothetical soul of the Romanian nation, constructed as inherently agrarian. It was also a building block in the system of power, expropriation, and exploitation at the heart of politically and legally enshrined anti-Semitism.[37] This was made explicit by Gruia in the explanatory report, where he clarified that the various bans directly aimed to Romanianize the economy and society as a measure of historical justice: "Romania belongs to Romanians only ... Our nation is a nation of peasants; peasants are its source, our nobility of land and blood."[38] Ultimately, being Romanian was simply defined as not being Jewish, as in the preamble of the June 8, 1940 Decree that banned marriages between Jews and Romanians by blood, and consequently defined a Romanian by blood as any Romanian citizen who was not Jewish.[39]

Implicit in Decree 2650 is the gendered construction of identity—the father's religion and blood were the primary criteria of ethnicity, and only women baptized and married to Christians were not considered Jewish. In

---

35   Ibid., 40.
36   Boia, *Cum s-a românizat România*.
37   Ian-Haney Lopez, *White by Law: The Legal Construction of Race* (New York: NYU Press, 1996).
38   FCER, *Evreii din România între anii 1940–1944* Vol. I, 43.
39   Similarly, Decree-Law 711 from 1941 forbade Jews to convert to Christianity and punished those who did.

other words, only women's blood could be "cleansed" by conversion.⁴⁰ Finally, the Decree also constructed Jewish and non-Jewish as ethical concepts: being "Romanian by blood" was a good to be inherently defended, while being Jewish was inherently immoral: there was a "moral, spiritual, and organic incompatibility between a Romanian by blood and those belonging to Judaism," conversion was an act of political opportunism if only the children were baptized, and "blood" was not to be understood as a physical component, but an ethical one (as Gruia explained, the goal was to avoid difficulties encountered in other European legal systems).⁴¹

Jewish Claimants before the Court: Resistance through Law

A basic typology of resistance ranges from overt and radical, through accommodation, and ultimately (and arguably) to mere oppositional state of being.⁴² Resistance through law is a type of overt, non-violent resistance, targeted and strategic (if collective, such as public interest litigation), or diffuse, at individual levels (micro-resistance that may or may not have a clear outcome). As a foundational element of the state apparatus, law generally sustains structures of domination, yet even under authoritarian conditions may provide openings and opportunities for resistance (that may also simultaneously be a form of accommodation to state power),⁴³ especially if the legal profession is independent and organized.⁴⁴

The cases discussed in this article are one form of resistance through law belonging to the broader category of infra-politics of resistance. It is highly likely they were coordinated—many of the claimants were lawyers themselves, and this was a relatively small community. It should also be understood alongside other types of Jewish legal resistance to Romanianization, such as the tens of thousands of petitions against expropriations and evictions throughout the country (and at least 950 in Timișoara between 1942 and 1944).⁴⁵

---

40 For an overview of the connections between gender and citizenship, see Maria Bucur and Mihaela Miroiu, *Birth of Democratic Citizenship. Women and Power in Modern Romania* (Bloomington, IN: Indiana University Press, 2018).
41 FCER, *Evreii din România între anii 1940–1944* Vol. I, 40–1.
42 Jocelyn A. Hollander and Rachel L. Einwohner, "Conceptualizing Resistance," *Sociological Forum*, 19, no. 4 (2004):533–554.
43 E.g. Rajah, *Authoritarian Rule of Law*; Richard Abel, *Politics by Other Means: Law in the Struggle against Apartheid, 1980–1994* (New York and London: Routledge, 1995); Waikeung Tam, *Legal Mobilization under Authoritarianism. The Case of Post-Colonial Hong Kong* (Cambridge: Cambridge University Press, 2013).
44 See Tam, *Legal Mobilization under Authoritarianism*.
45 Ionescu, *Jewish Resistance*, 147–60; ANR, Fond Curtea de Apel Timișoara, Inv. 1277.

Decree 2650/1940 established a very tight statute of limitations—three months—for claims for individuals "who are unclear about their Jewish status" (Article 19). This framing of the issue both shifted the burden on the individuals, and introduced the state as the ultimate arbiter of one's identity. The administrative court had jurisdiction over these cases. Modeled on the French system of public law, it had extensive law-making power through the power of judicial review of administrative action. During the five-year period examined here, the court functioned with a recurring cast of characters (the same individuals, in different roles): three-judge panels at the appeal level, a representative of the Public Ministry presenting the position of the state, and a rapporteur.[46] They were all men, all part of the legal fabric of the city. One of them was a member of the National Peasants' Party and was later identified as a legionary. Another judge was a founding member of the Rotary Club in the city.[47] Presumably, they knew personally many of the Jewish claimants, since many of them were lawyers.

During this period, at least 40 claimants came forward. They included lawyers, accountants, engineers, businessmen, retirees, filing for themselves and sometimes on behalf of their children. The vast majority of claims were requests to be declared Jewish category II, based on two types of reasons: having been decorated during the war, and equality of treatment between the Jewish inhabitants from Transylvania and Banat, and Wallachia and Moldavia. A second large category of cases were claims to be declared Christian. With very few exceptions (noted below), all these claims were rejected by the court.[48]

Citizenship and Utility: Less Discrimination as Reward

Decree-Law 2650 included in the slightly less discriminatory category II individuals who were injured or decorated during World War I. While Article 5/d explicitly mentioned individuals who actively fought for Romania, in Romania's wars, the next paragraph only mentioned individuals injured or decorated for acts of bravery during the war, with no other reference to type of war or side of the war. Transylvania, as part of the former Austro-Hungarian Empire, fought on the side of the Central Powers,

---

46 The names are listed at the beginning of all court decisions studied here. ANR, Fond Curtea Locală Administrativă Timișoara, Files 33/1940, 36/1940, 22/1944, 23/1944.
47 "Istoric Rotary Club Timișoara," https://www.rotarytm.ro/, accessed 3 December 2019.
48 ANR, Fond Curtea Locală Administrativă Timișoara, Files 33/1940, 36/1940, 22/1944, 23/1944.

while Romania was on the side of the Allies. The lack of clarity in the legislation gave cause of action to some of the petitioners, who asked to be declared category II because they were decorated during the war (such as a lawyer who had converted to Catholicism and had two separate claims).[49]

An accountant from Timișoara, also decorated during the war, argued that Decree 2650 did not specify which army: "the legislator intentionally intended participation in Romania's wars, which is normal, since the law wanted to reward those who are deserving and who did their duty and followed commands, regardless of the army in which they served, since this is entirely independent of the individual." The court rejected this interpretation and relying upon legislative intent and the explanatory report, concluded that Jewish category II was meant only for wars fought on behalf of Romania. The petitioner put forward a literalist interpretation of Decree 2650, but the court favored an original intent one.[50]

By contrast, a Timișoara merchant succeeded in having his WWI bravery claim accepted. Unlike the accountant, the merchant was decorated by the Romanian Ministry of War and also naturalized (on the basis of an individual statute) by a tribunal in Wallachia. Notably, the public ministry representative (the accuser before the administrative court) was not opposed to granting the request.[51] The only other similar claims admitted came from Jews from Wallachia who fought on behalf of Romania during the war and subsequently moved to Banat.

In 1943, Law 143 legally assimilated three main categories of Jews to ethnic Romanians: Jews who had volunteered to serve in the Romanian army and had fought on the frontline in the Second Balkan War and World War I; Jewish soldiers in the Romanian army who had been awarded citizenship during WWI for their bravery; and those who "proved themselves useful and faithful to the Romanian nation through their devotion and exceptional deeds or through their constant and praiseworthy activity."[52] Utility as a condition of citizenship goes back to at least the 1924 citizenship statute, which shortened time to citizenship for foreigners seeking naturalization if they proved they were useful to the nation (Article 8/a).

---

49   ANR, Fond Curtea Locală Administrativă Timișoara, File 33/1940, 2.
50   Ibid., 19–25.
51   Ibid., 50.
52   Ionescu, *Jewish Resistance*, 153.

Ethnicity, Citizenship, and Inequality

A second and far larger category of claims fundamentally questioned the *de facto* inequality of treatment of Jews from Transylvania and Banat, compared to those from Wallachia and Moldavia. The key historical distinction is that in Transylvania and Banat, Jewish emancipation was successful (through the Austro-Hungarian Law XVII from 1867). By contrast, the 1866 Constitution of Romania specified in Article 7 that only Christians could become Romanian citizens, a provision that signaled the acceptability of various anti-Semitic measures during the late 19th–early 20th century. It was only under pressure from international powers, which linked Romania's independence to amending Article 7, that Romania revised it in 1879 to allow access to citizenship regardless of religious beliefs, albeit on an individual basis. As a reward for participating in Romania's independence war against the Ottoman Empire, 888 Jews were thus granted citizenship, which was a very small proportion of the entire Jewish population at the time.[53]

The creation of category II by Decree 2650 as a less-discriminated against category is thus not accidental, as it builds upon Romania's history of discrimination. Neither is 1918 as the cut-off date: prior to 1923, only a very small minority of the country's Jewish population had full equality and citizenship rights, while the reverse was true in Transylvania and Banat, where full emancipation had been in effect for some time. The categorization thus achieved two goals: first, to reverse emancipation *de facto*, and second, to create new levels of discrimination between the Jewish inhabitants of Romania, specifically against those from Transylvania and Banat, for whom it was impossible under Article 5 of Decree 2650 to qualify as Jews category II, given the different regional historical contexts.

The struggle of Jewish claimants from the Banat to be recognized as category II is thus a struggle to preserve their fully equal citizen status, as it had been recognized since 1867. Claimants' histories and arguments before the court are revealing: a lawyer from Timișoara and his son, a veterinary medicine student, had been granted full citizenship under the 1867 Austro-Hungarian statute;[54] another lawyer from Timișoara and Subotica (in Vojvodina) talked about his grandfather, born in 1804 in Timișoara, who had been granted citizenship on the basis of the 1848 (first, short emancipation) and 1867 statutes in the Austro-Hungarian Empire, which (he argued) enjoyed full legal continuity after 1918.[55]

---

53 Victor Neumann, *Istoria Evreilor din România* (Timișoara: Amarcord, 1996), 171.
54 ANR, Fond Curtea Locală Administrativă Timișoara, File 33/1940, 26–27.
55 Ibid., 57–58.

A couple who filed their claim together explicitly relied upon the inequality between Jews from different historical regions: for Jews from Regat, individual naturalization was the only option before 1918, while for those from the Austro-Hungarian Empire, there were statutes in 1867 and 1879 that granted them citizenship as a group (emancipation). Individual naturalization was an option only for those that immigrated after 1879 to Romania, which paradoxically privileged them in 1940.[56]

Most claimants argued that the 1940 lawmaker did not intend to exclude all Transylvanian Jews from category II, or to discriminate between Jews from different regions. Other claimants took the argument a step further, such as a lawyer from Buteni who claimed a bigger right to citizenship of Jews from Transylvania and Banat compared to those from Regat, precisely because of the prior full emancipation.[57] Some claimants relied on the concept of legal continuity and asserted a pre-existing right (not creating new rights),[58] while yet a different group (including one of the very few women, a lawyer who became a criminal judge after 1948) claimed category II status on the basis of a 1903 Hungarian statute granting nationalization on an individual basis (in turn based on the 1867 statute).[59]

All of these claims were rejected, and none of the court's decisions veer from the following key literalist points: first, the legislator did not give Jewish inhabitants from the territories annexed by Romania after 1918 automatically category II status, but on the contrary required naturalization through "individual statute or individual legal provision." Second, "the concern is today, 1940, and regulating the statute of Jews in Romania based on Romanian laws, not foreign laws now abrogated." Third, as the petitioners became Romanian citizens by annexation, they could not rely on prior, foreign laws. Fourth, Decree 2650 created category II status based on "exceptional merits" particularly on the basis of fighting for Romania. Therefore, a Jewish individual from the annexed territories may be local/indigenous to Banat or Transylvania, but he could not claim that in his capacity as former Hungarian citizen, he contributed in any measure to Romania's independence, unification, or progress, therefore could not claim category II status.[60]

---

56 Ibid., 89.
57 ANR, Fond Curtea Locală Administrativă Timișoara, File 22/1944, 83–86.
58 Ibid., 183–187.
59 Ibid., 287–291, 292–295.
60 ANR, Fond Curtea Locală Administrativă Timișoara, File 33/1940, 29–32, 64–68, 95–99.

Fifth, petitioners had no *de jure* or *de facto* claim of inequality between Jews from old Romania and those from annexed territories, "and if such inequality exists, it is for good reason, as the legislator wants to reward those Jews who contributed to Romania's independence, unification, or progress." There was no inequality of treatment, the court argued, since category III includes all individuals, while category I includes all those who came after 1918: "therefore the legislator does not **distinguish** among Jews who are Romanian citizens on a regional basis, but creates a single system of **reward**—which is not the same thing—for a small part of the Jewish population that identifies with the aspirations of the Romanian nation and therefore gained the right to exceptional treatment by the Romanian state" (underlined in the original).[61]

The court's reasoning packages racist (in)justice in a tight formalist framework. At the heart of it is an understanding of Jews as foreigners who under the best of circumstances can "buy" their way in on a limited basis only (the reward for exceptional merits discussion). There is also a double legal burden, as Jewish inhabitants of Transylvania and Banat cannot benefit from prior Hungarian laws granting them full citizenship, but can certainly suffer because of them, since they had been Hungarian citizens and thus inherently suspicious. Clearly this burden does not carry through for Romanians or other minorities from those regions. If Jews from Transylvania cannot claim in any way to have contributed to Romania's progress or nationhood, could Germans or Hungarians? And are Romanians from Transylvania assumed to have automatically contributed simply by being Romanian?

This inequality of treatment also sheds light on the unraveling of the very meaning of citizenship: from a liberal understanding of citizenship as anointing membership in a community with equal rights and responsibilities belonging to all citizens regardless of ethnicity, language, religion, etc., to a duty-based, three-tiered concept of ethnic/racial citizenship. First-tier citizenship is racially-based and includes all non-Jewish citizens of Romania. Second-tier citizenship is reserved for category II Jews, is duty-based, maintains some rights, includes only a minority of Romania's Jewish inhabitants, and automatically excludes all Jews from Transylvania and Banat. As Romanian-ness was key to this political and ideological discourse, the exclusion of Banat and Transylvania's Jews, many of whom straddled identities, pointed to their double "foreignness," since many of them had partially assimilated to either German or Hungarian communi-

---

61   Ibid.

ties. Third-tier citizenship included the vast majority of the Jewish inhabitants of Romania. This third-class category of citizenship was heavily duty-based, stripped of key rights and privileges, in effect re-creating Jews as a barely tolerated, always under suspicion minority. Citizenship ceased to be the primary category organizing the relationship between individuals and the state, and was replaced by race/ethnicity, with citizenship subordinated to it.

Religion and Blood

A third category of claims before the court were requests to be declared non-Jewish/Christian. While religion was initially the formal criterion for creating "statutory Jews," in practice the religious criterion was used interchangeably with the blood criterion. Article 2 itself constructed Jewish identity as a broad net capturing both. Most of the cases in this category involved claimants from mixed Christian-Jewish marriages or claimants who converted to Christianity, and raised the following questions: is birth or upbringing determinative, and what is the impact of religious conversion? The court ultimately determined that blood, heredity, and in particular paternal heredity, was the ultimate criterion, and that when in doubt, there is a presumption of being Jewish.

In response to the petition of an engineer, born in 1892 and baptized Reformed at age seven, with parents baptized as well, the court found that the Decree (and explanatory report) conflated Jewish by ancestry and by religion. The court ruled that there could only be considered Christian the child who was baptized at birth, thus "**was never baptized under Judaism**" (underlined in the decision). Baptizing the child was an act of "political opportunism" that could not be overcome by the "implacable [Jewish] origin/ancestry." The intention of the legislator, in the eyes of the court, was to consider Christian only the child baptized at birth by already baptized Jews, since a key goal of the statute was "preventing the infiltration of the Christian community by Jews." The engineer, baptized at seven, was declared statutorily Jewish.[62]

Literalism and legal formalism occasionally provided a shield for Jewish claimants, as in the case of a city hall accountant fired for being Jewish. She was born Jewish, but married a teacher of Orthodox religion in 1909 and converted in 1921, so well before the 1939 statutory deadline. The court declared the firing illegal, found her Christian on the basis

---

62   Ibid., 33–42.

of Article 2/f of Decree-Law 2650 (baptized women married to Christians), and ruled in her favor on both reinstatement and ethnicity, on a strictly religious basis.[63] The case highlights the gendered construction of ethnicity and questions the predominant narrative of "preventing the infiltration of the Romanian community." The gendered nature of constructing ethnicity is also clear in the case of an engineer, also fired from his job as chief of the technical service for the county, also baptized, but who could not prove that his parents were baptized Christians (a question not raised for the accountant). The court declared him Jewish category III, and found that his firing "can, and should happen." Two significant differences from the accountant's case: gender, and religion of conversion.[64]

The court continued to struggle to reconcile the incoherent religion + blood + gendered definitions of Decree 2650. Conversion of a parent mattered only sometimes (if the marriage convention was that the children were to be born and raised Catholic),[65] but death of a parent when the child was small did not make a difference if the parent never converted, even if the child was born and raised Christian.[66] Later conversion, whether for petitioners or their parents, could not erase the "implacable ancestry/origin," as Decree 2650 intended to stop the "infiltration" of Jewish children into the Romanian community (keep "racial purity").[67] Illegitimacy meant that only the mother's religion at birth mattered, regardless of any subsequent changes (such as conversion or marrying the Christian birth father).[68]

Regardless of how creative the lawyers' arguments were, or how sympathetic the court seemed sometimes, ultimately almost all of these claims were rejected. These outcomes are worse than for expropriation and eviction cases, which had some success: by September 1943, approximately 10 percent of the National Romanianization Center decisions were reversed. These cases were decided by special panels within courts of appeal, enjoyed some autonomy, and sometimes decided in favor of Jewish plaintiffs. Ionescu suggests that this limited success through law was "facilitated by the ambiguous nature of legal provisions, which lacked clarity and consistency, and stipulated many exceptions," and therefore "enabled different interpretations of the same legal text."[69] The much

---

63   ANR, Fond Curtea Locală Administrativă Timișoara, File 36/1940, 10–13.
64   Ibid., 86–89.
65   Ibid., 122–125.
66   Ibid., 3–6.
67   Ibid., 148–152.
68   Ibid., 95–98.
69   Ionescu, *Jewish Resistance*, 147–57.

more consistent and negative results in the identity cases show how literalist and originalist judges operated under the cover of legal positivism to advance the racist ideology of the state.

Judge-made Identity

A fundamental problem facing the local administrative court and its docket of cases on Jewish identity was the lack of legal criteria for determining ethnicity. The only legislation that dealt with this issue was restricted to determining Jewish identity in the context of the Holocaust, which meant racializing it. Its mix of religious, blood, and ethical criteria might have functioned ideologically and politically by enlarging the category of who counted as Jewish under the law, but was otherwise incoherent. It was only a matter of time, moreover, before other claimants came forward asking for their ethnicity to be determined. Already in October 1940, the court rejected the claim of a civil servant who wanted to be categorized as German for lack of jurisdiction, stating that all it could do was find someone Jewish or Christian, but it could not inquire into ethnic origin otherwise.[70]

Yet it is the anti-Semitic legislation and the court's case law that established a modicum of principles, therefore constituted the basis for the post-1944 judge-made law on ethnicity. The late war ethnicity trials were explicitly decided on the racial criteria developed in the Jewish identity trials, thus reinforcing essentialist narratives. A clear example is the court's determination in the Jewish identity cases that ethnicity is established at birth, which subsequently became a cornerstone principle for all ethnic identity cases that came before it. One particular case decided on January 4, 1944, thus before the end of the war and not involving a Jewish identity case, was a watershed moment in how the local administrative court understood both its power and the construction of ethnicity.

The mayor of Arad refused to issue a German declaration of nationality to one of the town's inhabitants, who sued him. The claimant was born in 1915, an illegitimate child of a Roman Catholic mother, baptized Catholic at birth. His mother subsequently married his father, who was Jewish, in 1923. The mayor's refusal stemmed from this (retroactive) legitimation, from counting the father's ethnicity as more important than the mother's, and from an expansive understanding of his power to issue certificates of ethnic origin based on publicly known facts. The mayor was clearly engaged in his own attempt to construct ethnicity. The claimant

---

70   ANR, Fond Curtea Locală Administrativă Timișoara, File 36/1940, 34.

countered that legitimation through subsequent marriage only worked when the natural father was noted in the birth certificate, at birth; that prior case law established that for illegitimate children, the mother's ethnicity mattered and ethnic origin was established on the basis of parents' ethnicity at the time of the birth of the child; and finally, that once obtained at birth, ethnic identity could not be lost. The court overwhelmingly agreed and directed the mayor to issue the certificate of German ethnicity. It further clarified that ethnic identity was not a matter of private law open to contractual solutions, but a matter of public law that could not be resolved by the parties' agreement.[71] This decision shifted ethnicity from a personal to a state matter for all cases, not just those on Jewish identity.

The court reaffirmed this principle in another, similar German mother/Jewish father case, where the only difference was that the child was legitimate (thus the outcome was also different).[72] Here the court clarified the key principles for establishing ethnicity: that ethnicity is a fixed, unchangeable concept that is legally determined (an essentialist understanding of ethnicity), that it is not within the purview of an individual to determine their ethnic identity, that ethnicity begins at birth and can never be lost or changed, that ethnicity is pure, a zero-sum game (no case found mixed ethnicities or identities), and that ethnicity is a gendered concept insofar as the father's blood counts more heavily than the mother's. The court also moved quietly away from concerns of "racial purity" and "infiltration of Romanian community" seen in earlier cases (the year, 1944, when it looked like the Axis would lose the war, might have had something to do with this), in favor of some legal coherence and consistency.

The Game of Ethnicities

As the tide of the war turned, so did the cases that came before the court. As early as spring 1944, before Romania formally joined the Allies, the court started hearing cases on ethnic identity—claimants asking to be declared French, Czech, Hungarian, etc.—on a different statutory basis. A 1938 statute regulating, among others, the powers of local authorities, gave mayors the power to issue "certificates of notoriety" when so asked

---

71   ANR, Fond Curtea Locală Administrativă Timișoara, File 22/1944, 13–17.
72   ANR, Fond Curtea Locală Administrativă Timișoara, File 24/1944, 184–187.

by citizens.[73] Mayors' decisions were open to judicial review of administrative action, which became the main mechanism for cases on ethnicity other than Jewish. Two issues complicated these cases: standing, and the very concept of "certificates of notoriety."

By the time the court began to hear most of these cases, Romania had joined the Allies and all racial legislation was abolished. The 1923 Constitution was revived, and its formal equality provisions seemingly made ethnicity inquiries moot. Yet the court found that the vast majority of petitioners had standing because they had real, actual, legitimate reasons to sue. Suddenly moving away from formalism and literalism, the court took a (legal) realist approach and acknowledged that legislation "in force or not yet found unconstitutional" required citizens to prove their ethnic origin in their various dealings with the state. These included new measures against members of the German Ethnic Group, such as banning the use of radios for ethnic Germans and Hungarians, and forced labor by the same groups, among others. In a decision from October 24, 1944, the court determined that Article 5 of the 1923 Constitution "was not fully in force," and the petitioners had standing.[74] It is a rather extraordinary step for a local administrative court to virtually nullify the application of a constitutional provision, but one that is not incongruent with administrative courts' self-understanding of their roles and powers.

The court hit a more serious obstacle regarding standing with the adoption of the Nationalities Statute 86 from February 7, 1945, which directly banned inquiries into the ethnic origin of Romanian citizens (Article 2). The court became rather creative and continued to find standing based in part on original intent—the statute was meant to protect all Romanian citizens, so it could not be interpreted in a manner contrary to the intention of the lawmaker (cynically turning on its head the intention of the legislator to forbid inquiries into ethnicity because of prior anti-Semitic abuses). Other reasons also departed from legal formalism: if the court interpreted Article 2 in an "absolutely prohibitive manner," it would make it impossible for Romanian citizens targeted by various military and civil regulations to defend themselves, which would be "unfair and unjust" (for example, the Timiș prefect's order regarding mobilization for forced labor of ethnic Germans); finally, it was important to know one's ethnic origin in order to punish those who tried to avoid the law.[75]

---

73 These were distinct from certificates of nationality, which were issued on the basis of nationality registers, created by the 1924 citizenship statute and its implementation measures.
74 ANR, Fond Curtea Locală Administrativă Timișoara, File 24/1944, 245–254.
75 Ibid., 287–290.

Article 2 was amended on August 6, 1945 to allow for ethnic inquiries within a year from the date of the amendments. Romanian citizens could pursue declarations of nationality (ethnicity), only once, verbally or in writing, at city hall, otherwise declarations of nationality from the 1930 census (based on self-identification) remained valid. If one made no declaration in 1930 or 1945, and if no other nationality transpired from "acts or other facts," one's nationality was Romanian by default (!). Children followed the nationality of their parents: illegitimate children followed the mother's, children from mixed marriages followed the nationality of the father. Once they became legally adult, children had a year to declare whether they maintained their nationality or declared a new one. Finally, when one *chose* a nationality, they also had to declare the nationality recorded in the 1930 census. This may seem like the rebirth of subjective concepts of ethnicity, but state-assigned ethnicity is not fully gone, as "All Romanian citizens interested in the clarification of their old nationality (ethnic origin in the racial concepts of the past) can ask for city hall to investigate."

The petitioners' standing was overwhelmingly connected to avoiding forced labor, which the court sympathetically acknowledged as a real issue.[76] This was manifestly not the case for the Jewish claimants in the earlier cases, for whom acts such as conversion to Christianity were seen as illegitimate acts of political opportunism. The realist approach to interpreting standing rules reveals the court's sympathy towards this category of claimants, in contradistinction to the originalist, formalist approach used for the Jewish claimants. The outcomes of the cases reinforce the court's bias: most Jewish claimants lost, most others won (at least initially). This pattern confirms yet again, more subtly, that the Romanian community can encompass all but its Jewish members.

"Certificates of notoriety" complicated the issue even more, however, as the court was now forced to assess 'legally' and 'objectively' one's ethnicity, compared to public perceptions of one's identity, i.e. the whole village knows X as German or Hungarian. To solve this problem, the court initially added more criteria for determining ethnicity—family name, lan-

---

76 As early as fall 1944, ethnic Germans and Hungarians were mobilized for forced labor locally, later there were deportations in the Soviet Union.

guage, traditions, religion (Hungarians are mostly Evangelical, for example),[77] where one studied (e.g. France, despite the fact that this was common at the time),[78] devotion to one's community, one's behavior ("as always Hungarian"),[79] witness testimony, etc., before returning to heredity. The court also excluded some criteria, such as politics. In a May 1944 case challenging Timișoara mayor's decision to issue a certificate of German origin because the claimant could not prove that she was a member of the German Ethnic Group, the petitioner, a widow, argued that ethnic origin was a biological issue determined at birth, not dependent on membership in a political group.[80] The court agreed.

Other cases were significantly more complicated and forced the court to grapple with the concept of "notoriety." A Timișoara inhabitant sued the mayor for refusing to issue him and his father a certificate of French origin because both were "notoriously known as Hungarian." The claimant argued that his great-grandparents, married in 1799, were Catholics from Alsace-Lorraine settled in Banat as refugees after the 1771 German-French war, with a Magyarized family name, which did not, however, change its French origin. The court acknowledged first that Romanian law did not have rules for determining ethnic origin, and therefore would decide descendance based on common law ["normele dreptului comun"],[81] language, traditions and actions ["fapte"], education and culture, and feelings and attitudes. The claimant showed no proof that he was French, as neither history, nor name, nor witnesses were sufficient, and "notoriety" was not equal to "fame," but meant "knowledge, science" [cunoaștere, știință]. City hall did not undertake any investigations, therefore the mayor's decision to declare him Hungarian was "totally arbitrary," and the mayor could declare him neither French, nor Hungarian.[82]

By October 1944, the court had fully incorporated the requirement of an investigation by city hall, as well as its own field investigations and expert opinions, and had subsumed specific issues, such as last names, to

---

77   ANR, Fond Curtea Locală Administrativă Timișoara, File 24/1944, 315–319.
78   Ibid., 287–290.
79   Ibid., 339–343.
80   Ibid., 194–198.
81   Common law here in the sense of general principles, body of law, as opposed to special norms, provisions (*lex generalis* versus *lex specialis*).
82   In the only dissenting opinion I found, the dissenting judge argued that both claims should be rejected for lack of standing, in light of the constitutional principle of equality before the law. The reasoning in the dissenting opinion did not resurface. ANR, Fond Curtea Locală Administrativă Timișoara, File 24/1944, 245–254.

biological ascendance.[83] It also explicitly refined its key consistent holding, namely that since there were no norms regarding ethnic origin, the court had to follow its precedent, which indicated that ethnicity was obtained at birth and could never be lost, and that for legitimate children, the father's ethnicity carried the day, while for illegitimate children, the mother's. Most importantly, the court was willing to examine ascendance on the paternal side for as far back as it took to establish an uncontroversial origin.[84]

The case that epitomizes the struggle to define ethnic identities after the repeal of racist legislation, however, was a surprising class action law suit from March 1945. The villagers of Tomnatic (northwest corner of today's Timiș county), more precisely 879 of them, sued the Tomnatic city hall for refusing to issue them certificates of French, Czech, or Romanian origin. The 1930 census did not record any French speakers, and the Ministry of Internal Affairs considered them German, thus subject to forced labor orders (but suspended these orders pending the trial). The mayor, Nicolae Pierre, initially adopted a constructionist approach, arguing that ethnicity could change, politics mattered for these changes, and in Tomnatic the original French specificity had been absorbed by the local German culture. Following his own investigation, he eventually decided not to oppose the lawsuit. The villagers argued that ethnic origin could not be confused with nationality or native tongue, that it was biological and could not be changed or lost through political opinion or renunciation. Their lawyer proposed three principles for determining ethnicity: biological, with equal parental contributions; historical (French and German heritages combined, French blood stronger than German!); and legal. The latter meant that with no clear legal criteria for establishing ethnicity, and *reasoning by analogy from the abrogated racial legislation*, the ethnic origin of Romanian citizens was determined by their parents. The Tomnatic villagers' parents were mostly German and French, but since the German blood was merely a "component" of the French blood, the French ethnicity prevailed.

The villagers also (re)constructed the genealogy of the village: a 1937 county history book by Samuil Borovszky documenting the initial French colonization, nationality of the initial church, school and administration, numerous family trees preserved by the church, the original list of French colonists from 1774, and the 1927 census where most of the claimants declared themselves French. This was not a cheap undertaking.

---

83   Ibid., 255–261.
84   Ibid., 287–290.

On August 13, 1945, the local policeman arrested 141 people from Tomnatic, including the local shopkeeper and others (among them, the mayor's relatives), who were collecting 1,000 lei per person for the costs of the trial. The total seized was 73,000 lei (given the rampant inflation, this was not necessarily a lot of money), and the policeman thought the money was meant for a bribe.[85]

The court undertook its own investigation and hired a Timișoara doctor to determine the equality of physical and intellectual contributions of the parents regarding ethnic identity. Following the investigation, 34 villagers gave up their claims, and 133 needed more evidence. The court ultimately decided on 712 claims, and held that an individual's identity was determined by two factors: citizenship/indigeneity [indigenat], obtained on the basis of objective, positive legal criteria; and nationality, which signified an individual's belonging to a nation through birth or assimilation, on the basis of descendance or on the basis of feelings of attachment continuously demonstrated by the individual (biological criteria united with subjective criteria). Romanian law, like its French model, considered citizenship synonymous with nationality (*jus soli*), and "Romanian" and "Romanian citizen" had been used interchangeably. The 1924 citizenship statute almost completely eliminated the word "citizenship" and replaced it "with nationality," but terms such as "ethnic origin," "race," "nationality," "Romanians by origin" also continued to be used. For ethnicity, language, religion, and traditions mattered, and once obtained, ethnic origin could not be lost.

The court also ruled that the father's ethnicity was determinative for legitimate children, and the mother's for illegitimate children, since scientifically there was no proof that the mother's contribution was higher than the father's, and to avoid practical difficulties. The court evaluated other evidence, such as the evolution of family names since 1774, including on cemetery stone heads, changes in the use of language from French to German, and the impact of political changes, but nonetheless ended up in the same place, namely blood. Language, held the court, was only one of the factors that determined ethnicity, which could not be lost even if the language was. The loss of language, speculated the court, was probably due to forced denationalization of inhabitants of the Austro-Hungarian Empire, intermarriages with the Germans, and being far away and not in touch with the villages of origin in France. Surrounded by Germans, over time the French settlers of Tomnatic lost their own language in favor of German.

---

85   ANR, Fond Legiunea de Jandarmi Timiș-Torontal, inv 611, File 261/1945, 1–26.

The court thus found that 439 of the petitioners were French, 222 petitioners were French, Czech or Romanian but only on the mother's side, and in 47 cases there was no French connection.[86] The win of the Tomnatic villagers was temporary, however. While they were spared from forced labor in the immediate aftermath of the decision, the 1951 deportations to Bărăgan (forcibly relocating individuals living close to the Yugoslav border and others considered politically undesirable to eastern Romania) took no note of the decision or the villagers' ethnicity.[87]

Conclusion

Between 1940 and 1945, the Timișoara administrative court actively constructed the concept of ethnic identity. While the racial statutes of 1938–1942, and in particular Decree-Law 2650 laid out some criteria for determining Jewish identity, the court's piecemeal, originalist, formalist interpretation eventually created ethnic identity as an essentialist, primordial, gendered category—ethnicity was assigned at birth, inherited from one's ancestors, unchanging, immutable, fixed.[88] It was not of one's choosing, and there could be only one (there was no such thing as mixed ethnicities). The claimants mostly mobilized instrumental understandings of ethnicity—ethnic identity as a tool, resource for gaining resources,[89] to negotiate their status and as a shield against abusive state policies.

This was a particularly difficult endeavor in a region where mixed identities had historically been prevalent. The court's attempt to set boundaries in an ethnically fluid region succeeded precisely because of the peculiar intersection of law and politics, as the latter redistributed power and resources through ethnically-based channels. Assigning fixed identities, both before and after August 1944, functioned as a mechanism of power, a way to determine inclusion in and exclusion from the community on all levels, from political (citizenship) to economic and social, such as specific resources (jobs, property, etc.). The ultimate goal, as numerous interwar politicians proclaimed, was to establish an ethnic hierarchy with Romanians at the top and Jews at the bottom. The court's decisions also

---

86 ANR, Fond Curtea Locală Administrativă Timișoara, File 24/1944, 404–421.
87 Smaranda Vultur, "The Role of Ethnicity in the Collectivization of Tomnatic/Triebswetter (Banat Region) (1949–1956)," in *Transforming Peasants, Property, and Power: The Collectivization of Agriculture in Romania (1949–1962)*, eds. Constantin Iordachi and Dorin Dobrincu (Budapest: Central European University Press, 2009).
88 Yang, *Ethnic Studies*, 42.
89 Ibid., 46.

functioned as a mechanism for forcibly creating a single Jewish identity (despite the historical diversity of the Jewish communities of Romania), and within it, two sub-categories: those who "identify with the aspirations of the Romanian nation" and thus deserved to be partially rewarded and included in the community, and the rest. The judicial refusal to accept multiple identities even after the fall of the Antonescu regime bolstered essentialist narratives of ethnicity and maintained nation-state building efforts.

More than half of the Jewish claimants were lawyers, and most likely they knew each other and probably the judges. Their presence indicates clear and conscious efforts to mobilize and resist through law. Since they all lost, it is unclear whether they were informally encouraged or deterred from filing suit. They were also part of a much larger petition movement from the Jewish community through political and legal channels, which suggests a strategic, multi-pronged approach. The court treated lawyers differently from non-lawyer claimants. Non-lawyer claims were dealt with swiftly (within three months), while most lawyer claimant cases lingered for four years (filing a lawsuit did not stop the implementation of anti-Semitic legislation, including disbarring).

Not all Jewish claimants had lawyers, while all the post-1944 claimants did. In all cases, and despite the lawyers' best efforts, most interpretations remained strictly and literally within the four corners of the law, and not a single one questioned the justice or fairness of the legislation itself. Court decisions, similarly, and particularly given the stakes, are written in a cold, dehumanizing, legal formalist style devoid of compassion or any hint of justice.

The authoritarian nature of the regime itself does not seem to have had much of an impact on the court's decisions or outcomes. Rather, the formalist, positivist self-understanding of the court in a broader context of continuous, autochthonous anti-Semitism resulted in an attitude, at best, of "supreme [legal] indifference" to the Jewish claimants (as Livingston describes Italian lawyers and judges during the same time period),[90] and at worst, of complete collusion with the anti-Semitic goals of the political regime. This was not inevitable, as shown by the post-August 1944 decisions, where the court suddenly found its legal realist legs and discovered concern and justice for claimants attempting to avoid forced labor

---

90 Livingston, *The Fascists and the Jews of Italy*.

and later deportation, most likely because Germans had historically been viewed significantly more favorably than other minorities.[91]

All decisions, however, showcase the ability and willingness of authoritarian regimes to move past mere instrumental, blunt uses of the law, and to deploy law's constitutive functions. The administrative court was the site for the construction of identities, rewriting of history and meaning of community (Are Jews part of the community? What does the Romanian nation stand for? Is it defined by exclusion?), and selective convergence of history and memory (for example, for the Tomnatic villagers), fulfilling or dashing the symbolic expectations of those who sought its protection.

---

91   See, for example, Boia, *Cum s-a românizat România*; Cristian Cercel, *Romania and the Quest for European Identity. Philo-Germanism without Germans* (London: Routledge, 2019).

Writing History Through Trials: The Case of the National Peasant Party

*Monica Ciobanu**

Abstract: *This article provides a comparative account of two criminal trials that addressed the role played by the National Peasant Party (PNȚ) in national history. The focus is on the ability of legal trials to construct historical narratives. The first was conducted in 1947 by the newly-established communist regime and resulted in the legal ban of the party. In 2015, the narrative was entirely reversed in court. The PNȚ was presented as a fully democratic actor. Alexandru Vișinescu—a former commandant of the Râmnicu-Sărat prison where prominent party leaders were subjected to repression— was sentenced for crimes against humanity. The sharp differences between these two legal proceedings—a Soviet-style show trial versus legal action that was oriented to providing some redress for the victims of communism—is emphasized. But the conclusion is that criminal trials in general fall short in providing historical lessons and that retrospective justice does not necessarily produce reconciliation or accountability.*

The role of criminal trials in bringing measures of accountability and justice in the aftermath of human rights violations represents an important topic of inquiry for scholars of transitional justice. Yet, there is also a substantial body of scholarship that acknowledges courts as places where moral and historical justice are dispensed. Numerous past and more recent examples, including the trial of Adolf Eichmann in Jerusalem, trials involving high-level officials of the fascist Vichy regime in France, the prosecution of crimes of the apartheid regime in South Africa and genocide in the former Yugoslavia, or indictments against former communist officials in post-communist Europe, show how courts may easily be transformed into sites of remembering.[1] The publicity and emotionally charged

---

* Monica Ciobanu holds a PhD in Sociology from the Graduate Faculty of the New School for Social Research and is Professor of Criminal Justice at Plattsburgh State University of New York. I am grateful to my co-editor for this special issue, Mihaela Șerban, and to two anonymous reviewers for their useful comments on an earlier version of this article.
1 For the relationship between political trials and the judicialization of history see Jens Meierhenrich and Devin O. Pendas (eds), *Political Trials in Theory and History* (Cambridge: Cambridge University Press, 2016). For the role of criminal trials in

atmosphere in which these legal proceedings are conducted can also transform them into conduits of "state sponsored history."

This politicization and historicization of courts can also be found in Romania. Whether following the 23 August 1944 coup against the authoritarian military regime led by Marshal Ion Antonescu, which subsequently resulted in almost half a century of communist dictatorship, or after the 1989 popular uprising that initiated the country's transition to democracy, the functions of judges and historians have become frequently intertwined. One of the most relevant cases involves the pre-war National Peasant Party (PNȚ). Its leaders, ideology, record of governance during the interwar period and its role during the Antonescu regime have twice become the subject of heavily publicized criminal trials. First, in 1946 the newly established communist authority used the so-called "Tămădău escape," which involved a failed attempt by several prominent party leaders to escape political persecution by fleeing abroad, as a justification to legally ban the PNȚ. Organized as a show trial, the fabricated accusations of treason and fascism were later incorporated in an officially sanctioned communist historiography. Over sixty years later, on 24 July 2015 the Supreme Court of Appeal in Bucharest sentenced Alexandru Vișinescu—a former commandant of Râmnicu-Sărat prison from 1956 to 1963—to twenty years for crimes against humanity. It was in Râmnicu-Sărat that some of the most prominent PNȚ leaders were subjected to harsh and violent repression. In the absence of living witnesses who had experienced this treatment, the testimonies of others, including family members, provided the basis for a general indictment of the communist system that went far beyond a single defendant. Quite unlike 1947, both prosecutor and judge presented the PNȚ and its leadership as true believers in democracy and

---

the creation of the historical memory of the Nazi Holocaust, together with Hannah Arendt's controversial *Eichmann in Jerusalem: A Report on the Banality of Evil* (New York: Viking Press, 1963), see also Donald Bloxham, *Genocide on Trial: War Crimes, Trials and the Formation of Holocaust History* and *Memory* (Oxford: Oxford University Press, 2001) and Devin O. Pendas, *The Frankfurt Auschwitz Trial, 1963–1965: Genocide, History and the Limits of the Law* (Cambridge: Cambridge University Press, 2005). See Richard J. Golsan (ed), The *Papon Affair: Memory and Justice on Trial* (New York and London: Routledge Press, 2000, translations by Lucy B. Golsan and Richard J. Golsan) for the trials of the post-war Vichy regime in France. For the post-communist countries in Europe see Uladzislau Belavusau and Alexandra Gliszczynska-Grabias (eds), *Law and Memory: Towards Legal Governance of History* (Cambridge: Cambridge University Press, 2017). Also, for the use of law in the context of the genocides in former Yugoslavia and post-apartheid South Africa, see Nicola Henry, *War and Rape: Law, Memory and Justice* (London: Routledge Press, 2011) and Rita Kesselring, *Bodies of Truth: Law, Memory and Emancipation in Post-Apartheid South Africa* (Stanford, California: Stanford University Press, 2017).

praised them for their instrumental role in the 1918 act of national unification. The historical narrative had then been entirely reversed.

This article analyzes these two trials comparatively with an emphasis on how the participants attempted to manufacture a historical narrative of the National Peasant Party both during and after communism. The Tămădău trial could easily be described as a classic case of a political trial whose principal goal was to eliminate a political enemy and to consolidate the foundation for a communist order.[2] The legal banning of the PNȚ from all political activity and the sentencing of its leadership in November 1946 was immediately followed by the pursuit of vigorous measures and policies of Soviet-style communization. In contrast, the Vișinescu trial had a clearly restorative purpose of bringing some measure of compensatory justice for the victims of communism. The defendant, however, who had retired from his office in 1978 and was indicted for crimes committed more than half a century ago, was seen by the few surviving political prisoners and their descendants as the embodiment of the darkest period of communism associated with gulag repression and Sovietization. In that sense, the Vișinescu case belongs to the domain of retrospective criminal justice. Unlike transitional justice that focuses on purging the new democracy of any criminal elements from the previous regime, retrospective justice addresses abuses committed at least a generation ago that are still alive in the memory of some parts of society.[3]

However, despite these significant differences, in both trials the courtroom was used as a venue for expressing historical trauma and collective suffering at the hands of the bourgeois or the communist governments, respectively. Both trials benefited from outside courtroom publicity and attempted to assume non-legal pedagogical functions in providing moral and political lessons in history for present and future generations. As Jeffrey Alexander puts it, both trials produced "trauma-dramas" that had as principal protagonists some public figures representing the leader-

---

2   See Otto Kirchheimer, *Political Justice: The Use of Legal Procedures for Political Ends* (Princeton, New Jersey: Princeton University Press, 1961) and Jens Meiernich and Devin O. Pendas, "The Justice of My Cause is Clear, but There's Politics of Fear: Political Trials in Theory and History", in *Political Trials in Theory and History*, eds. Meierhenrich and Pendas, 1–64.

3   See Eva-Clarita Pettai and Vello Petai, *Transitional and Retrospective Justice in the Baltic States* (Cambridge: Cambridge University Press, 2014). For criminal trials and transitional justice see Agata Fijalkovski and Raluca Grosescu (eds), *Transitional Criminal Justice in Post-Dictatorial and Post-Conflict Societies* (Cambridge: Intersentia, 2015).

ship of the PNȚ both before and after 1989.[4] Given this focus on historical justice the following questions arise: To what extent do retrospective post-communist trials differ in their ability to produce "state sponsored history" compared to Stalinist show trials? More broadly, how successful are courts in establishing a historical record of the past? How relevant are these trials for issues relating to historical memory, justice and identity in Romania?

To explore these questions, first the historical and political contexts and their established legal instruments under which the defendants were tried are presented. Analysis of the actual legal proceedings follows and is focused on the relation between questions of guilt, ideological rhetoric and constructing a historical narrative. Last, the use of law as an instrument for legitimizing officially sanctioned history in Romania is considered.

The Tămădău Trial: The Soviet Consolidation of the Jurisprudence of Terror

The trial of the most prominent leaders of the historical interwar PNȚ in November 1947 resulted in sentences for the most severe crimes, including treason, ongoing support and participation in the destructive and anti-national activities of the 1940–1944 fascist dictatorship. The alleged plot to illegally overthrow the government with the external support of Western capitalism and imperialism was tacked on.[5] As "enemies of the people," unworthy of hard-working citizens who labor for a parasitic bourgeoisie, the defendants were portrayed as symbolizing greedy industrial capitalists and landowners who had exploited Romanians for decades.[6] The emphasis on these qualities clearly suggests the political motivation of a court whose goal was to eliminate a political enemy, whether real or

---

4 See Jeffrey Alexander, "On the Social Construction of Moral Universals: The Holocaust from War Crimes to Trauma Drama", in *Cultural Trauma and Collective Identity*, eds. Jeffrey Alexander, Ron Eyerman & all (Berkeley, Los Angeles: University of California Press, 2004), 196–263.

5 For the full text of the sentence see "1947 nov. 11, ședința de după masă. Sentința" in *Procesul lui Iuliu Maniu: Documentele Procesului Partidului Național Țărănesc*, Marcel-Dumitru Ciucă (ed), vol. III, Sentința (Bucharest: Editura Saeculum I.O., 2001), 5–380.

6 Foucault defines social enemies as a distinctive group of criminals who exercise violent power on the rest of the society "through the position they occupy in the process of production by their refusal to work." See Bernard H. Harcourt (ed.), *Michel Foucault, The Punitive Society: Lectures at the Collège de France, 1972–1973* (New York: Palgrave MacMillan, 2015, translated by Graham Burchell), 26–27.

imagined.[7] Articulated in a court of law, it was typical of the early stages of the dictatorship of the proletariat when violence becomes the main and only source of revolutionary law.[8]

However, the Tămădău legal case could properly be understood only in the complicated context that predated and followed the 23 August 1944 royal coup against Marshal Ion Antonescu's dictatorship. Antonescu came to power in 1940 when Romania was allied with Nazi Germany in its conflict with the Soviet Union. Initially the war was popular among Romanians. Especially after Bessarabia and Bukovina, annexed by the Soviet Union in 1940, were reclaimed in 1941, Antonescu enjoyed both popular support and the tacit backing of some segments of the historical parties, both the PNȚ and the National Liberal Party or PNL.[9] The results of the 2 March 1941 plebiscite showed an overwhelming popular support for Antonescu's policies. However, as the military campaign expanded further East and the army later became engaged in an aggressive war against its traditional allies, Great Britain and then the United States, the leader of the PNȚ—Iuliu Maniu (1873–1953)—began organizing clandestine operations involving secret services of both to extract Romania from the Axis alliance.[10]

Yet, anti-fascist resistance was weak and divided between the bourgeois parties and the PCR. The PCR, which at the time counted less than 1,000 members, was unpopular due to its subservience to Soviet communists and their specific position on Bessarabia and Bukovina.[11] As a result, the PNȚ and other anti-fascist groups were reluctant to accept the PCR in an alliance.[12] For their part, British officials were ambivalent towards Maniu, whom they perceived as inefficient, weak and unwilling to

---

[7] Meierhenrich and Pendas, in "The Justice of My Cause is Clear", 57–59 classify such trials as both political and destructive.

[8] See Vladimir Ilych Lenin, *The Proletarian Revolution and the Renegade Kautsky* (New York: International Publishers, 1934).

[9] Together with Bessarabia and Bukovina, ceded to the Soviet Union in 1939 as a result of the Ribbentrop-Molotov pact, Romania also lost northern Transylvania to Nazi-occupied Hungary and Southern Dobruja to Bulgaria in 1940.

[10] Dennis Deletant, *British Clandestine Activities in Romania during the Second World War* (Basingstoke: Palgrave Macmillan, 2016).

[11] See Vladimir Tismăneanu, *Stalinism for all Seasons: A Political History of Romanian Communism* (Berkeley: University of California Press, 2003).

[12] See 20 December 1942, Bucharest "Scrisoare CC al PCR adresată lui Iuliu Maniu, președintele PNȚ îndemnînd la adoptarea unei atitudini comune față de problemele păcii și războiului implicînd România", in *Istoria Partidului Național Țărănesc: documente, 1926–1947*, eds. Vasile Arimia, Ion Ardeleanu, Alex. Cebuc (Bucharest: Editura Arc, 2000), 206–207.

cooperate with their Russian ally.[13] Antonescu himself was also reluctant to submit to what he thought were disadvantageous terms with the Allies in early 1944. This, coupled with the fear of the historical parties that the PCR was taking over, had prompted Maniu (in alliance with liberals, social-democrats and communists) to persuade King Michael to arrest Antonescu on 23 August.

Both before and after Maniu was considered the most popular and influential politician in the country. He had earned his nationalist reputation as leader of the National Party (PN) for his role in urging the 1918 creation of a much enlarged Great Romania. During the interwar period, Maniu established himself as a political maverick. In 1921, he merged the PN with the left-wing Peasant Party in 1921, then led by Ion Mihalache (1882–1963). Mihalache and his party advocated for a peasant state. The new party—the PNȚ—became a left-leaning party representing mainly the interests of the rural middle-classes and continued to retain its Transylvanian nationalist ethos rooted in Christian democratic principles. It also established itself as the main competitor to the Liberal Party (PNL) that advocated on behalf of the industrial urban bourgeoisie. But Maniu remained de facto in control until 1947 while a genuine mystique began to gather about him.[14] The PNȚ's interwar record included an overwhelming victory in the 1928 elections and then its return to power from 1932 to 1933.[15] Yet due to either internal divisions or to the international economic depression of the 1920s, the party was not able to live entirely up to its electoral promises. Some of these failures, and especially the shortcomings of the 1929 land reform, the repression of workers strikes in 1929 and 1933 and the 1937 electoral pact with the Iron Guard were overplayed in the 1947 trial and used to incite some segments of the society against the PNȚ.[16]

Eight days after the 1944 coup, Soviet troops entered Bucharest. In this context, the provisions included in the Armistice signed on 12

---

13   Dennis Deletant, "Shattered Illusions: Britain and Iuliu Maniu, 1940–1945", in *Journal of Romanian Studies* 1, no. 1 (2019): 53–74.
14   Several laudatory biographies of Iuliu Maniu have been published in Romania after 1989. Some of the most significant include Gabriel Țepelea (ed), *Iuliu Maniu în fața istoriei* (Bucharest: Hans Seidel, Editura Cartea Românească, 1993), Apostol Stan, *Iuliu Maniu, naționalism și democrație: biografia unui mare român* (Bucharest: Editura Saeculum i.O., 1997) and Cicerone Ionițoiu, *Viața politică și procesul Iuliu Maniu*, vol 1, *O jumătate de secol 26 octombrie–11 noiembrie* (Bucharest, 1997).
15   See Ioan Scurtu, *Istoria Partidului Național Țărănesc* (Bucharest: Editura Enciclopedică, 1994, second edition). From 1938 to 1940, during the royal dictatorship of Carol II political parties (including PNȚ) were banned from public life.
16   Scurtu, Istoria Partidului Național Țărănesc, 225–226.

September 1944 regarding the punishment of war criminals,[17] carried out under the authority of the Allied Control Commission (that included the Soviet Union, the United States and Great Britain), forced Romania to succumb to Soviet military control. Under the pretense of de-Nazification and with the direct assistance of Soviet commissars, the emerging communist regime began a witch-hunt against all political and social groups that were or could at the time oppose the country's communization. In compliance with Armistice conditions, a care-taker government led by General Constantin Sănătescu in August/September began internment of German and Hungarian citizens in labor camps.[18] Although the 1923 Constitution was reinstated, its democratic freedoms and civil rights provisions were actually undermined by the addition of an article that gave the Council of Ministers discretionary powers and by the provisions of the Armistice agreement seeking to punish those responsible for inflicting national disaster. It punished those responsible for installing Antonescu's dictatorial regime in 1940 and for involving Romania in a military alliance with Nazi Germany. However, as officials of the Ministry of Interior and the security police were almost entirely retained in office, communists, the PCR and their Soviet backers were increasingly dissatisfied, leading to changes in the government.[19] Sănătescu had no choice but to accept Vishinski's order to reshuffle his government and appoint a significant figure in the PCR, Teohari Gerorgescu, as deputy minister of the interior. This concession, however, failed to ensure his political survival and a new government led by general Nicolae Rădescu was formed. Known as the last democratic government until December 1989, Rădescu's was short-lived and lasted only two months in 1944–5.

Eventually, as a result of Anglo-American inaction and Soviet pressure, the King was forced to accept another government in March 1945. Unlike his predecessors, the new prime minister Petru Groza (a landowner, left-wing agrarian and prominent lay member of the Orthodox Church) was willing to adopt a subservient position in carrying out Soviets orders. Groza defied the authority of the King, who now refused to counter-sign any legislation, and illegally pursued coercive measures

---

17 It is estimated that during the war as many as 250,000 to 400,000 members of the Jewish community were killed under the jurisdiction of the Romanian state. See Radu Ioanid, *The Holocaust in Romania: The Destruction of Jews and Gypsies under the Antonescu Regime, 1940–1944* (Chicago: Ivan R. Dee, 2000).
18 See Hannelore Baier (ed.), *Departe, în Rusia, la Stalino* (Bucharest: Fundația Friedrich Ebert, Academia Civică, 2003, Romanian translation by Werner Kremm).
19 See Dennis Deletant, *Communist Terror in Romania, Gheorghiu-Dej and the Police State: 1948–1965* (London: Hurst & Company, 1999), 56.

against the historical parties. The inclusion in the so-called coalition government of the National Democratic Front (FND) of the two dissident factions from the PNȚ and PNL, represented by Anton Alexandrescu and Gheorghe Tătărescu, was merely symbolic. The FND also included besides the PCR, the Ploughmen's Front led by Groza, a dissident faction in the Social-Democratic Party and other communist groups.

The first political trials were initiated in 1945 by the newly established People's Tribunal and indicted several military commanders involved in the 1941–1942 massacres of the Jewish population in Odessa, then under Romanian control. A year later, Ion Antonescu himself was tried, found guilty and executed for war crimes, crimes against the peace and treason. But as Cosmin Cercel shows, the court was dominated by communists which, instead of focusing on crimes committed against citizens in general, emphasized the theme of a country colonized and the oppression of the Romanian peasant forced into an unjust war against a friendly eastern neighbor.[20] In fact, after March 1945 these vague accusations were made possible by revised legislation. Decree-Law no. 312 of April 1945 that established the framework for punishing war criminals was so broadly conceived that it allowed discretionary punishment of many who held or played secondary roles in the Antonescu administration.[21] At the same time, the communist newspaper *Scânteia* called for the prosecution of those morally responsible for the establishment of a fascist dictatorship and wartime losses. Those targeted were particularly Maniu and Brătianu (the PNL leader) and journalists who allegedly supported extremism in bourgeois publications. As the Council of Ministers continued to hold the upper-hand in these courts, those who agreed to collaborate with the PCR were spared from being put on trial. This was the experience of Alexandru Petrescu, the presiding judge in the Tămădău trial, who, after agreeing to conduct all the political trials, was removed by Sănătescu from the list of war criminals.

What seems to be distinctive about this period is the coexistence and overlap between multiple forms of transitional justice involving both trials mounted against war criminals and fascist elements (including the Iron Guard) and trials against the historical parties. But by using vague accusations of fascism against the latter, the PCR manipulated the process of denazification to instill fear and achieve domination though law. As the

---

20 See Cosmin Sebastian Cercel, "Judging the Conducător: Fascism, Communism, and Legal Discontinuity in Post-War Romania" in *Towards Legal Governance of History*, eds. Belavusau and Gliszczynska-Grabias, 25–26.
21 See Ion Bălan, *Regimul concentraționar din România*, 1944–1964 (Bucharest: Fundația Academia Civică, 2000), 50–54.

newly emerging power, the PCR used the courts to educate the public, or in Foucault's terms, the party was sovereign in establishing monopoly over truth and knowledge.[22] These show trials were conducted in parallel with a campaign of intimidation and mass arrests of members and supporters of the opposition parties, the anti-communist resistance movement and the clergy. In fact, the first arrests began in 1945 and targeted the members of the extremist right-wing Iron Guard known as the Legionary movement. For a brief period, the Guard was Antonescu's coalition partner from September 1940 to February 1941 and had been responsible for widespread violence, including pogroms against the Jewish minority. Antonescu ultimately expelled them from the government.[23]

Before the November 1946 elections prominent PNȚ members were also arrested in order to preempt their candidacy for public office. Groza's efforts to undermine the party in the elections also included physical attacks against its members and sympathizers, the replacement of ballots, banning of PNȚ's newspaper *Dreptatea* and propaganda against Maniu by the communist-dominated media.[24] But despite acts of violence and intimidation exerted by the PCR, it was estimated that the PNȚ had significantly outnumbered the communists at the polls. However, the official results declared an overwhelming victory for the PCR and gave the PNȚ only 32 seats in the legislature. Although there is no consensus regarding the PNȚ's real gains, Corneliu Coposu (Maniu's personal secretary at the time and after 1989 head of the party) claimed later the results were reversed in the communists' favor.[25] Nonetheless, the elections were officially ratified by the King. The following year in March through May hundreds of

---

22 Michel Foucault, *The Archeology of Knowledge* (New York: Pantheon Books, 1972).
23 For a history and the ideology of the Iron Guard see Roland Clark, *Holy Legionary Youth: Fascist Activism in Interwar Romania* (Ithaca: Cornell University Press, 2015).
24 Fűrtös and Bârlea (eds.) *Alegerile parlamentare din 19 noiembrie 1946. De la memoria colectivă la cercetarea istorică*, and Virgil Țărău and Ioan Marius Bucur, *Strategii si politici electorale în alegerile parlamentare din 19 noiembrie 1946* (Cluj-Napoca: Centrul de Studii Transilvane, Fundația Culturală Română, 1998).
25 See Doina Alexandru, *Corneliu Coposu, Confessions: Dialogues with Doina Alexandru* (Boulder: East European Monographs, distributed by Columbia University Press, New York, 1998, English translation by Elena Popescu), 37–39. Whatever the real numbers were, it is evident that the PCR had fraudulently claimed the results. The gross irregularities were noted at the time by foreign diplomats in Romania. See the memoir of the US diplomat Berry Y. Burton, Cornelia Bodea (ed.), *Romanian Diaries, 1944–1947* (Iași: The Center for Romania Studies, 2000).

political opponents (principally PNȚ members and supporters) were arrested despite Maniu's protests to the American legation.[26]

In this context, Maniu decided that the only viable alternative left for the party, and for the democratic opposition, was to send a group of prominent PNȚ members outside the country to lobby for their interests. Together with Mihalache, the group included Nicolae Penescu, the secretary general and his wife; Nicolae Carandino, the chief editor of the party's newspaper *Dreptatea* and his wife; and deputy Ilie Lazăr and Dumitru and Eugen Borcea. They were apparently to be flown from Tămădau airfield (forty six km from Bucharest) to Istanbul by two pilots. However, "the escape" was in fact orchestrated by the secret services that sent two pilots allegedly to assist Maniu in his plan.[27] Unlike the rest of the escapees, the two were quickly released after their arrest. However, instead of being charged with an attempt to illegally cross the border, the party, which included Maniu and several political and military figures, was accused of treason, espionage, attacks to the state sovereignty by attempting to provoke a civil war, and complicity to an imperialist-capitalist plot against the Soviet Union and its socialist allies.

Their fate was already determined before the trial. The toxic propaganda published by major communist newspapers attempted to mobilize the working class in public meetings against criminals, fascists and terrorists.[28] At the same time, the political education section of the PCR's Central Committee urged party activists to show no mercy to Maniu and his clique.[29] The legal proceedings were carefully prepared and intimate portraits of each of the defendants emphasized strengths and weaknesses that could be used against them during interrogation and (in some cases) to pit them against each other.[30] This strategy worked in two cases

---

26 See Gheorghe Onișoru, *Operațiunea Tămădău: desființarea Partidului Național Țărănesc* (1947) (Bucharest: Institutul Național pentru Studiul Totalitarismului, 2008), 35–38.
27 The escapees realized right away when they arrived at the airport and saw the size of the plane (too small to accommodate all of them) that they had been trapped. See Paul Lăzărescu, (ed.), Nicolae Carandino, *Nopți albe și zile negre* (Bucharest: Civic Academy Foundation, 2017), 74–75.
28 Dorin Dobrincu, "Contribuția presei la dizolvarea PNȚ" in *Căderea Cortinei, Analele Sighet 5*, ed. Romulus Rusan (Bucharest: Fundația Academia Civică, 1997), 646–657.
29 See "Teze pentru campania în jurul procesului PNȚ—pentru uzul activiștilor și îndrumătorilor. Secția de educație politică a CC al PCR, septembrie 1947" in *Procesul lui Iuliu Maniu*, ed. Marcel-Dumitru Ciucă vol. 1, Ancheta, 145–153.
30 Arhiva SRI, dosar 40.001. vol. 14, "Caracterizările acuzaților, întocmite conform indicațiilor de mai sus, pentru a-i servi anchetatorilor", in *Procesul lui Maniu* ..., ed. Marcel-Dumitru Ciucă vol. I, 95–118.

involving Penescu and Vasile Serdici who, during the trial, blamed Maniu for transforming the party into his personal fiefdom and for shifting it away from its initial leftist ideology into an extremist right-wing direction. The defendants were subjected to late-night lengthy and harsh interrogations. While in custody, Maniu was isolated from other defendants. He took a dignified position during the proceedings and took full responsibility for the failed escape.

A total of nineteen individuals were indicted in connection with the Tămădău case. Together with Maniu and those who had tried to flee (Mihalache, Carandino, Penescu, Lazăr), two other groups of defendants were also implicated. The first included several former high-level officials from the Ministry of Foreign Affairs who allegedly conspired with Maniu and a capitalist imperialist Britain and United States against Romanian national interests and those of the Soviet Union. A second group of retired military officers (some of whom were part of the party's military education establishment) was also charged on equally serious grounds. They were tried for attempting to provoke a civil war and to overthrow the government by force in alliance with "terrorist armed groups" such as *Sumanele Negre* and *Mișcarea Națională de Rezistență*. It was true that especially after the stolen 1946 elections Maniu continued to inform Western embassies of Groza's government violations of the provisions of the December 1945 Moscow agreement, signed by the foreign ministers of the US, USSR and UK, that should have guaranteed civil liberties. It was also accurate that some PNȚ leaders had contacts with leaders of the armed resistance movement. However, these groups were by far too disparate, heterogenous and under constant threat of being exposed, to overthrow the regime.[31] In fact, some of the partisans serving harsh sentences in regime penitentiaries were brought in to testify against the accused. Also, given the international context following the Yalta agreement and the extensive powers held by the PCR consolidated with Soviet military backing, it could hardly be the case that a coherent coordinated conspiracy like this could have ever even been put into effect. Still, the court managed to fabricate all accusations and to link them together with the respective conspirators into a single act of national betrayal. The defense was weak and mostly consisted of appointed counsel. At least in one case, the defense attributed the accused's guilt to his decadent bourgeois education and

---

31   Monica Ciobanu, "Reconstructing the History of Early Communism and Armed Resistance in Romania," *Europe-Asia Studies*, 66, no. 99 (November 2014):1452–81.

upbringing.³² Many of the defense witnesses either failed or were unwilling to testify on their behalf. As a result, all nineteen were found guilty and the PNȚ leaders were sentenced to hard labor and lengthy prison terms.³³ Both Maniu and Mihalache died in prison. This scenario approximates a classical model of political trial which, as Shklar points out, represents little more than the instrument of a totalitarian system to effect a permanent revolution.³⁴

Despite the decapitation of the PNȚ's leadership, the regime was still fearful of its local and youth organizations that remained active clandestinely. Other trials were subsequently conducted that led to many imprisonments.³⁵ The PCR's attack on democratic institutions culminated with the forced abdication of King Michael in December 1947. Thus, after a short and convulsive transitional period that had begun in 1944 and ended in 1947, the PCR finally had full control of the legal system, allowing it to develop the archipelago of prison facilities and work colonies that was to house 600,000 political detainees and 200,000 administrative internees.³⁶ The last of them were released in 1964.

Law No. 16 from January 1949 broadened even further the range of acts considered crimes against state security and introduced the death penalty. As Kevin McDermott and Matthew Stibbe pointed out, the mass repression of the Stalinist terror in Eastern Europe was aimed at all potential antagonistic segments in the population, any alternative centers of authority (political or religious), and to find scapegoats for the failures of the newly installed communist governments.³⁷ Romania was no exception and throughout the 1950s such political trials continued to serve these goals. Whether they were targeting historical parties, religious

---

32 This was the case of Victor Rădulescu Pogoneanu's lawyer who presented him as the typical bourgeois intellectual doomed to choose the wrong path. See *Procesul lui Maniu* ..., Marcel-Dumitru Ciucă vol. IV, 231–238.
33 *Procesul lui Maniu* ..., Ciucă vol. IV, 371–378.
34 Judith N, Shklar, *Legalism: Law, Morals and Political Trials* (Cambridge, Massachusetts: Harvard University Press, 1986), 144. Also see Philippe Nonet and Philip Selznick, *Toward Responsive Law: Law and Society in Transition* (New Brunswick, New Jersey: Transaction Publishers, 2001), 44–46.
35 Gheorghe Onișoru, *Operațiunea Tămădău: desființarea Partidului Național Țărănesc* (1947), 122, and Petre Țurlea, *PNȚ: tentative de reînființare după 1947* (Bucharest: Editura Historia, 2007).
36 Romulus Rusan, *Cronologia și geografia represiunii comuniste în România* (Bucharest: Civic Academy Foundation, 2007).
37 Kevin McDermott and Matthew Stibbe, "Stalinist Terror in Eastern Europe: Elite Purges and Mass Repression," in *Stalinist Terror in Eastern Europe*, eds. Kevin Dermott and Matthew Stibbe (Manchester and New York: Manchester University Press, 2000), 12.

denominations, former legionaries, or communist officials who were deemed to deviate from the party line, it was through secrecy, torture, intimidation and false confessions that the accused were always found guilty and subjected to exemplary punishment. However, the use of officially sanctioned terror could not entirely remanufacture a historical narrative aligned with the PCR's ideology and interests. Through acts of remembering, both during and after communism, the surviving members of the PNȚ and their descendants were able to keep alive a different historical account that emphasized its democratic traditions and the courage and patriotism of their leaders. Below, I will discuss how these private and clandestine memories were incorporated in measures of retroactive justice.

The Vișinescu Trial: Retrospective Justice and Historical Remembrance

To understand the intricacies of the Vișinescu trial as a case of retrospective justice, some background regarding the PNȚ and its clandestine leadership activities after 1964 until 1989, and then its post-communist political performance during the democratic transition is necessary. I argue that the convergence of three factors seems to explain this form of reckoning with the past. First, the active and persistent remembering of the PNȚ past promoted by political prisoners during and after communism played a major role. Second, the immediate context following the 1989 overthrow of the regime and the ensuing political polarization between former communists and anti-communist forces elevated the PNȚ (renamed the National Peasant Christian-Democratic Party–PNȚCD) as the main player in the political opposition. Last, the shift from the militant anti-communism of civil society into electoral rhetoric promoted since mid-2000s by institutional actors formerly linked with the communist regime resulted in long overdue but symbolic forms of historical redress.

Upon their release from state detention facilities in the early 1960s, political prisoners continued to be subjected to threats, harassment and surveillance at the hands of Securitate. Many were blackmailed or coerced into becoming informers. But by the mid-1960s and early 1970s, the PCR's leadership under Gheorghe Gheorghiu-Dej, and then more vigorously under his successor Nicolae Ceaușescu, attempted to move away from mass terror and to cultivate some measure of popular legitimacy.[38]

---

38 See Michael Shafir, *Romania, Politics,* Economy *and Society* (Boulder: Lynne Rienner Publishers, 1985), 41–42.

Official state historiography began to rewrite the history of the PCR and its leaders and portray them as rightful heirs to a historical national tradition.[39] In contrast, the pre-war parties and movements including the PNȚ were represented as condemned to oblivion by both history and the people.[40] Yet recently released high-profile political prisoners could easily have served the purposes of the state. If the regime coopted them to serve in either a political or professional capacity, the government could use it as evidence of successful ideological reeducation of the enemies of socialism. Among those targeted was Corneliu Coposu, Maniu's former personal secretary, whose family background and early upbringing were strongly influenced by interwar cultural traditions in Transylvania.[41] However, his uncompromising position impressed his former party colleagues, who considered him as Maniu's de facto successor.

A group of approximately a hundred of these pre-war party members continued to maintain communication with each other after their release.[42] But whether attending birthday parties, funerals, or meeting at Coposu's house, the secret police was always hovering in the background.[43] Several, including Ion Diaconescu, Ion Bărbuș, Gabrielescu, Cicerone Ionițoiu, Nicolae Ionescu-Galbeni, and Gabriel Țepelea were to hold key party or government positions after 1989. But before that they were aware of constant surveillance. They chose to write secret diaries and memoirs and engage in an underground strategy of resistance.[44] In these

---

39 See Katherine Verdery, *National Ideology Under Socialism: Identity and Cultural Politics in Ceaușescu's Romania* (Berkeley: University of California Press, 1991).
40 See Mihai Fătu, *Sfîrșit fără glorie: PNȚ (Maniu) și PNL (Brătianu) în anii 1944–1947* (Bucharest: Editura Șiințifică, 1972).
41 See Marin Pop, *Monografia familiei Coposu: între istorie și memorie* (Zalău: Editura Caiete Silvane, 2014).
42 See Ion Diaconescu, *După temniță* (Bucharest: Nemira, 2003), 38–39.
43 Coposu's extensive Securitate file (including his family and inner circle) housed at CNSAS files reveals vast information regarding Coposu, his PNȚ friends and acquaintances, family members and others including dissidents, foreign visitors, and communists who had fallen in disgrace. Their private lives, views regarding the internal and external political developments, tapped phone conversations in Coposu's home had been recorded for over twenty five years (1965–December 1989). (CNSAS: Dosar I 100562, Fond Operativ, four volumes; D (Documentar) 00002, four volumes; I 0149087 (DAPL), 37 volumes).
44 Several memoires written before December 1989 include the following: Doina Alexandru (ed), *Corneliu Coposu. File dintr-un jurnal interzis. 1936-1947, 1953, 1967-1983* (Vremea: Bucharest, 2014); Dan Berindei (ed), *Ioan Hudiță, Jurnal politic ianuarie–24 august 1944* (Bucharest: Roza Vânturilor, 1997); Constantin Ticu Dumitrescu, *Mărturie și document*, vol. 1, Partea I, *Recurs la memorie* (Bucharest: Polirom, 2008); Gabriel Țepelea, *Amintiri și evocări* (Bucuresti: Editura Fundației Culturale Române, 1994); Augustin Vișa, *Din închisorile fasciste în cele comuniste* (Institutul pentru Analiză si Strategie Politică Iuliu Maniu, Colecția 'Problemele

writings and in some public appearances, Coposu and others contradicted the official version of the August 1944 account that attributed the royal coup to an armed insurrection led by the PCR. They also emphasized Maniu's and the party's role in the 1918 movement for national unification and other intricacies of interwar history, such as their relationships with the communists and the legionaries. In some cases, however, these activities triggered a sharp response from the authorities, including arrests and interrogations. Nonetheless, the party continued informally to maintain itself and ensure its survival and Coposu was to become known as a major anti-communist figure in both Romania and the West.

This underground activity resulted in the party's return to the forefront of national politics immediately after the overthrow of the regime as the National Peasant Christian-Democratic Party (PNȚCD). For the next six years, it became the dominant force in the anti-communist coalition of political parties and civic associations. The power vacuum left by the collapse of the regime and the uprising that, with over 1,000 dead, led directly to the execution of Ceaușescu and his wife, gave former unreformed communists led by Ion Iliescu the opportunity to seize power. Predictably, very little reckoning with the communist past was undertaken. Instead, the focus of criminal trials and memorialization had become what happened in the December revolution. While Romania by 2004 had initiated the second largest number of transitional judicial proceedings in the whole formerly communist region at just under 5,000 investigations leading to trial, a majority of them addressed cases that occurred during the overthrow of the regime and not prior to it.[45] However, these trials failed both in establishing any foundational narrative of the revolution and in achieving swift successful prosecutions.[46] The few cases involving communist officials similarly failed. This was the case of the penal investigations initiated by the Association of Former Political Prisoners (AFDPR) in 1991 against two high-level officials (Alexandru Drăghici and Alexandru Nicolschi) and then in 2000 against Gheorghe Crăciun (a former commandant of Aiud Prison from 1958 to 1964). All three died before their cases could be concluded.[47] The only legal redress achieved by the PNȚ

Timpului': Bucharest, 1997); Ion Diaconescu, *Temnița, destinul generației noastre* (revised edition) (Nemira: Bucharest, 2003).

45 See Lavinia Stan, *Transitional Justice in Post-Communist Romania* (Cambridge: Cambridge University Press, 2013), 30.

46 Raluca Grosescu and Raluca Ursachi, "Transitional Trials as History Writing: The Case of the Romanian December 1989 Events" in *Transitional Criminal Justice in Post-Dictatorial and Post-Conflict Societies*, eds. Fijalkowski and Grosescu, 69–100.

47 Raluca Grosescu and Raluca Ursachi, *Justiția penală de tranziție: de la Nuremberg la post-comunismul românesc* (Iași: Polirom, 2009).

was symbolic. In October 1998, the Supreme Court of Justice annulled all the convictions of the PNȚ escapees and others in the 1947 trial, virtually all of whom were dead now.[48]

For their part, Coposu and his party together with the reestablished PNL, the AFDPR, former dissidents and other civic groups attempted to manufacture a narrative of December 1989 as the "unfinished revolution." They demanded retribution for the crimes committed by the communist regime and justice for the victims. Eventually in 1996 (a year after Coposu's death), the heterogenous alliance of the National Democratic Convention (CDR) seized power on an anti-communist platform. But as Korycki argues, political parties that turn to the past are prone to be absorbed with moral judgement, tend to personalize guilt and polarize the electorate.[49] This was the case with the PNȚCD. After four years of inefficient governance, ongoing squabbles with its allies and its uncompromising attitude towards opponents, it was severely sanctioned by the electorate and vanished from politics.[50]

However, even after PNȚCD's electoral defeat in 2000, the historical era of gulag-style repression continued to influence public debates. But unlike the 1990s and early 2000s when the historical narrative of Romanian Stalinism was articulated primarily through the lived experience of its protagonists, since mid-2000s it was now incorporated in remembered history. A variety of groups and individuals of different political orientations including liberals, heirs to the PCR, right-wing religious groups with legionary affinities began to adhere to the narrative of the gulag as part of a broader national history of victimization and resistance. State-sponsored measures of historical redress initiated after 2014 illustrated this trend.[51] But the legal proceedings initiated after 2006 by the Institute for the Investigation of Crimes of Communism, later renamed as the Institute for the Investigation of Crimes of Communism and the Memory of the Romanian Exile (IICCMER)—an official body charged with investigating human rights violations committed before 1989—were not concluded. The socialist criminal code of 1969 (persisting until 2014) never contained any legal definition of crimes against humanity. At the same time, the amnesty

---

48 Ciucă, *Procesul lui Iuliu Maniu* …, vol. 3, part 2, 433–457.
49 Kate Korycki, "Memory, Party Politics, and Post-Transition Space: The Case of Poland," *East European Politics and Societies and Cultures*, 31, no. 3 (August 2017): 518–44.
50 See Lavinia Stan, "From Riches to Rags: The Romanian Christian Democrat Peasant Part," *East European Quarterly*, XXXIX, No. 2 (June 2005): 179–227.
51 Monica Ciobanu, "Remembering the Gulag: Religious Practices and Representations," in *Justice, Memory and Redress in Romania: New Insights*, eds. Lavinia Stan and Lucian Turcescu (Newcastle, UK: Cambridge Scholars), 214–234.

laws passed by Ceaușescu in 1988 and again by Iliescu in January 1990, in conjunction with a fifteen year statute of limitations built into the criminal code, severely stalled any further legal investigations. It seemed then that justice for the abuses and crimes committed during the most repressive years of communist rule would remain unfinished business. But as Grosescu showed in a recent study, the IICCMER's own sustained efforts, and especially of two jurists (Oana Soare and Valerian Stan), both well acquainted with international law, resulted in the incorporation of the UN's crimes against humanity clause in the new criminal code.[52]

It was in this context that on 24 July 2015, for the first time since the fall of the communist regime, a successful indictment and a finding of guilt was brought against a former official responsible for mass Stalinist repression in the 1950s and early 1960s. The Supreme Court of Appeal in Bucharest upheld the sentence of ninety year old Alexandru Vișinescu (1925–2018)—the commandant of Râmnicu-Sărat prison from 1956 to 1963—to twenty years imprisonment for crimes against humanity. Among the inmates housed in Râmnicu-Sărat twenty-one were leading members of the PNȚ, including its older founders Ilie Lazăr (1895–1976), Ion Mihalache (1882–1963), and Victor Rădulescu Pogoneanu (1891–1962), as well as younger members such as Corneliu Coposu (1914–1995), Ion Diaconescu (1917–2011) and Ion Bărbuș (1918–2001), who played an active role in the party's revival after 1989. Although many of Vișinescu's victims were prominent public figures, such as members of the interwar PNL, clerical leaders of various religious denominations and top communist officials in influential positions after the 1944 coup, the focus of the proceedings was dominated by the memory of those connected to the PNȚ.[53] In fact, two of the three civil parties in the trial—Anca-Maria Cernea and Elena Iacob—were directly related through family ties with the PNȚ group. The third, Nicoleta Eremia, was the widow of Ion Eremia (1913–2004), a former army general in 1952 who advocated for reforms after Stalin's death and had gained a reputation as a novelist.

During the reading of the final verdict, prosecutor Mioara Moșoiu made numerous references and read into the court record parts of memoirs and other accounts by well-known political prisoners, as well as excerpts from secret police documents housed in the *National Council for*

---

52 Raluca Grosescu, "Judging Communist Crimes in Romania: Transnational and Global Influences," *International Journal of Transitional Justice*, 11, no. 3 (November 2017): 282–303.
53 Dosar Nr. 3896/2/2014, 2103/2014, Curtea de Apel București/secția I penală/ sentința 1 penală nr. 122, 28–39.

the *Study of Securitate Archives* (CNSAS).[54] It is important to note that in 2013, Andrei Muraru (the director of IICCMER at the time) had filed a criminal complaint against him without a real dossier but based on a scholarly publication that he himself had commissioned.[55] It was then left to the judge to undertake the reconstruction and the interpretation of historical sources regarding the institutional mechanisms of early communist repression in general, and of Vișinescu's record during his tenure at Râmnicu-Sărat prison in particular. This transfer of expertise from the historian to the judge has considerably transformed the proceedings into a case of retrospective justice. In the absence of living witnesses, the memoirs of Vișinescu's victims, the second-hand recollections of those who knew them, and the archival sources were all that was left to bear witness. These sources provided graphic details of the physical and mental degradation resulting from torture inflicted by Vișinescu and his staff against inmates. This treatment amounted to nothing less than the slow destruction of the country's old political elites. As head of the detention facility, Vișinescu had been more than overzealous in implementing the official policy of suppression. In the sentence pronounced by the presiding judge, Carmen Veronica Găină stated that the defendant had intentionally inflicted a slow death against all *recalcitranți* detainees transferred to Râmnicu-Sărat in 1957 after organizing a hunger strike in Aiud prison. Her vivid description of the methods used against political prisoners reinforced the image of Râmnicu-Sărat as a place burned into their memories. It was where inmates were locked in cells in such extreme isolation that, according to Coposu and others, upon release they had to relearn or rediscover the art of speech.[56] Complete isolation and the prohibition of

---

54 The following memoirs, interviews and historical writings about Râmnicu-Sărat prison include: Ion Eremia, *Insula Robinson* (Bucharest: Fundația Academia Civică, 2014); Mihai Godo, *Iezuit. Nu câinele comuniștilor* (Oradea: Editura Ratio et Revelation, 2014); Cicerenoe Ionițoiu, *Viața politică și procesul lui Iuliu Maniu* (Bucharest: Libravox, 2003); Dorin Ivan, *Experimentul Râmnicu-Sărat* (Râmnicu-Sărat: Editura Irineu Mihălcescu, 2005); Mihai-Emil Marinescu, *Prin ungherele iadului comunist: Râmnicu-Sărat* (Bucharest, 2007); Apostol Stan, *Ion Mihalache: destinul unei vieți* (Bucharest: Salecului, 1999); Gheorghe Pătrașcu, *Zile de încercare și de har: amintiri din închisoare* (Roman: Editura Serafică, 2007); and Augustin Vișa, *Din închisorile fasciste în lagărele și închisorile comuniste* (Augustin Vișa: Karograf, 2002). For a list of the archival documents used as evidence during the trial see Andrei Muraru, *Vișinescu, torționarul uitat: închisoarea, crimele, procesul* (Iași: Polirom, 2017), footnote 42, 303.
55 Dumitru Lăcătuș, "Râmnicu-Sărat," in *Dicționarul penitenciarelor din România comunistă (1945–1967)*, ed. Andrei Muraru (Iași: Polirom, 2008), 439–453.
56 Monica Ciobanu, "The Vișinescu Trial: A Case of Retrospective Justice or Historical Memory?", paper presented at the Annual Convention, *Law and Society Association*, Washington DC, May 2019.

all contact between inmates or anyone or anything else (apparently even the spiders in the cells were killed by the guards) were particularly debilitating. Physical abuse: throwing cold water on the sick and old to force them out of bed (Mihalache and Pogoneanu), beatings for small disciplinary violations were frequent and indiscriminately applied. Valentin Cristea, a witness during the trial, recounted that he was completely isolated for attempting to communicate in Morse code with fellow prisoners.[57]

Their suffering, which seemed even to surpass the horrors of the Soviet gulag, symbolized the widespread suppression of the nation by an alien foreign power. Only someone as innately violent as Vișinescu—a man of limited education whose upward mobility was owed to the Minister of Internal Affairs (MAI) early policies of recruitment—could become the instrument of such repression.[58] With no survivors of the Râmnicu-Sărat prison (except Valentin Cristea), it was left to the assembled descendants as witnesses to reconnect with what was now a distant past, of which they had no direct experience.[59] It appeared that the courtroom was transformed into a dramatic stage for "public remembering ... in depicting the past as a series of traumas and injustices."[60] In incorporating the work of memory activists represented by journalists and civil society groups, the act of historical remembrance had become the basis for retrospective justice. In this fashion, retroactive justice became a part of what Jan Assman has called "cultural memory",[61] constituting the basis for historical justice.[62]

There is no doubt that these allegations represented an accurate account of the abuses inflicted at the hands of Vișinescu. Primary archival material produced by the MAI at the time confirm these allegations. However, the trial failed in providing accountability for the human rights

---

57 Dosar Nr. 3986/2/2014, 58–68.
58 See Dumitru Lăcătușu, "Alexandru Vișinescu—O Biografie," *Articole de Istorie*, 8, No. 1 (2015): 218–35.
59 Some of the descendants of political prisoners incarcerated in Râmnicu-Sărat included Anca-Maria Cernea, Mihaela Bărbuș, Ionuț Gherasim, Florin Vișa, Cornelia Manor, Nicoleta Eremia, and Elena Iacob. Apart from Nicoleta Eremia (the widow of Ion Eremia, a former army general in 1952 who advocated for reforms after Stalin's death), the others were related through family ties with the PNȚ. Cernea, Ieremia and Iacob represented the civil parties in the trial.
60 Stina Lőytőmäki, *Law and the Politics of Memory: Confronting the Past* (London and New York: Routledge Press, 2015), 122.
61 See Jan Assman, *Cultural Memory and Early Civilization: Writing, Remembrance and Political Imagination* (Cambridge: Cambridge University Press, 2011).
62 See Klaus Neumann and Janna Thompson (eds), *Historical Justice and Memory* (Madison, Wisconsin: University of Wisconsin Press, 2015).

violations perpetrated by the two main responsible institutions, i.e. the Ministry of Internal Affairs (MAI) and the General Directory of the Penitentiaries (DGP) under which Vișinescu performed his duties. Both institutions blamed each other and denied any wrongdoing by claiming that at the time the justice system was entirely subordinated to the party-state.[63] At the same time, testimonies of some family members and journalists elevated these acts of cruelty to a typical "trauma-drama" court narrative. For example, the story involving the death of Ioan (Jenică) Arnăutu, aged 36, after force-feeding by Vișinescu had a powerful effect on the audience and the presiding judge.[64] Equally powerful and accusatory were video documentaries showing interviews with Coposu and other PNȚ members. Lucia-Hossu Longin, the documentary journalist especially known for *Memorialul Durerii*, also used a television-style dramatic technique during her expert testimony. She recalled the bitter cold inside the prison during a visit with her crew in the early 1990s when the cameras almost froze up.

As for Vișinescu, initially he attempted to project a calm demeanor at the trial and to exercise his right to remain silent. But as the trial progressed and incriminating evidence against him emphasized the accuracy of the indictment, his self-confidence became increasingly shaky. Perhaps he came to realize that the trial was genuine and not a simple charade as it initially appeared to him. The final reading of the sentence provoked a strong emotional response from Vișinescu. In a somewhat ironical twist, he presented himself as a mere victim of the regime which had simply used someone like him, a poor orphan who had no choice but to obey state orders. He begged the court for mercy and sought compassion from the judge in saying that he has been nothing less than a servant of the state all his life. It seemed that the relationship between victimizers and victims had been reversed. If in 1947 it was the bourgeois capitalist class that oppressed the working proletariat, now it was bureaucratic socialism that had abused it!

Political Trials: Unfinished Lessons in History

Given that the final act rendered by a judge in any trial is to establish a verdict of guilt or innocence against a defendant on behalf of the political authority of the state, it is arguable that all trials are ipso facto political. There is, however, a fundamental difference between how non-demo-

---

63 Muraru, Vișinescu ..., 386–388.
64 Mihaela Bărbuș and Anca-Maria Cernea, personal communication, 26 May 2017.

cratic and democratic regimes conduct political trials. While the former is entirely disconnected from any due process, in the case of a constitutional order "it is not the political trial itself but the situation in which it takes place and the ends that it serves that matter."[65] Yet, when prosecutors, judges, attorneys, and witnesses transform the courtroom into a stage where political and ideological views are expressed, then offenders and victims cease to be everyday individuals. Both inside and outside the court emotions run high. The general public, which for the most part is neither well acquainted nor fully invested with the case, is expected to absorb and internalize some lesson of history. The narrative may be so compelling that it seems that a painful past is under scrutiny and is to be reckoned with in the courtroom. It is precisely such theatrics as these that are used in the service of public understanding of the past for the future that constitutes the core of political trials.[66]

As already shown, during the two PNȚ trials, both non-democratic and democratic regimes invest the legal system with pedagogical functions. In both cases, the stories narrated in court sought to provoke among the public outrage towards the defendant(s) and result in empathy or perhaps a sense of identification with the victim(s). In order to project a strong message to the audience, prosecutors, judges and witnesses engage in a persuasive type of communicative language that operates according to a simplistic distinction between criminals/victims, traitors/heroes, good and evil. In 1947, Maniu, Mihalache and others were demonized as selfish, corrupt and manipulative bourgeois politicians with no regard for the toils of ordinary people. In these interpretive terms, the Tămădău escape was nothing more than a last traitorous act against a citizenry beaten down by decades of PNȚ inspired economic exploitation and fascist oppression. During the indictment, after first accusing the defendants of treason and hating the people, second prosecutor Stanciu continued to attack: "on the morning of July 14, when the Romanian peasant arises at sunrise to plough ... to make bread for those who steal documents from the Ministry of External Affairs, the so-called peasant, who is not a peasant, Ion Mihalache ... was not leaving for harvesting but was

---

65 Shklar, *Legalism* ..., 144–145.
66 See the following: Meierhenrich and Pendas, ibid.; Mark Osiel, *Mass Atrocity, Collective Memory, and the Law* (New Brunswick and London: Transaction Publishers, 2012); Yasco Horsman, *Theaters of Justice: Judging, Staging and Working Through in Arend, Delbo, Stanford* (California: Stanford University Press, 2011); Austin Sarat and Thomas R. Kearns (eds), *Writing History and Registering Memory in Legal Decisions and Legal Practices* (Ann Arbor: University of Michigan Press, 1999).

leading the Tămădău group."⁶⁷ He also described Maniu as a traitor without any feeling for the people starving in the aftermath of the war.⁶⁸ Thus, an exemplary sentence in the name of people's justice and not of the court could only be fair. This message was amplified by an audience of three hundred and fifty who were brought in to express their outrage loudly against those they defined as class enemies.⁶⁹ Some of the defendants themselves adopted a similarly dramatic tone. For example, Penescu's bombastic lecture was aimed at strengthening his defense by self-criticism.⁷⁰

Over six decades later the narrative was reversed. Several of the alleged traitors in the Tămădău trial were presented as victims of a regime that had viciously attacked them as enemies of the people. A major shift in interpretation suggests significant weaknesses in the legal system's ability to dispense compensatory justice by engaging in retrospective truth-telling. As Todorov argues, "historical truth is not the same as judicial truth, which recognizes only two values: guilt or innocence, black or white, yes or no."⁷¹ This was clearly the case in 1947. In violation of the 1923 constitutional provisions, which were formally reinstated after Antonescu's removal in August 1944, the court characterized the PNȚ's political opposition to the PCR and communist ideology in general as treasonous. This inaccurate accusation constituted the basis for manufacturing a thoroughly biased narrative of the PNȚ as a fascist organization both before and after the war. In the aftermath of de-Nazification policies promoted by the allied victors following the war, these criminal charges were instrumental in establishing a weak PCR as legitimate. But both historical analysis and personal memoirs documented the strained relationships between some elements of the party (which included Mihalache) and the Iron Guard in the interwar years. Inaccuracies in respect to the party's alleged support for Antonescu's regime were eventually corrected. In fact, a significant number of prominent leaders, including Carandino, Lazăr and Vișa sentenced in the Tămădău trial, were interned by Antonescu for their anti-fascist activities. A distorted interpretation of the electoral pact signed in 1937 by Maniu with the Iron Guard and then contacts between the PNȚ and the legionary group from Transylvania represented by

---

67 "Rechizitoriul procurorului Alexandrescu", in *Procesul lui Iuliu Maniu* ..., Ciucă, vol. 2, part 1, 139.
68 Ibid., 131–132.
69 Carandino, *Nopți albe și zile negre*, 90.
70 Ciucă, *Procesul lui Iuliu Maniu* ..., vol. 2, part 1, 160–188.
71 Tsevetan Todorov, "Letter from Paris, Salmagundi, Winter/Spring 1999," in *The Papon Affair: Memory and Justice on Trial*, ed. Richard J. Golsan, 221.

Horațiu Comaniciu after 1942 were also grossly overplayed in 1947. Both the context and the complexities of these political agreements between the two parties were willfully ignored. The 1937 pact included other parties and political organizations that joined forces to preempt Carol II from undermining constitutional democracy. As for Comaniciu, he represented only a marginal wing of the legionary movement that was banned in 1944. Subsequently and only briefly, a small portion of its membership joined the parties represented in the National Democratic Bloc (BND).[72]

Both the clandestine efforts of the surviving PNȚ members undertaken before 1989 and then their contributions to post-communist historiography to rehabilitate both the party and Maniu have been discussed earlier. However, these historical accounts should also be interpreted in relationship to the political circumstances under which they were produced. After 1989, the party's record and its leadership were reconfigured within an electoral context distorted by political polarization. In the 1990s and after, several of the key players in the PCR during the Dej era, including Silviu Brucan, Alexandru Bârlădeanu, Corneliu Mănescu became major figures in the FSN and fierce opponents of the PNȚCD.[73] Thus, the PCR's record could easily be combatted by an oversimplified representation of the PNȚ's interwar ideology. By 1933, together with Maniu's democratic wing opposing Carol II's authoritarian tendencies, a conservative nationalist group predisposed to concessions towards the King, and a group advocating the peasant state led by Mihalache, were in dispute over their differences.[74] Maniu's political choices and actions both before and after the war, and especially his refusal to preside over the 1944 government had also been justified as a proper decision at the time.[75] The relationship between him and Codreanu was similarly downplayed by some historians and memorialists who omitted Maniu's empathy with Codreanu's patriotic feelings.[76]

---

72 Rebecca Ann Haynes, "Without the Captain: Iuliu Maniu and the Romanian Legionary Movement after the Death of Corneliu Zelea Codreanu," *Slavonic and East European Review*, 97, no. 2 (April 2019): 334–336.
73 Monica Ciobanu, "Romanian Communists under Gheorghe Gheorghiu-Dej: Legitimation before 1965 and Its Memory as Opposition to Ceaușescu" in *Historical Memory of Central and East European Communism*, eds. Agnieszka Mrozik and Stanislav Holubec (New York: Routledge, 2018), 221–241.
74 Ioan Scurtu, *Istoria Partidului Național Țărănesc*, 221.
75 For a more critical analysis of Maniu see Mihai Pelin, *Iluziile lui Iuliu Maniu* (Bucharest: Editura Viitorul Românesc, 2000).
76 Rebecca Ann Haynes, "Reluctant Allies? Iuliu Maniu and Corneliu Zelea Codreanu against King Carol II of Romania," *Slavonic and East European Review*, 85, no. 1 (January 2007): 106–127.

This one-sided historical interpretation influenced the proceedings of the Vișinescu trial. During testimony, the descendants of Râmnicu-Sărat prisoners were vocal in emphasizing that their parents and grandparents were, as members of the PNȚ, defenders of democratic values and opposed both communism and fascism. In fact, one of the civil parties openly stated that the memory of victims of communism should not be monopolized by extremist groups and individuals sympathetic to the legionary ideology.[77] Yet, both the demographics and the political orientations of the many who were detained until 1964 in Râmnicu-Sărat and elsewhere represented a more diverse segment of the population and were not limited to either members or sympathizers of the PNȚ or the Legionary movement. Vișinescu himself exercised and abused his authority against different groups of inmates. Prior to his tenure at Râmnicu-Sărat (1956–1963), he gained a reputation for cruelty during his time as chief of the bureau of inspections in Jilava prison in 1950 to 1952 and then as political deputy chief for Mislea prison (a facility for women political prisoners). Aurora Dumitrescu, who had several encounters with Vișinescu in both prisons, testified at the trial and revealed disturbing details of his treatment of women (one who was pregnant).[78] However, Vișinescu was only prosecuted for crimes committed from 1956 to 1963.

These limitations were noted and challenged by some historians with expertise on the topic. For example, Cosmin Budeancă from IICCMER was critical of the way the memories of Râmnicu-Sărat told by political prisoners came to be transmitted by others and presented as sensationalist stories in court.[79] The most notable examples include Vișinescu's killing of Mihalache and participation in the squad that executed Antonescu. Although the judge dismissed these claims, other historians criticized the court's knowledge of history, IICCMER's deficient historical counsel and the narrowness of the case.[80]

---

77   Mihaela Bărbuș and Anca-Maria Cernea, personal communication, 26 May 2017.
78   Aurora Dumitrescu, personal communication, 5 July 2011.
79   Cosmin Budeancă, personal communication, 23 May 2017.
80   See Mircea Stănescu, "Inculparea torționarilor comuniști: noi ficțiuni, vechi realități" (11 February 2015), https://mircea-stanescu.blogsopot.ro/2015/02/inculpare-tortionarilor-comunisti-noi.html, accessed 10 January 2020 and Dumitru Lăcătușu, 23 "Note și consemnări de la procesul lui Alexandru Vișinescu" (23 April 2015). www.contributors.ro/reactie-rapida-note-si-consemnari-de-la-procesul-lui-alexandru-visinescu-sedinta-din-22-aprilie-2015/, accessed 10 January 2020.

Conclusion

Despite its shortcomings, the 2015 trial brought to justice a defendant who had clearly engaged in human rights violations. In contrast, the Tămădău trial had exclusively relied on fabricated accusations against the defendants with the purpose of permanently banning a political opponent from public life. It was a typical show trial conducted in the aftermath of the war by the communist government, with Soviet backing. As an example of retrospective justice, the Vișinescu trial was genuinely motivated by the intention to provide some measure of historical redress for victims of communism. Yet, given that the voices of only one group of descendants was heard, the trial failed to provide an adequate historical lesson, nor did it contribute to a dialogue between advocates or authors of different memories. As Osiel put it, "When victims claim a monopoly over the meaning of the event—it defies the purpose of discursive democracy that requires people to engage in a civil exchange or competing views."[81] As it is, it appears that a retrospective form of justice is more likely in a public debate to maintain conflicted and painful memories of the past. Unlike legal forms of transitional justice effected in the immediate aftermath of human rights violations, retrospective justice also seems less likely to emphasize institutional accountability and instead, interprets guilt in individual terms.

In Romania, three decades after the collapse of communism the issue of reckoning with the past remains central to the politics of the present. Electoral competition is still symbolically divided between former communists or the heirs of the PCR and the anti-communists or the democrats. The legacy of the Iron Guard continues to provoke major controversies. As for the PNȚ, although no longer a significant political player, its legacy is still much disputed. Second and third generation descendants continue to advocate on its behalf from a civic platform. Conflicts over the right to legal ownership over the PNȚCD are also currently unfolding. In 2017, a small group of formerly active members from the 1990s gathered to reestablish an authentic PNȚ against a group of impostors who they claimed had hijacked it.[82] Given that multiple histories are constantly revised and rewritten by historians and non-historians alike, it is unlikely that the Vișinescu trial represents the final word in the dispute between the PNȚ and the successor communist regime.

---

81 Osiel, *Mass Atrocity, Collective Memory, and the Law*, 150.
82 Florin Pușcaș, "Partidul Național Țărănesc Maniu-Mihalache pregătește primul congres", Stiripesurse.ro (29 May 2017), https://www.stiripesurse.ro/partidul-na-ional-aranesc-maniu-mihalache-pregate-te-primul-congres_1198996.html, accessed 10 January, 2020.

Restitution Reversal or "Re-nationalization"? An Analysis of Law, Property, and History Through the Case of the "Szekely Mikó" High School in Transylvania

*Emanuela Grama**

Abstract: *In 2002, the Reformed Church in Transylvania requested the retrocession of the Reformed Szekely Miko high school in Sf. Gheorghe/Sepsiszentgyörgy, Covasna's capital city. The state restitution commission at that time approved the return. In 2012, a court invalidated the initial restitution decision, accused the members of the former commission of fraud, and requested that the Church return the building to the city authorities. A close reading of the legal arguments that each party employed to justify or reject the restitution reveals competing temporalities of law and visions of history. This paper analyzes the long and tense debates around this case of property restitution-reversal, to further explore several interconnected phenomena: broader ideologies about the relationship of historical, ethnic, and property rights in contemporary Transylvania; the political mobilization of Romania's ethnic Hungarians around property restitution; and the ways in which negotiations around property propelled more conservative elites to the leadership of Transylvanian Hungarians and enabled them to strengthen their ties with their kin-state, Hungary.*

Introduction

"No one will carry the building on their back to Bucharest," the prefect said.[1] As the representative of the Romanian government in a county where ethnic Hungarians represent three quarters of the county's population, the prefect was trying to assuage the rancor and frustration of the region's ethnic Hungarians. Their reaction was triggered by a 2012 court

---

* Associate professor of anthropology and history, Carnegie Mellon University, Pittsburgh, USA. I would like to thank the editors of this special issue, Monica Ciobanu and Mihaela Şerban, as well as the journal editor, Peter Gross, for their comments on earlier drafts. My gratitude also goes to Britt Halvorson, who offered comments on previous drafts and copyedited the final version.
1 "Prefectul Codrin Munteanu: Tema 'renaționalizării' Colegiului Szekely Mikó este falsă," July 24, 2012, *Mesagerul de Covasna*.

decision regarding the property status of the Mikó high school in Sfântu Gheorghe/Sepsiszentgyörgy, Covasna's capital city. The school had been established in the late 19th century as a religious institution affiliated with the Reformed Church, one of the historically Hungarian churches in Transylvania.² The building was nationalized in 1948. The Reformed Church officially claimed it back in 2001—after the government issued legislation for the restitution of ethnic and religious property and established a governmental commission to oversee these restitution cases. In 2002, the Reformed Church submitted its request to the commission, who approved the transfer of the school from state control to Church jurisdiction.

However, the case was reopened in 2010 in the form of a criminal investigation, which concluded that the restitution was a fraud, that the commission members committed a crime, and that the Church must return the high school to the city authorities. The decision sparked waves of protests among Transylvania's Hungarians, leading them to call the restitution reversal a "re-nationalization" launched by the state, and to search for justice outside Romania's borders. Needless to say, they found no solace in the prefect's assurance that the building would remain part of the city, as the property of the community. On the contrary, the ethnic Hungarian leaders perceived "the Mikó case" as a clear political intervention, meant to fracture their ethnic community from within.

This paper analyzes the tense debates around this case of property restitution-reversal, to further explore two interconnected phenomena: the political mobilization of Romania's ethnic Hungarians around property restitution; and the ways in which negotiations around property propelled more conservative elites to the leadership of Transylvanian Hungarians, and enabled them to strengthen their ties with their kin-state, Hungary. This paper argues that the Mikó case has helped the conservative voices among the Transylvanian Hungarian leadership become more visible and gain more political clout at home, among Transylvanian Hun-

---

2   The Hungarian historical churches in Transylvania include the Roman-Catholic, the Reformed Church, the Evangelic-Lutheran, and the Hungarian Unitarian. 94% of those who belong to the Reformed Church are ethnic Hungarians. As a religious institution, The Reformed Church in Romania is composed of two eparchies, the Királyhágómellék/Oradea Reformed Church District in the Banat region, and the Transylvanian Reformed Church with its seat in Cluj-Napoca. In this paper, for the purpose of simplification, I use "the Reformed Church" or "the Church" to refer to the Transylvanian Reformed Church. It was this church that petitioned the Romanian state for the restitution of the Mikó high school. I must note that all of the Hungarian historical churches officially supported the position of Transylvania's Reformed Church: that the reversal of the restitution was unlawful.

garians, while creating new allegiances with Orban's government and enticing the region's Hungarians to support Orban's divisive rhetoric.

There is, however, something more poignant and revelatory about the debates around the Mikó case. A close reading of the legal arguments that each party employed to justify or reject the restitution reveals competing temporalities of law and visions of history underlying these arguments. The courts adopted a legally formalist perspective on property rights, by considering exclusively the information recorded in the land registry as the ultimate legal proof. The Church and its proponents, however, invoked a more heterogenous array of laws and documents that they asserted to be legal proofs of their property rights (over the Mikó high school). Thus, the Church underscored an understanding of property rights as grounded in and validated by a nexus of religious loyalties, ethnic allegiances, and claims for historical rights echoing former negotiations of power between the Hungarian nobility and the Habsburg empire. The second argument of this paper is that the legal controversy around the Mikó high school sheds light on how Transylvania's Hungarians have appealed to nostalgic renditions of a 19th-century multicultural Central Europe in order to claim a new visibility for themselves as "Europeans," and less as Romanian citizens.

In my analysis, I draw on a wide range of sources, including newspaper articles, online discussions about the Mikó case, public commentaries made by various parties involved in the case, as well as legal documents, such as several court decisions, an excerpt from the land registry, and petitions for and against the restitution and articles from Hungarian- and Romanian-language newspapers (all available online). I have tried to take into account many perspectives about the Mikó case, shared by different parties (religious leaders, city authorities, state officials, ordinary citizens of both Romanian and Hungarian ethnicity), and to set each of these views within their cultural and political context. My aim is to untangle broader ideologies about the relationship of historical, ethnic, and property rights in contemporary Transylvania.

The Reformed Church in Transylvania: A Short History

In Transylvania, the ethnic Hungarians' identification with the Reformed Church is steeped in a history of struggle for political and religious autonomy. In the 17th century, the Reformed Church managed to gain a dominant position in the autonomous Transylvanian principality, under the leadership of a series of princes who belonged to this church. To fight back against both secular modernization and imperial hegemony of the

Habsburg empire, the Reformed Church in Hungary embraced "an explicitly ethnic nationalism," promoting itself as the exclusive representative of the "Magyar religion."[3] Following the 1867 Compromise, which led to the transformation of the Habsburg empire into the Austro-Hungarian dual monarchy, Hungary's liberal politicians helped the Reformed Church compensate in symbolic power for what it did not have in material assets. The 19th-century political elites promoted this church as being "more 'national' than Catholicism could ever be," making it thus into a symbol of a free Hungarian nation.[4]

These elites' dreams of a fully autonomous Hungary whose geographical borders would match those of its historical kingdom were shattered by World War I and the subsequent Treaty of Trianon, signed in 1920. Following the Treaty, pre-1918 Hungary lost two thirds of its former territory and population.[5] Various regions, formerly Hungarian territory, were incorporated in its neighboring countries. Romania received most of the Banat region and all of Transylvania. After the inclusion of Transylvania in Greater Romania, the Reformed Church regarded itself as the sole protector of a Hungarian ethnic identity. The Romanian state, however, tried to undermine the Reformed Church—alongside other religious denominations.[6] Transylvania's historic churches (Roman Catholic, Reformed, Lutheran, and Unitarian) criticized the state for encroaching on the autonomy and property of the religious communities.[7]

After the Communist Party officially came to power in 1947, the Reformed Church, like other religious denominations (with the exception of the Orthodox Church) was marginalized and its property nationalized, a particularly painful loss being the confiscation of their schools. This is why the Church viewed the end of communism in 1989 as the potential return to its pre-1945 *status quo*, and hoped that the postcommunist

---

3   Paul Hanebrink, *In Defense of Christian Hungary: Religion, Nationalism, and Antisemitism, 1890–1944* (Cornell University Press, 2000), 9.
4   Hanebrink, *In Defense of Christian Hungary*, 18.
5   "Treaty of Peace Between The Allied and Associated Powers and Hungary And Protocol and Declaration, Signed at Trianon June 4, 1920."
6   In parallel with the religious reform, the interwar Romanian state also pursued land reform. Launched in 1921, the reform aimed, in principle, to endow peasants with more economic autonomy by dividing large latifundia owned by aristocratic families. However, the Bucharest-based government used the reform to weaken the Transylvanian Hungarian aristocracy, who owned most of the estates in Transylvania. Stefano Bottoni, *Transilvania roșie. Comunismul român și problema națională 1944–1965* (Editura ISPMN, 2010), 38.
7   Horatiu Pepine, "Americanii critică legea cultelor din România," Radio Deutsche Welle, January 4, 2007.

authorities would return the Church property formerly nationalized by the communist state. It turned out that they had to wait much longer.

This was partly because the ex-communist politicians who came to power after 1989 viewed property restitution as their own poker game: they would give away only specific parts of state property only if they gained something from these restitutions. Postponing restitution was a way for the state to signal, indirectly, that an ethnically homogenous Romanian "nation" was the only politically viable community. Consequently, the ethnic and religious minority communities had to wait until the state cared to hear their restitution claims. In the end, it was pressure from abroad—especially from the European Union and other Western states, such as Germany and the USA—that made this state suddenly lose its deafness and begin issuing laws for property restitution.

Property Restitution in Postcommunist Romania

Legal scholars distinguish between three forms of property arrangements: common property, collective property, and private property. The first is represented by the concept of the "commons," which identifies a resource that, in principle, should be available to all members of a society (such as a park). This inclusivity and availability to all should be guaranteed by rules that prevent anyone from gaining exclusive access to that resource. In a collective property system, it is the community as a whole that decides on how an important resource is used. In contrast to common property, a resource deemed "collective property" is not necessarily available to all, but the representatives of that specific community collectively decide on who will use it and how. Private property differs from both common and collective forms because it is centered on individual decision-making (be that of a person, a firm, or a family) and exclusivity. In such a system, the person who has property rights over an object has full control over it—and could invoke those rights to transfer the use rights over to another person, while retaining the property rights.[8]

These differences become blurrier if we place them in the context of a state. In this case, state property, which is a distinct form of collective property, differs from private property, which could also encompass common and collective property that the state actors do not control. This distinction is particularly important in the postcommunist context, where both individuals and communities, including ethnic and religious com-

---

8   "Property and Ownership," last revised March 2020, *Stanford Encyclopedia of Philosophy*, https://plato.stanford.edu/entries/property/.

munities, called for the restitution of the pre-1945 individually- and collectively-owned assets that the communist state had confiscated through nationalization.

In principle, the Romanian postcommunist authorities should have treated equally all the claims for property restitution made by both individuals and groups, including ethnic and religious communities.[9] No matter if the assets in question had been owned individually or collectively, the communist state eventually confiscated all of them by 1960.[10] Consequently, the postcommunist government should have returned all of these assets to their former owners—ideally under similar legal conditions and as soon as possible. That did not happen. Instead, for more than a decade after the end of communism, the Romanian authorities strategically postponed the restitution of both individual and collective property. They kept it as convoluted and ambiguous a process as possible with an eye to using it for their own benefit, both as a source of self-enrichment and for gaining more political clout.[11]

In 1999, the Romanian government issued Ordinance 93 on the restitution of buildings formerly owned by ethnic minorities. But the ordinance also had some caveats. For instance, if after the nationalization, the new users of the buildings did extensive reconstructions or extensions (more than 50%), then the buildings were considered new and would remain state property. Some local authorities exploited this caveat, by invoking prior renovation or attempts for reconstruction to reject resti-

---

9   There is a fast-growing literature on property restitution in post-1989 Romania. For an analysis of the politics of land restitution, see Katherine Verdery, *The Vanishing Hectare: Property and Value in Postsocialist Transylvania* (Cornell University Press, 2003). For arguments about property rights as human rights, and the tense negotiations between national and European courts (such as the European Court of Human Rights), see Monica Ciobanu, "Recent Restorative Justice Measures in Romania (2006–2010)," *Problems of Post-Communism*, 60 (2013), 45–57; Lavinia Stan, "The Roof over Our Heads: Property Restitution in Romania," *Communist Studies and Transition Politics* 22 (2006): 180–205; Mihaela Șerban, "Regime Change and Property Rights Consciousness in Postcommunist Romania," *Law & Social Inquiry* 2018, 43(3): 732–763 and *Subverting Communism in Romania: Law and Private Property 1945–1965* (Lexington Books, 2019). For the cultural effects of the restitution of nationalized houses, and changes in ideologies and practices of kinship, see Liviu Chelcea, "State, Kinship and Urban Transformations during and after Housing Nationalization." PhD diss., University of Michigan, 2004. For strategic devaluation of historical houses as a tool to prevent their restitution, see Emanuela Grama, *Socialist Heritage: The Politics of Past and Place in Romania* (Indiana University Press, 2019).
10 Decree 218/1960 declared as state property "goods of any kind under state control or custody not reclaimed within two years ... regardless of how they had come into the state's possession." Mihaela Șerban, email communication, April 24, 2020.
11 Verdery, *The Vanishing Hectare: Property and Value in Postsocialist Transylvania*.

tution. In response to protests from the ethnic communities, the government amended the ordinance and passed a new law in 2004. Law 66/2004 granted the restitution of *all* buildings that belonged to the ethnic communities and were confiscated between 1940 and 1989. It stated that the ethnic communities could also reclaim the nationalized buildings that underwent renovations, reconstructions, or extensions, but that they would have to retroactively pay for those improvements. However, the implementation of law 66 remained arbitrary. By early 2017, the ethnic German community received only eight restitutions in kind and compensation for three other cases, out of the 136 that they had requested.[12] In 2012, the party of Romania's ethnic Hungarians—the Democratic Alliance of Hungarians in Romania/Uniunea Maghiarilor din Romania, UDMR henceforth)—pointed out that the restitution of the property formerly owned by the Hungarian community continued to be cumbersome, that many claims remained unsolved, and requested that the Romanian government implement a faster and simplified procedure.[13]

In 2002, the government passed law 501 on the restitution of religious property. However, the law did not satisfy the expectations of all Christian denominations. The Hungarian-speaking churches in Romania (Reformed, Unitarian, Roman Catholic, and Lutheran) declared this law "flawed and ineffectual" and denounced "refusals to execute ... verdicts establishing property rights of churches ... and even bad faith interpretation of legal provisions."[14] In 2005, the United States Congress officially called on the Romanian government to "provide fair, prompt, and equitable restitution to all religious communities" and noted that Law 501/2002 was adopted "without consultation with the affected religious communities, [did] not effectively meet the needs of those communities, contain[ed] numerous legal deficiencies, and [was] delayed in its implementation."[15]

Both laws for the restitution of property to ethnic minorities (ordinance 66/1999) and religious denominations (501/2002) signaled that the government treated the restitution of individual and collective property as distinct issues. Other laws regulated the restitution of individual

---

12   126 restitution claims were solved, with 51 rejected, 28 cancelled by the petitioner, and 37 redirected to other authorities. "Răspuns ANPR la cererea deputatului FGDR Ovidiu Ganț," 27 February 2017.
13   They also noted that other political factions in the parliament fought against the restitution in kind, and attempted instead to pass a new law that replaced restitution with financial reparations. UDMR, "Program electoral, 2012–2016."
14   "White Book on Church Property Restitution in Romania," Transylvanian Reformed Church, Cluj, 2016, 10.
15   H. Res. 101, in the House of Representatives, May 23, 2005.

property.[16] This complex and often convoluted legislation made it even more difficult for the claimants to figure out which law they should invoke to support their case, leading to more confusion and delays that further decelerated the restitution process. The EU representatives noted that this cumbersome legislation was an impediment instead of an incentive for the restitution, and warned the Romanian government that if they did not expedite the restitution process, they could compromise Romania's plans to join the Union in 2007.

To comply with the EU's ultimatum, the government passed a new law in 2005. Law 247/2005 consolidated the previous legislation on property restitution in one act. The new law thus signaled a shift in the perspective of the state regarding property and its restitution. Prior to law 247, the state made a legal separation between different kinds of property (ethnic, religious, and individual) and different assets (buildings, land, forests, etc.). With the new law, the state actors wanted to signal that they would be treating the restitution of any kind of property the same way, and that they would no longer discriminate between different kinds of petitioners. Law 247/2005 proved to be effectual inasmuch as it helped the Romanian authorities signal their alleged obedience to the EU's directives and their willingness to become "Europeans."

In reality, many restitution claims submitted by the ethnic minorities and their churches continued to drag on for years. In 2016, Transylvania's Reformed Church published an English-language report about the current status of the restitution requests made by Transylvania's historical churches—that is, the churches to which the majority of the ethnic Hungarians have historically belonged. The report argued that the restitution process became stagnant once Romania achieved its international goals: to become part of NATO and then the EU.[17] Likely meant to appeal to politicians and other supporters abroad and rally their support, the report pointed out that the state authorities had not yet solved many

---

16 In 2001, the parliament passed Law 10/2001, which provided for the restitution in kind of the buildings confiscated by the state between March 6, 1945 and December 22, 1989, as well as those taken by the state in 1940 from their Jewish owners. One of the purposes of Law 10/2001 was to acknowledge the complaints of many former owners who found themselves unable to retrieve their properties because the former tenants had already bought them at preferential prices (following Law 112/1995). For a discussion of the parliamentary debates and the convoluted process of the application of Law 10, see Șerban, "Regime Change and Property Rights Consciousness," and Stan, "The Roof over Our Heads." See also Liviu Damșa, *The Transformation of Property Regimes and Transitional Justice in Central Eastern Europe: In Search of a Theory* (Springer, 2017).

17 "White Book On Church Property Restitution in Romania," 43.

requests, and that even when the central officials approved some restitutions, the local authorities postponed the restitution de facto—and that sometimes the courts even reversed earlier restitutions, such in the case of the Mikó high school.

The "Mikó Case" as a Legal Controversy

The much debated reversal of the restitution of the Mikó high school in Sf. Gheorghe, a city with a predominantly ethnic Hungarian population, has revealed how property and property rights are intertwined with political struggles.[18] In this section, I will describe the parties involved in the struggle over the high school, summarize some of their arguments, and clarify the chronology of the conflict. The Mikó high school was built at the end of 19th century, with funds that came partly from the local authorities and partly from the inhabitants of the city of Sepsiszentgyörgy (located then in the Austro-Hungarian monarchy).[19] The local count Imre Mikó contributed a major donation, supplemented by small donations from other residents and loans contracted by the local authorities (to be paid back also by the residents via local taxes). The majority of the town inhabitants belonged to the Reformed Church, and the Church established the curriculum and administered the high school.[20] However, the high school had juridical autonomy and the records in the land registry showed that it was the high school, and not the Church, that had property rights over the building (and other assets). The Reformed Church continued to administer the high school and its curriculum throughout the interwar period, until it was confiscated by the communist state in 1948.[21]

---

18   For an analysis of ethnicity, property and nationalism, see, for instance, Verdery, "Transnationalism, Nationalism, Citizenship, and Property."
19   Tímea Bakk-Dávid, "Kié a Mikó: a református egyházé vagy a háromszéki székelyeké?" June 29, 2020, http://itthon.transindex.ro/?cikk=9751. A note on sources: I translated the Romanian-language sources and I relied on Google Translate to read the Hungarian-language sources. I thank Dániel Kálmán, a native Hungarian speaker, for checking my translations.
20   In 1880, the large majority of the town population was Hungarian: in a total of 6,221 inhabitants, 6,086 were Hungarians, 32 Romanians, 76 Germans, and 27 "others." Source: http://www.kia.hu/konyvtar/erdely/erd2002/cvetn02.pdf.
21   See the historical summary in the text of the sentence issued by the Buzău county court on June 28, 2012. Criminal Sentence no. 715 of June 28, 2012, File no. 13020/200/2011, the Buzău Criminal Court, The 17-page single-spaced document offers a detailed summary of the case, including a summary of the depositions of the three committee members accused of abuse of power. In the paper, I will henceforth refer to this document as "the 2012 court decision."

During communism, it remained a high school, but the official teaching language switched back and forth from Romanian to Hungarian according to the political agenda of the communist state.[22] After the end of the communist regime, it took back its pre-1945 name, the "Szekely Mikó" high school, and returned to Hungarian as its original teaching language. In addition to this public high school, the Church opened its own confessional (Reformed) high school, in a different section of the same building. (Even though there are two distinct high schools in the same building, in this paper I use "the Mikó high school" to refer to the entire building.)

As previously mentioned, in 1999 the government passed Ordinance 83 regarding the restitution of property to ethnic groups. The ordinance was accompanied by an appendix, which initially included 36 buildings that "had belonged to the ethnic minorities and had become state property through enforcement, confiscation, or nationalization."[23] In December 2000, through a governmental decision, 37 more buildings were added to the list. The Mikó high school was one of them. Soon thereafter, in February 2001, the Reformed Church requested the Mikó building from the city council of Sf. Gheorghe, noting that the Mikó building was part of the buildings that the state had confiscated from the Reformed Church (confirmed by the appendix to ordinance 83/1999).[24] In March 2001, the city council, formed mostly of ethnic Hungarians elected locally, officially agreed with the restitution.

The Church also submitted its request to the state commission that dealt specifically with the restitution requests placed by ethnic minorities (established according to ordinance 83/1999). The ordinance mentioned that the commission should consider the requests for the restitution of "buildings ... and residential land that had belonged to the communities (organizations, *religious denominations*) of the citizens of the national minorities in Romania" (my italics, article 1). The members of the commission that analyzed the Reformed Church's request were: an ethnic Hungarian who was the representative of the Ministry of Public Affairs, an ethnic Romanian representing the Ministry of Justice, and another ethnic Hungarian standing for the Reformed Church. Even though the Mikó

---

22 "Proiect de dezvoltare," Mikó high school, October 16, 2014.
23 "Ordonanța de urgență nr. 83/1999 privind restituirea unor bunuri imobile care au aparținut comunităților cetățenilor aparținând minorităților naționale din România," in *Monitorul Oficial*, Partea I nr. 266 din 10 iunie 1999.
24 Initially, ordinance 83/1999 had one annex. In 2000, the government authoritized an additional annex with other buildings, including the Mikó high school. "Hotărâre nr. 1334 din 14 decembrie 2000 pentru completarea anexei la Ordonanta de urgenta a Guvernului nr. 83/1999 ...," *Monitorul Oficial* nr. 698 din 27 decembrie 2000.

building was included in the appendix of properties that had been nationalized, ordinance 83 required that the commission verified the legal status of each of the items (buildings) on that list (article 2, point 3).

Per ordinance 83, the commission was to issue their final decision only after they received the confirmation regarding the legal situation of a specific building from the Ministry of Public Administration. The commission asked the Ministry to confirm that the Mikó high school had been nationalized as Church property. The latter, however, responded that the Mikó building was part of "the private domain of the state," as an educational institution, and that consequently it fell under the jurisdiction of Law 20/2001.[25] But the commission ignored the note from the ministry, deciding instead to grant the Reformed Church property rights over the Mikó high school. (More specifically, the commission granted property rights to the Eparchy of the Transylvanian Reformed Church, not to the local Reformed church in Sfântu Gheorghe. For simplification, I will refer to the Eparchy as the Reformed Church or the Church.)

In sum, different parties, and even distinct state actors, perceived differently the legal status of the Mikó building. One state institution (the Ministry of Public Administration) viewed the building as individual property. The Church, however, alongside the restitution commission, regarded it as a form of collective property that had belonged to the ethnic Hungarian community, and consequently should be returned to this ethnic group.

Following the commission's decision, in July 2002, the city council of Sf. Gheorghe officially returned to the Church all of the assets that had belonged to the Mikó high school prior to nationalization, and the legal authorities recorded the Church as the new owner in the land registry. The Church was legally obliged to allow the Mikó high school to continue using the building, but it began charging the city council rent (the high school remained a state institution, administered by the Ministry of Education).[26]

Once they received the Mikó building, the Church petitioned for the restitution of another building. This second building, located a ten-minute walk from the high school, used to function as the student dormitory. During communism, state authorities rented the apartments in that building to some state employees, including high school personnel.[27] A few

---

25 The 2012 court decision (Buzău).
26 The 2012 court decision (Buzău).
27 Tímea Bakk-Dávid, "Kié a Mikó: a református egyházé vagy a háromszéki székelyeké?", June 29, 2009. http://itthon.transindex.ro/?cikk=9751. After the end of communism, as state tenants, they became eligible to purchase their

families, all ethnic Hungarians, became apartments owners in that building—at least, until 2002, when the Church received property rights over the Mikó high school, and implicitly the former dormitory. Once that happened, the Church informed these families that their apartment purchase was no longer valid, and that they had to move out. When they refused and insisted on their property, the Church brought them to court.[28]

In 2004, the local court in Sf. Gheorghe rejected the Church's request for the eviction of the owners, but the Church appealed this decision, and opened another lawsuit in the Covasna regional court. The latter acknowledged the Church's claim of property, and requested that the previous purchases of apartments be declared void. The three families appealed, in turn, and the trial moved to a third court (Brașov). In 2006, this third court confirmed the decision of the Covasna court that the Church was the new owner, and declared it final. The case seemed to be closed in favor of the Church.

But one of the apartment owners refused to give up. A retired accountant with many connections in the city, he decided to peruse the local archives and libraries in search for documentation about the history of the Mikó high school and its relation to the Reformed Church.[29] He collected no less than 638 documents, which he used to prove that the Reformed Church had never had property rights over the assets of the Mikó high school. Initially, he showed these documents to the Church's representatives, hoping that both parties could reach a compromise: that the Church would allow the former owners to keep their apartments, and, in exchange, the owner would forget about the controversial restitution. The Church, however, rejected his proposal. According to the owner, the Church Bishop told him that he (the owner) could not report the Church to the Romanian authorities because that would go against the interests of the Hungarian community—and implicitly, of the owner as a member

---

apartments—per Law 85/1992. Even though this building was much older than communist apartment buildings, the city council placed it in the same category, because it had initially been built with funds from the community.

28 "Curtea de apel Brasov, Decizia civilă nr. 187/R, dosar 44/R/2005, 15 martie 2006," Available at https://drive.google.com/file/d/0B5TNc8kJUS3gZmdkYUFG N1RTNXM/view. I thank the writer with the blogname of "BurePișta," who discussed the legal intricacies of the Mikó case in an extensive blog post, and who kindly shared links to the original court documents (posted on-line in full). See blog post of February 2, 2015, at https://maghiaromania.wordpress.com/2015/02/02/juristu-blogului-cazul-Mikó-dreptatea-si-teoria-relativitatii/.

29 I must note that this man had a controversial reputation in the city, having been a highly-placed communist official before 1989. See posts by "nodeki" and "reccsman," on September 8, 2012), available at https://maghiaromania.wordpress.com/2012/09/02/colegiul_szekely_Mikó_/#comment-8122.

of that community. Failing to reach an agreement with the Church, in 2007 the owner reported the case to the Anti-Corruption Prosecutor's Office.[30] The Anti-Corruption Office began investigations, which lasted a few years.[31] They interviewed the members of the 2002 restitution commission, the owner who made the complaints, and the representatives of the Church.

In 2010, the Prosecutor's Office issued their verdict: they recommended that the three members of the 2002 restitution commission be judged in a criminal trial and that the Reformed Church be withdrawn its property rights over the Mikó high school.[32] The trial began in a regional court (Buzău). In 2012, this court pronounced the commission members guilty of abuse of power and fraud against the state, and sentenced each of them to three years in prison with execution.[33] The court also required that the Church pay back the rent they had received from the city council during the years after the 2002 restitution.

The Reformed Church contested the decision, presenting it as a form of re-nationalization rooted in the state's nationalism. They appealed the decision, and the trial reopened in a different court (in Ploiești). A wave of protests accompanied the court's decision. In September 2012, around 25,000 people came to Sfântu Gheorghe to show support for the Church

---

30   Bakk-Dávid, "Kié a Mikó?" June 29, 2009.
31   There had been previous complaints against the restitution, such as the one made by the prefect of the Covasna county. See "Către Ministerul Administrației, în atenția Domnului Ministru Octav Cozmanca," October 17, 2002, signed by prefect Horia Grama (no connection to the author). In July 2002, a few months after the commission granted property to the Church, the then prefect contacted the government to notify them that the restitution was illegal. The prefect was a member of the Social Democrat Party and was appointed by the government then dominated by the same party, PSD. However, the authorities ignored this notification. Documents issued on August 13, 2018, by Prefectura Covasna to Dan Tanasa, per his request for accessing public information. While I do not share Tanasa's views of the Mikó case, I thank him for sharing the sources on-line (available at scrib.com). Another possible explanation of the state authorities' decision to not follow up the Covasna prefect's petition was the context of the 2000 national elections. In 2000, the former communists, who formed the Social Democracy Party of Romania (PDSR, in Romanian), returned to power as part of a political coalition (which in 2001 became one party, the Social Democratic Party, PSD). The ex-communists relied on the Party of Romania's Hungarians (UDMR) and its supporters to win the elections (even though UDMR did not join the government as a coalition partner). Stephen M. Saideman, R. William Ayres, *For Kin or Country: Xenophobia, Nationalism, and War* (Columbia University Press, 2008), 162.
32   Ministerul Public, Parchetul de pe lângă Înalta Curte de Casație și Justiție, Direcția Naționala Anticorupție, Serviciul Teritorial Brașov, "Rechizitoriu, 22 December 2010," available in full at http://erdelyiopcio.blogspot.com/2015/01/a-Mikóitelet.html.
33   The 2012 court decision.

and challenge what they viewed as an outrageous "injustice."³⁴ The protests, organized by the Hungarian historic churches, brought the leaders of these churches together with hundreds of pastors, leaders of the party of Romania's Hungarians, and other ethnic Hungarians from around the country, as well as some Hungarians from abroad. The participants wore a black band, meant to signify their mourning for the loss of the high school, and they also placed a black flag on the façade of the Mikó building. The protests continued throughout September and early October 2012. In October, on the day before the trial would resume in Ploiești, the pastor of the local Reformed Church called for the city's ethnic Hungarians to form a living chain around the Mikó high school. People of all ages came to show their support: older men and women were standing next to young families with toddlers. Some brought signs that read: "Return what you stole! Where is justice? Where is truth?"³⁵

The Church's bishop declared that the verdict was a "clear derision of justice and equity," which caused "severe material and moral detriment to the Transylvanian Reformed Church." He noted that the fine imposed on the Church was absurd, given that the church had already invested significant funds in the modernization of the high school.³⁶ The leaders of the other Hungarian historical churches in Romania supported the Reformed bishop's strong criticism. In a shared statement, they declared that the condemnation of the commission members was akin to "an authentic show trial" from the Stalinist period. They considered the decision "an attack against Hungarians in Transylvania," which signaled "the beginning of an imminent re-nationalization process, harkening back to the days of communism." And they concluded that "the rule of law in Romania is a sham, a lie, and an illusion."³⁷

The political representatives of the Hungarian community in Romania immediately rallied behind the Church leadership in condemning the court decision. While ethnic Hungarians from all across Romania were travelling to Sf. Gheorghe to protest the Romanian authorities, a

---

34   "Circa 25.000 de maghiari au protestat la Sf. Gheorghe," September 1, 2012, *Adevarul*.
35   "Élő lánc a Székely Mikó Kollégiumért," signed by pastor Imre Sánta, October 1, 2012, https://www.sepsiszentgyorgy.info.
36   In English, in original. More exactly, the sum invested by the Church was 2,9 million lei. "Resolution of the Transylvanian Reformed Church District's General Assembly regarding the Romanian State's Re-nationalization of the Szekely Mikó Reformed High school in Sepsiszentgyörgy/Sfântu Gheorghe," July 6, 2012, http://regi.reformatus.hu/data/attachments/2014/11/27/SzMK_ugy_EN.pdf.
37   These are excerpts from the English-language statements. "Statement," signed by the leaders of the Hungarian Historic Churches of Transylvania, July 11, 2012, http://regi.reformatus.hu/data/attachments/2014/11/27/SzMK_ugy_EN.pdf.

representative of the party of Romania's Hungarians in the European Parliament declared that the Mikó case was not solely "an attack against the entire Hungarian community," but also a signal that the Romanian government would fully abandon restitution in kind to the churches and to houses of worship of other religious denominations. He added, "not all of the cities with buildings that had already been returned to their former owners are led by Hungarians [that is, by a city council dominated by ethnic Hungarians]. Such a decision leads the way to the renationalization of all church property, ... not only of the [confessional] schools."[38]

During this time, the Romanian state authorities tried to distance themselves from the case, pointing out that a decision rests with the court and emphasizing the separation of judicial from political power. In 2012, after the first court decided that the Church must return the building to the city council, while the case was still litigated, the county prefect emphasized that the Mikó building would become part of the city's patrimony, as a public good. Claiming that he tried to diffuse tensions in the community, the prefect highlighted the difference between "the state," seen exclusively as the Bucharest-based central authorities, and the city as the locality of the public patrimony. He noted that there were "two possibilities: that the building would be owned either by the Reformed Church, or by the high school itself, and not by the Romanian state." As I already mentioned in the introduction, the prefect dismissed the Church's accusation about the building's re-nationalization by saying: "No one would carry the building on their back to bring it to Bucharest. It would not become the property of the Romanian state."[39] Another Romanian politician, the head of the regional office of the Social Democrat Party, and the former prefect of Covasna, rejected the Church's interpretation of the Mikó case as a violation of ethnic rights, noting that, because of the mostly ethnic Hungarian composition of the city council, it represents strictly a conflict **within** the Hungarian community—"a Hungarian-Hungarian issue"—and therefore cannot be viewed as a conflict between the Romanian state and the Hungarian community.[40]

But the question of who had property rights over Mikó was not simply a "Hungarian-Hungarian" issue. In fact, despite the former prefect's remarks, the state had the instruments to legally take back the

---

38 Sógor Csaba, "Intergrupul pentru Minorități din PE a adoptat o rezoluție în cazul Liceului Székely Mikó, 2012-09-13," http://sogorcsaba.eu.
39 "Tema 'renaționalizării' Colegiului "Szekely Mikó" este falsă, afirmă prefectul de Covasna," July 24, 2012,
40 "PSD Covasna: Cazul "Mikó" este o problemă maghiaro-maghiară, statul roman e acuzat pe nedrept," September 7, 2012, *Mesagerul de Covasna*.

building—and the Church and its supporters knew that. According to law 213/1998, the government could pass a governmental decision whereby a building or any other good was transferred from the "private domain" to "the public domain" of the state (article 8). If a building became part of "the public domain" then it could not be further sold, or inherited by potential users, or returned—that is, it could no longer be the object of a restitution claim (article 11).[41]

In 2012, the Church and two of the members of the commission appealed the first verdict (issued by the Buzău court). The trial resumed in another court (Ploiești). In 2014, this court partially amended the 2012 decision, deciding to suspend the prison sentences for the commission members and to cancel the fine on the Church. However, the court kept the previous charges of fraud and abuse of power levied against the members of the 2002 restitution commission, and maintained that the Mikó assets remain state property (administered by the city). However, the 2014 court decision included the following caveat: "currently, the owner of the building is the Romanian state, but ... the building may be legally returned to that person or community that proves that they had property rights over the building, or that they are the successor of such an owner."

This caveat gave new hope to the Church representatives.[42] They decided to re-submit their claim to the special commission for the restitution of ethnic and religious property (part of the National Authority for Property Restitution).[43] In 2016, this state commission met with the representatives of the Church and discussed the case, but in the end, it decided that the building would remain in the city's public patrimony.[44] Once again, the Church appealed the commission's decision and the case was reopened in 2016 in yet another court. Once again, the Church lost its case. It appealed again and the case moved to the National High Court of Justice. In 2018, the High Court rejected the appeal, and issued a final decision that the building would not be given back to the Church.[45] In 2019,

---

41   "Lege nr.213 din 17 noiembrie 1998 privind proprietatea publică și regimul juridic al acesteia."
42   In 2014, the Church brought the case to the European Court of Human Rights, but I could not find any source that would offer further clarification about the current situation of the case with the ECHR.
43   Within this institution, there is a special commission for property restitution in charge with the claims made by the ethnic and religious groups.
44   National Authority for Property Restitution, notifications regarding the meetings of April 21, 2016, and May 31, 2016. http://www.anrp.gov.ro.
45   "Eparhia Reformată din Ardeal pierde DEFINITIV procesul cu Guvernul României în cazul clădirii Colegiului Szekely Mikó," November 23, 2018, *Mesagerul de Covasna*. The article quotes the decision 4087 of November 22, 2018: "The High Court

in a separate case involving a larger number of state bureaucrats formerly accused of corruption, the National High Court of Justice found the members of the 2002 restitution commission not guilty and acquitted them.

Following the 2014 court decision, which restated that the Mikó building must be returned to the city authorities, the Church declared: "Our former trust and faith in the rule of law has vanished. Our entire community, 700,000 people, have been unjustly abused, called liars, impostors, and greedy. This is not about the property of a building or the lack thereof, but about a moral injury of our dignity."[46] In another statement, they maintained that it was "ours to regain the buildings that we are legally entitled to and to value the inheritance of our forebearers according to their wishes. It is us who [should] administer their patrimony, and for the use of our community."[47] Their comments conveyed a deeper frustration. In the Church's view, and its supporters, the reversal of the restitution was equivalent to an erasure of their history—and in this particular case, of the historical relationship between the Reformed Church and the Hungarian community.[48]

However, the Reformed Church and the conservative faction of UDMR (the party of Transylvanian Hungarians) also gained significant traction from this legal defeat. In fact, they have managed to turn property loss into political capital both inside and outside of Transylvania's Hungarian community. Their comments and protests gained them not only heightened visibility at a European level, but also in Viktor Orban's Hungary.[49]

Almost immediately after the High Court issued the final decision regarding the Mikó high school, in November 2018, the Hungarian minister of foreign affairs made an official visit to Romania. In his declaration following the visit, he made no allusion to the Mikó case or other controversies regarding property restitution. Instead, he said that "the best news" was that the Romanian authorities accepted Hungary's proposal to launch a program of economic development in Transylvania, aimed specifically at the ethnic

---

    rejects the appeal made by the Reformed Church in December 20, 2016 as unfounded. [The decision is] final."
46 Raluca Pantazi, "Reacție fără precedent a Bisericii Reformate din România după renaționalizarea clădirii unui colegiu din Sfântu Gheorghe," November 27, 2014, https://www.hotnews.ro.
47 "Noul caz Mikó—Dosarul cu numărul 498," December 24, 2016, https://adevarul.ro/news/societate/noulcaz-Mikó-dosarul-numarul-498.
48 Horațiu Pepine, "Problema Colegiului Szekely Mikó," August 30, 2012, *Deutsche Welle*. See also the discussions on the blog: https://maghiaromania.wordpress.com/2012/09/02/colegiul_szekely_Mikó_/.
49 I could find any official comment made by representatives of the EU institutions, and the European Court of Human Rights has not issued any decision on it (as far as I know).

Hungarians.⁵⁰ The Orban government has supported several Hungarian communities in neighboring regions, but Transylvanian Hungarians have received the largest financial backing (approximately 145 million Euro every year starting in 2016). With this money, the Hungarian community has built new stadiums, kindergartens, schools, and universities, and established a regional Hungarian-language mass media (newspapers, websites, and TV stations). The largest beneficiary of Hungary's backing, however, has been Transylvania's Reformed Church.⁵¹

In an interview, the episcope of this Church emphasized only the benefits of the Hungarian support. He compared the situation of Transylvanian Hungarians minority with a child whose parents had divorced one hundred years ago (an allusion to the 1920 Trianon Treaty)—implying that Romania's Hungarians have been deprived of rights and agency, being thus reduced to the status of a dependent child. The episcope referenced the Mikó case as a startling example of the Romanian state's disregard for minority rights, pointing out that the decision regarding the restitution reversal has been cited by other courts as a precedent in "similar cases"—though he did not clarify which cases.⁵²

The episcope alluded to a new strategy of political and economic mobilization. That is, if the Romanian authorities refused to return the assets previously owned by the Hungarian community and churches, then Transylvanian Hungarians would rely on the financial assistance and the additional citizenship that the Hungarian government offered to their co-ethnics outside Hungary's borders. In sum, the ethnic Hungarians would turn to Hungary's help to compensate for what they viewed as property "theft" committed by the Romanian state.⁵³

---

50   "Visita oficială a domnului Péter Szijjártó Ministrul Comerțului Exterior și al Afacerilor Externe al Ungariei la București," November 9, 2018, https://bukarest.mfa.gov.hu
51   Akos Keller-Alant, "Living like in Hungary: Orban bankrolling Romania 'ethnic parallelism'," January 30, 2020, Balkan *Insight*.
52   He recalled that out of 700–750 buildings that the Reformed Church had requested, only 40 percent was returned, with the other cases being suspended or rejected. "Episcopul Ardealului: 'poate ar fi mai bun un primar român cinstit' la Tg Mureș, decât să se bată ungurii între ei," *Radio Europa Liberă Romania*, October 13, 2019, translated excerpts from the interview (in Hungarian) that the episcope gave to *Kronika*, Transylvania's Hungarian-language daily.
53   As soon as Viktor Orban and his party returned to power after the 2010 election, the Hungarian government passed the double citizenship law, which allows ethnic Hungarians living outside Hungary to apply for Hungarian citizenship. In 2016, the number of the ethnic Hungarians living in Romania who held dual citizenship (Romanian and Hungarian) was more than 515, 000. Source: https://www.hotnews.ro. In 2019, the Hungarian vice prime-minister declared that 1,1 million

Here we begin to see why the initial restitution of the Mikó high school, and later, the reversal of that restitution, became particularly powerful rhetorical tropes for the leaders of Transylvanian Hungarians. In these discourses, the Mikó case symbolized injustice (in the form of harassment of ethnic Hungarian politicians), disregard of the Transylvanian Hungarians' history, the Romanian authorities' lack of knowledge of and unwillingness to understand the historical ties between religious and political institutions within this ethnic community, and more importantly, a denial of property rights understood as ethnic rights.

The Mikó High School as Inalienable Property

The equivalence that the religious and political leaders of Transylvanian Hungarians made between the right to private property and ethnic minority rights (the rights to express and practice one's ethnic identity) must be understood through the broader significance that the Mikó building carried as a material, tangible source of group identity—what anthropologist Annette Weiner called an "inalienable possession" that a group imbues with collective meaning and, therefore, plays a role in reaffirming that group's identity.[54] The Reformed Church claimed ownership over the building by stating that the Church was "the only successor of the reformed schools in Transylvania, and consequently of the Mikó reformed high school."[55] The Church reclaimed the high school because they viewed it as their exclusive prerogative to create, reify, and protect the ethnically Hungarian community. For instance, a woman who attended Mikó in the late 1990s noted that it was the Church that took care of the high school when the Romanian state did not:

> All of the desks in the high school were replaced by desks sent from Holland and Germany—as donations to the Reformed Church. We are talking about 25 classrooms, not just a few. In the same year [1998–1999] [the high school received] computers, also through donations. That the high school belonged to the Reformed Church helped tremendously, because they relied on donations [to compensate] for what the state did not want or could not do.[56]

---

ethnic Hungarians became Hungarian citizens—out of approximately 3 million living outside Hungary. Source: https://www.dcnews.ro.
54 Annette Weiner, *Inalienable Possessions: The Paradox of Keeping-while-Giving* (University of California Press, 1992)
55 "Sentința civilă nr 228, February 6, 2003, Judecătoria Sfântu Gheorghe," page 2. Documents issued on August 13, 2018, by Prefectura Covasna to Dan Tanasa. www.scribd.com
56 Comment by Emese Török, September 2, 2012, https://maghiaromania.wordpress.com/2012/09/02/colegiul_szekely_Mikó_/.

During the prolonged court case, the question of what constituted "resources" became an issue of debate. In the opinion of the criminal court that reviewed the restitution case in 2012, "resources" meant exclusively financial contributions and did not entail revenues of any kind, including property rights. The court presented the multiple sources of funding critical to the establishment of the school and its buildings (including the students' dorm): the city council opened a bank credit first in 1873, and a second one in 1890; the land was offered by the city community; almost 3,000 members of the community made individual donations, including a substantial donation offered by count Mikó Imre.[57] In addition, the Hungarian state contributed annual funds to the school. At the same time, the court emphasized the legal separation between the school and the Church. It mentioned a contract between the high school and the Reformed Church, in which the two parties agreed to exchange some land—yet another proof, in the court's view, that the high school functioned as a separate legal entity. Relying on these contracts, the judge concluded that "the school was the owner of its patrimony," legally independent from the Church, which had not invested financially in the school.

The Church, backed by the city local authorities and the UDMR (the party of Transylvanian Hungarians), rejected an understanding of "resources" as solely finances. Instead, it counterposed this view with a more encompassing and heterogenous notion of collective support for the school, in which the school was a vessel of cultural identity made possible by the efforts of the entire ethnic community. This view was also echoed by more recent accounts, such as this story of origins published in a 2014 report of the Mikó high school: "The project was commissioned and paid for by Count Mikó Imre. The residents of the Szekely county brought the construction materials in their carriages. The city donated the land.[58]"

The understanding of property that emerges from this narrative is very different from a view of property rights set within the framework of legal formalism, one where these rights are exclusively determined by only one legal fact: the name that appears in the land registry. The narrative offers instead a story of origins that extolls the high school as collective property, built by the local community. In their restitution claim, the Reformed Church highlighted this collective history of local effort and labor. Even though the Church was not recorded in the land registry as the owner of the high school, in their view the school was built with the

---

57   60,000 forints in 1876, according to the 2012 court decision, page 10.
58   "Liceul Teoretic "Székely Mikó." Proiect de dezvoltare. Aprobat în Consiliul Profesoral din 16. 10. 2014." Available at https://isj.educv.ro/sites/default/files/pdipas-1461100716.pdf.

purpose of continuing and reinforcing the ethnic community gathered around its church.

When the school was built at the end of the 19th century, the local community, formed mostly of ethnic Hungarians, overlapped with the national community, as the region was then within the borders of the Hungarian kingdom (as part of the Austro-Hungarian Dual monarchy). Between 1867, the signing of the compromise between Austria and Hungary, and 1918, the end of the empire and Transylvania's inclusion in Greater Romania, the Hungarians in the Hungarian kingdom enjoyed exclusive political rights that were not available to the other ethnic groups in the empire. At that time, the local community was mostly ethnically Hungarian, and a significant part of them belonged to the Reformed church.[59] Between 1870 and 1876, out of the approximately 5,000 total inhabitants, a number that likely included also children, more than 2,500 people contributed individual donations to the establishment of the school.[60] 380 people offered building materials.[61] As far as the Mikó high school was concerned, there were no obvious tensions between the Hungarian state and the Reformed church because they viewed each other as complementary mechanisms of ethnic identity-making.[62]

Following Transylvania's inclusion into Greater Romania, the ethnic Hungarians found themselves to be the largest minority in the country. Instead of an ally, as the Hungarian government used to be for the Reformed Church, the Romanian state became an enemy. Consequently, the Church attempted to protect its autonomy in relation to the interwar Romanian government. Even though they had to deal with new politics and laws, they also tried to keep in place their pre-1918 status quo. This history comes across in their restitution request. To justify their claim, the church emphasized that post-1918 it maintained a relation with the school that entailed both supervision and ownership, similar to the one it

---

59 Before the 1877 administrative reform, Sepsiszentgyörgy/Sfântu Gheorghe was the largest town in the land of Három szék. Based on the census done in 1869, the population of Három szék was 11,3% Romanian (12,435), 88,3% Hungarian (97,197), 0,2% German (223), and 0,2% others (200). In 1869, the distribution of the religious denominations within the population of Három szék was the following: 45,5% Reformed (50,097), 35,1% Roman Catholic (38,685), 12,5% Orthodox (13,890), 4,3% Unitarian (4,689), 2% Greek Catholic (2,228), 0,2% (German-speaking) Lutheran (192), 0,3% Jewish (271). http://www.kia.hu/kony vtar/erdely/erdstat/erdstat1.pdf.
60 The 2012 court decision mentions 2,579 individual donations, made between 1870 and 1876, including the largest one from count Mikó Imre (page 10).
61 Bakk-Dávid, "Kié a Mikó: a református egyházé vagy a háromszéki székelyeké?"
62 See historian Paul Hanebrink's argument that the Reformed Church in Hungary was as a paragon of ethnic nationalism. Hanebrink, *In Defense of Christian Hungary*.

had had from the beginning during the time of the Austro-Hungarian empire. To support this claim, the Church's lawyers prepared a legal argument that relied on a mixture of laws from the pre-1920 (Hungarian) and post-1920 (Romanian) jurisprudences, as well as strategically selected documents that they presented as valid legal sources.

In the next section, I analyze distinct temporalities of law underlying the competing claims over the Mikó high school. I examine how each party (the Church's lawyers and the prosecutor) tried to suture different historical periods and geographies in one legal continuum or, on the contrary, emphasize their differences. I also analyze the tension between the specific laws and legal facts that each party invoked to ground their property claims—a conflict that stems from competing views of what is "the law." By examining the arguments brought by each party, I discuss the particular visions of history that informed the parties' legal reasoning, and explain why there could not be a simple answer to the question of who owns the Mikó school.

Competing Legal Orders and Fluid Historical Time

One of the pastors interviewed by the anti-corruption officers during the 2010 investigation complained that these officials had "no idea about the whole denominational school system," and no willingness to try to understand it. The pastor argued that the Church's property rights over the high school was similar to "the ownership of the parish of Sepsiszentkirály and the church: it was also built by the community, yet it belongs to the church."[63] He was alluding to an argument that the Church kept invoking during the debates: that Church law was not subordinated to state law, and therefore the high school was part of the church property. In other words, the high school was equal to a parish because both institutions were sites of religious education and community-making.

The debates about who had property rights over the Mikó high school can be understood through a broader discussion about "what is law," and how different actors identify and make sense of what stands for "legal facts" and "legal actions" at the intersection of state law, historical customs, and local histories of interacting with official authority. Specifically, I argue that the debates about the "Mikó case" can be interpreted through the tension between what theorists call "legal formalism" and "legal pluralism." Legal formalism is grounded in the claim that there is only

---

63 See interview with pastor János Bustya in Bakk-Dávid, "Kié a Mikó," June 29, 2009. http://itthon.transindex.ro/?cikk=9751.

one possible legal interpretation of the law, that what constitute "legally significant facts" and legally accepted sources should not be a matter of debate, and that the judge's verdict should not be influenced by other considerations of moral or political nature.[64] If we view the process of property restitution in postcommunist Romania through the lens of legal formalism, it becomes reduced to one pivotal question concerning only one legal source: what is the name or institution recorded in the land registry? The land registry becomes thus the exclusive proof of property rights. This perspective informs the decisions issued by the courts that judged the Mikó case following the investigations opened by the anti-corruption prosecutor.

We can better understand the Church's point of view if we analyzed it through the prism of legal pluralism. Very simply put, "legal pluralism" denotes a mixture of distinct legal orders and bodies of law that different ethnic, economic, religious groups comply with even though they are included in one polity. Legal plurality was a "simple fact of life" in many premodern empires, before the rise to power of allegedly more homogenous nation-states.[65] In the case of the states that emerged from the partition of the Austro-Hungarian Empire, despite these states' attempts to establish a stricter legal centralization, the religious and ethnic minorities continued to abide by former legal views and practices of the defunct empire.[66] Such loyalty was particularly prevalent among Transylvania's ethnic Hungarians, who viewed the integration of the region in Greater Romania as a political betrayal and actively fought for their ethnic and religious rights with the interwar Romanian state. Putting the religious legal order above the state legal order was only one form of political resistance. It was this history that informed the Church's view: that the postcommunist state must grant the Church property rights over all of the Reformed schools previously nationalized.

---

64 Brian Leiter, "Legal Formalism and Legal Realism: What Is the Issue?" (University of Chicago Public Law & Legal Theory Working Paper No. 320, 2010).

65 Karen Barkey, "Aspects of Legal Pluralism in the Ottoman Empire," in Lauren Benton and Richard J. Ross, eds., *Legal Pluralism and Empires, 1500–1850* (New York University Press, 2013), 83–107, 83. The literature on legal pluralism is extensive, but critical readings include, in chronological order: Sally Merry, "Legal Pluralism," *Law & Society Review* (1988): 869–896, Lauren Benton, "Historical Perspectives on Legal Pluralism," *Hague Journal on the Rule of Law* 3, no. 1 (2011): 57–69; Lauren Benton and Richard J. Ross, eds., *Legal Pluralism and Empires, 1500–1850* (New York University Press, 2013).

66 Natasha Wheatley is the first historian to focus on legal pluralism and the temporality of law in the Habsburg empire. See her dissertation, *Law, Time, and Sovereignty in Central Europe: Imperial Constitutions, Historical Rights, and the Afterlives of Empire* (Columbia University, 2016), and her forthcoming book, *The Temporal Life of States: Sovereignty at the Eclipse of Empire*.

When the Church representatives kept invoking, time and again, the canonic law, or the Church law, to justify why the high school was property of the Church as a historically confessional school, they implicitly pointed out that they observed and obeyed by a legal order of their religious community that functioned at the margins of the legal hegemony of the state. They invoked a history of intertwined economic relations, religious identities, and ethnic community-building to argue that the "living law" that informed how the Hungarians in the Covasna region used and understood the legal status of the Mikó high school was different from the legal regime of the interwar Romanian government.[67]

In what follows, I analyze the arguments prepared by the Church's lawyer and contrast them with those outlined in the 2012 court decision.[68] The lawyer argued that the court's "artificial argument disregards the provisions of church law, the law in force at the moment of registration, and the law in force at the time of nationalization."[69] In his view, the court decision ignored "the ecclesiastic law of the church," which regards these schools "as autonomous structures belonging to the body of the Church," and not as "separate legal entities or as legal persons." He stated that "the law in force at the time of the land registration (the law of the Austro-Hungarian Monarchy in Transylvania) never gave legal personality to these schools." Finally, he noted, the property status is signaled by the school's name: it is mentioned that it is a reformed school, therefore "the reference to the Church indicates the owner, and the word 'school' officially fixed the purpose of the property." These arguments point out two things: 1) that there was a separation between church law and civil law, that the former was distinct, and not subordinate to the latter (the state law), and 2) that all of the schools carrying the name "reformed" in the title had implicitly been owned by the Reformed Church before nationalization.

---

67 Eugen Ehrlich coined the concept of "living law" in 1913 in order to convey the ways in which the inhabitants of Bukovina, a multi-ethnic province in the Austro-Hungarian empire, constantly negotiated between different ethnic customs, laws of the land, and the imperial legal order. Anthropologist Sally Engle Merry revived Ehrlich's concept in her discussion about legal pluralism in colonial societies. See Merry, "Legal Pluralism," 874.
68 The lawyer is also a professor of law at Sapientia University, a private Hungarian-language university in Cluj, established and sponsored by the Hungarian government.
69 Emőd Veress, "Post-Communist Restitution of the Nationalized Reformed and Roman Catholic Church Property in Romania," *Acta Univ. Sapientiae, Legal Studies* 7 (1), 2018, 109–121. (The journal is published by Sapientia university, where Veress is a law professor.)

These arguments, however, are problematic for two reasons. First, the Reformed Church did lose ownership of some of its schools due to lower resources from a diminishing congregation. Historians of the Reformed Church in Transylvania noted that due to the impact of Counter-Reformation in Transylvania, supported by the Habsburg monarchy, the Reformed church chose to "voluntarily transfer schools to the [Hungarian] state," in the second part of the 19th century.[70] In 1867, at the time of the compromise between Austria and Hungary, and the expansion of the Hungarian state bureaucracy, the Reformed church had 587 schools; by 1918, the moment of Transylvania's inclusion into the Greater Romania, the church had only 175 schools.[71] That is, if all of the 587 schools presumably kept their initial purpose, more than 400 were either functioning as autonomous institutions, or became part of the patrimony of the Hungarian state, which was later seized by the Romanian state following the 1920 Trianon Treaty. Even if the Reformed Church build new schools after 1918, in an effort to bolster language learning and religious education to preserve Hungarian ethnic identity, they still did not gain back the other schools that they had lost.[72] Second, the argument that the court ignored "the ecclesiastic law of the Reformed church" did not matter, because in the Protestant/Reformed tradition, and in contrast to the Roman-Catholic canonic law, the church law is subordinate to the state law, as the Reformed Church recognizes "the supremacy of the state."[73]

As I mentioned earlier, the Church's lawyer argued that the legal practice at the end of 19th century and beginning of the 20th required that the land registry mentioned the function of the estate and the name of the user, which was the school, but that the user did not have legal status, being part and parcel of the Church as an institution. The lawyer also cited a 1911 law, passed by the Hungarian Ministry of Justice, that allowed the Church to claim ownership of the estates and buildings whose records in the land registry initially mentioned their purpose and users. The Church could not justify why they did not use that 1911 law to reclaim legal

---

[70] John Butosi, "The Reformed Church in Romania—in a Historical Perspective," *Reformed Review* 60 (Winter 1987): 116–142, 128. Unfortunately, Butosi does not cite the sources for these numbers. He was a pastor of the Reformed Church, so I presume that he had access to some internal documents of the Church.
[71] Butosi, "The Reformed Church in Romania," 127, 128.
[72] Between 1918 and 1928, "the number of Reformed elementary schools increased from 175 to 370 in the Cluj-Napoca (Kolosvar) District alone; in the Oradea (Nagyvarad) District the number came to be over 500." Butosi, "The Reformed Church in Romania," 131.
[73] For a general discussion on "canon law," see https://www.britannica.com/topic/canon-law.

ownership of the school at that time, and change the records in the land registry.[74] In sum, the lawyer grounded his arguments in a particular understanding of property rights—that of the legal system of the pre-1918 Hungarian state—to justify that the Church's property claims over the high school were still valid between 1918 and 1948.

The lawyer did so by "stitching" together the pre-1918 and post-1918 historical periods—that is, an imperial time and a national time. For instance, in order to show that they kept a similar relationship of ownership with the school after 1918, the Church also used as another proof the 1937 yearly handbook (*anuarul*) of the school. The document mentioned that "the church had the right of support and supervision of the school via the General Committee and the Board, which had jurisdiction over the immovable property."[75] In other words, the Church emphasized that even after 1918 it kept a *de facto* control over the school (though not *de jure*). By making this claim, the Church pointed out that the school remained in the ethnic community, and that the Church continued to be the representative of the local ethnic Hungarians, still a majority in the city but a political minority in the interwar Romanian state.

To counter the Church's arguments, the court in the 2012 trial called upon Romanian jurisprudence of the interwar period. It cited a 1938 law regarding the unification of procedures concerning the land registry; the law stated that "if the record in the land registry mentioned a real right vested in a person, it is assumed that the person has that right."[76] Given that there were no changes made in the land registry, the name in the land registry—the Reformed Szekely Mikó high school—was implicitly the name of the owner, and that remained the legal status until 1948, when the school became nationalized.

To reject the Church's arguments, the court relied on the laws of a different time and a different political geography: the laws passed by the interwar Romanian state. According to the latter (see the 1938 law

---

74 "Cazul Mikó: exemplul model al stopării retrocedării imobilelor în România—SINTEZĂ," November 8, 2018. https://hirado.hu/2018/11/08/cazul-Mikó-exemplul-model-al-stoparii-retrocedarii-imobilelor-inromania-sinteza/.
75 Sentința civilă nr 228, February 6, 2003, Judecătoria Sfântu Gheorghe, pages 4–5. Included in the documents that the office of the Covasna prefect made available to Dan Tanasa. Available at www.scribd.com.
76 The court cited article 32 of Law decree 115/1938. Here is the definition of "real right": "*jus in re*, under civil law, more commonly referred to as a real right or right in rem, is a right in property, known as an interest under common law. A real right vests in a person with respect to property, inherent in his relation to it, and is good against the world." Henry Campbell Black, *A Law Dictionary* (West Publishing Company, 1910), 678.

mentioned above), the Mikó school functioned as a legal entity on its own, able to use its ownership right. From this perspective, the school no longer could be conceived as part of the broader network of the Church, who had assets all across Transylvania. When the court declared that the school had been a separate legal entity before the 1948 nationalization, the judge implicitly diminished its importance as a symbol of the ethnic Hungarian community of Reformed denomination.

What is remarkable was that neither party mentioned a law issued in the interwar period that was directly relevant to a discussion about church property: the law of religions, which the Romanian state passed in 1928. Transylvania's historic churches, including the Reformed Church, viewed the law as the state's encroachment on their autonomy and property. According to the law 54/1928,[77] the state agreed to financially support the churches, but it also imposed a stricter control of the government on religious organizations and their customs. The state restricted the ability of the churches to acquire property (especially land and real estate) (Article 23). The law also stipulated that the legal status of all of the buildings (churches, parochial houses and other assets) administered by the churches must be verified against the land registry. If the land registry confirmed that the buildings were the property of the churches, they remained so. However, if the land registry revealed that the buildings were the property of an individual or private institution, they remained the property of that specific institution, but the local community was entitled to use them (in original, *posesiunea comunității locale*). If the private individual or institution no longer existed, the buildings became state property, and the local community gained use rights over them (Article 39).

According to Law 54/1928, the Mikó high school belonged to itself, and therefore could be used by the local community, because the owner was recorded in the land registry as "the Mikó high school," and not "the Reformed Church." Moreover, law 54/1928 made moot other previous laws. That is, all of the laws that the Church's lawyer invoked to emphasize a history of property rights that the Church purportedly carried into the post-1918 era were no longer valid. In sum, two laws (54/1928 and 115/1938) clarified that the Mikó building (and its student dormitory) were formally private property but that the local community—and not just the ethnic community—could use them. De facto, the building was then a form of local collective property.

---

77   For Law 54/1928, see http://licodu.cois.it/?p=10407&lang=en, last access 28 July 2020.

Still, the last modification made in the land registry prior to the 1948 nationalization is dated 1900—that is, when it mentioned that "this building was the property of the Mikó high school of Reformed confession, following the merger of estates no. 1063/1900." At that moment, the city was part of the Hungarian kingdom (in the dual monarchy), and the high school was considered the property of the Hungarian state. However, no change was made in the land registry, following the Romanian state's issuing of Law 54 in 1928. Neither the high school's leaders, nor the local city officials chose to modify the land registry to legally acknowledge that the building had become part of the collective property of the city. This detail could be indicative that the leaders of the local community, formed mostly of ethnic Hungarians, continued to abide by their own understanding of the living law of the land—a land in which the local community continued to view the Hungarian-language Reformed high school as an extension of the Church and implicitly a site of political and cultural resistance against an increasingly encroaching Romanian state.[78] The nationalization of 1948 is also indicative of how the communist state officials did the nationalization—they did not bother to check in the land registry, but simply relied on local common knowledge—and that information was that the Church had property rights over the high school, and therefore the Mikó building should be nationalized together with the other Church property.

One interpretation of this situation is that after 1918, the local community continued to rely on customs and regulations that they had developed as part of the Hungarian kingdom, and that they kept alive despite the shift to the Romanian administration. This history of legal pluralism—the tension between the state law and the living law that the Hungarians of Sf. Gheorghe abided by—informed the conflicts emerging during postcommunism. It was this knowledge—that lived law competed with the state law—that prompted the Church's 2001 restitution request and the decision of the commission members (two of them ethnic Hungarians) to approve the restitution.

Conclusion

The recent contestation of the Mikó court decision, and the current protests of ethnic Hungarians must therefore be understood as a conflict over history, and over varying ways of understanding and valuing property in

---

78 In 1930, out of 11,989 inhabitants of Sf. Gheorghe, there were 8857 Hungarians, 2211 Romanians, 209 Germans, 281 Jews, 197 Roma, 61 Ukrainians, 17 Slovaks, and 4 Serbs (by their declared ethnicity, not their mother tongue). http://www.kia.hu/konyvtar/erdely/erd2002/cvetn02.pdf.

relation to ethnic identity and ethnic rights. The 2012 court decision for the reversal of the 2002 restitution has triggered so much rancor among Transylvanian Hungarians because they viewed the decision as an erasure of their ethnic history, and a dismissal of the role that the Reformed Church had historically played as a cultural and political leader of the community. To assert its claim over the school, the Church invoked an origins story, the establishment of the school through the collective effort of the community, and the legal practice of a particular time and place: Hungary at the end of the 19th century, as a polity that was still part of the Austro-Hungarian empire, but that had gained significant autonomy over its internal affairs following the 1867 Compromise. By having the school separated from the church, the court made irrelevant what the ethnic Hungarians valued most: the historical link between education, religious freedom, and preservation of ethnic identity.

This is why the Church insisted that the building should be returned to the community who built it. The only actor that would guarantee that the building would be used solely according to the wishes of the ethnic community would have been the Reformed Church—and not the city council, which, even if it currently has a majority of ethnic Hungarian members, does not represent the interests of the ethnic community, but of the city as a whole. To compensate for this loss, the leader of Transylvania's Hungarians turned again to Hungary. In January 2019, just two months after the High Court pronounced the reversal of the restitution of the Mikó building as final, the episcope of the Reformed Church declared that they had bought ten hectares in the city of Sfântu Gheorghe where they would build a campus for a new Hungarian-language university. The project is fully sponsored by the Hungarian government.[79]

---

79 In January 2019, Hungary allocated 4,13 billion forints (approximatively $1,383,300 at the currency exchange rate of Sept. 2019) for the building of a university campus in Sf Gheorghe. https://hirado.hu/2019/01/07/fundatia-sapientia-construieste-un-campus-universitar-la-sfantugheorghe/.

Institutional Memories and Transgenerational Dynamics: The House of Terror and the Memorial of the Victims of Communism and of the Resistance

Simona Livescu

Abstract: *This article provides an insight into the twenty-first century politics of institutionalized memory in two former communist countries, Romania and Hungary, as illustrated by their respective human rights memorial museums' practices of documenting communist era abuse. After discussing the ways in which the two museums under consideration here inscribe themselves into the red and dark tourism phenomena, the article focuses on acts of over-remembering and misremembering that affect the politics of museal representation, highlighting the emotional communities created by these museums as well as the incomplete representation of the victim-victimizer rapport. In doing so, the article argues that institutionalized museal interventions into recent collective national and regional memories are representative of the still undecided legacy of communism in East and Central Europe.*

In 2010, the Federation of International Human Rights Museums was created with the understanding that all museums dealing with human rights violations and histories shared similar challenges in terms of dealing with "difficult, politically-loaded and controversial subjects." One of the Federation's stated aims is to change the traditional ways in which human rights museums around the world operate.[1] Its 2014 Taipei conference

---

[1] Human rights museums moved away from traditionally "authoritative master narratives and prescriptive vantage points of historiography," to include "diversified and sometimes even incompatible narratives;" increasingly, they "are entrusted with a new mission of community formation, making individual and collective audiences recognize themselves as subjects of rights and, thus, contributing to the democratization of culture and society." J. Andermann and S. Arnold-de Simine, "Introduction: Memory, Community and the New Museum," *Theory, Culture & Society*, 29, no 1, (2012): 6–9. For more on the evolution from traditional to modern and postmodern museum, see Timothy Ambrose and Crispin Paine, *Museum Basics* (Routledge, 2012); Tony Bennett, *The Birth of the Museum: History, Theory, Politics* (London: Routledge, 1995). Paul Williams, *Memorial Museums: The Global Rush to Commemorate Atrocities* (New York: Berg Oxford International Publishers, 2007); Élise Dubuc, "Museum and University Mutations: The Re-

explored the social impact of such museums, issuing the official dictum, "museums make a social contribution to the democratization of nations by encouraging free debate and confronting authoritarian versions of the truth."[2] A major aspect of the democratization process in Eastern Europe after 1989 was a reckoning with the history and legacy of the communist dictatorships in the region. This article provides a glimpse into the 21st century politics of institutionalized memory in two of the countries of the former communist bloc, Romania and Hungary, with regards to their respective human rights memorial museums documenting the abuses under communist rule. In both countries, private initiatives and the post-communist governments of the 1990s financed the establishment of museums dealing with the legacy of communist dictatorships and their gross human rights violations. However, the politics of organized remembering—to paraphrase Milan Kundera—differ in each case and the question of what exactly collectivities forget whenever they remember remains, in both cases, a pervasive one. The post-memory of a community is transferred to a second generation that appropriates the memory of a traumatic past as its very own, as Marianne Hirsch observed.[3] While this transfer of memory happens in various ways, memorial museums commemorating the victims and teaching audiences about their tragic fate are part of the memory work of those concerned with revealing large-scale abuse.

Why do museums of national mourning remain still vivid and significant in the collective memory, even though their audiences wish they would rather dispose with or forget the gruesome history their exhibits evoke? Is it because of the secrecy of the deeply disturbing images of abuse, which, at last unearthed from the obscurity of the past, are now in the open for everyone to comprehend? Is it because these museums offer concrete evidence of the pain existent only in memory? Researchers argue that we should see institutions of memory as "savings banks for our souls," because

> we regard institutions of memory as [being] important to our collective well-being. Accordingly, we must begin to discuss the preservation of these organizations not because they add to the quality of life, or to lifelong learning opportunities, or to informal education venues (though they do all that). But because, without them, we come apart.[4]

lationship between Museum Practices and Museum Studies in the Era of Interdisciplinarity, Professionalisation, Globalisation and New Technologies," *Museum Management and Curatorship*, 26, no. 5, (2011):497–508.
2   Federation of International Human Rights Museums, https://www.fihrm.org/resources/past-conferences/conference-2014/, accessed on 5 May 2020.
3   Marianne Hirsch, *Family Frames: Photography, Narrative, and Postmemory* (Boston: Harvard University Press, 1997).
4   Elaine Heumann Gurian, "Savings Bank for the Soul," *Reinventing the Museum* (Lanham, Maryland: AltaMira Press, 2012), 136–7.

We are also told, "memory has *force*;" it is "the medium through which the past makes demands on us," and these demands "speak to us of episodes in our history to which we now have to respond."[5] The force of memory is of concern to political leaders, publicists, and activists "keen to mobilize action in the real world. It is also why disputes over memory are carried on with such intensity and vehemence: the participants recognize that memory *counts*."[6] The story of national victimhood is not completed, even if the dark story of abuse, violence, and death has been apparently thoroughly covered. What are the social-educational effects of this collective story of past trauma? To what extent is this part of the social suffering story incorporated by museum sightseers into their lives? Beyond the political capital acquired by the founders and administrators of human rights museums, is there a different sort of legacy that escapes structures of power? Is there another social effect worth capturing, or, better said, a story that writes itself?

This article investigates acts of mis-remembering and over-remembering in the representation of the recent communist past in Romania and Hungary, as reflected in two of their human rights museums. Before deploying these critical terms, I include a brief review of the two countries' exit from communism in 1989, background information for both museums and their founders, as well as their explicit aims. Further, this article explores how the human rights museums discussed here inscribe themselves into the red and dark tourism phenomena. Examples of over-remembering and misremembering will be based on field observations from the author's successive visits to each museum; recent scholarship dealing with the remembrance of violent political past; visitors' comments about the two museums on social media; handouts from the Sighet Memorial Museum and the House of Terror; and discussions and correspondence with the museums' staff. The article closes with a comparative discussion of these museums' roles, pinpointing both weaker and stronger aspects in their respective politics of memory.

Romania and Hungary: Regime Change and Transitional Justice Paths

In both Romania and Hungary, national reconciliation and transitional justice—namely, efforts to deal politically and legally with the recent past as well as open public discussion about widespread human rights abuses

---

5   Ross Poole, "Misremembering the Holocaust: Universal Symbol, Nationalist Icon or Moral Kitsch?" *Memory and the Future* (London: Palgrave Macmillan, 2010), 32.
6   Poole, "Misremembering the Holocaust," 32.

—became part of their local discourses after 1989. The work of collecting, recording, publicizing, and collectively transmitting recent national memory in an institutionalized form instantly became a contested enterprise due to intense politicization. This politicization affected issues of recognition and documentation of past abuse, which automatically brought into the domain of public debate issues like responsibility, collaboration, lustration, legal persecution, and rewriting of national history, to name only a few. Public testimony by victims of past abuse and archival evidence of unlawful surveillance, imprisonment, interrogation, and torture often contrasted with the steady advancement of former human rights abusers in the new political system.

The politicization of national memory in both countries was the product of the transfer of political power from communist to post-communist governments. In the 1940s, communist rule began in both Romania and Hungary with "massive arbitrary arrests, show-trials of predetermined outcome, prison and labor camps, a ruthless secret political police orchestrated by NKVD agents, and 'liberating' Soviet troops."[7] Despite this initial similarity, communism in Hungary and Romania evolved along relatively different paths. In 1956, after the Soviets crushed the Hungarian revolt against the country's communist rulers and their Soviet allies, its communist leadership was obliged to work with citizens to "transform communism into a local grown, liberalizing variant."[8] Thus, the abortive Hungarian Revolution helped install what historian Laszlo Varga calls a soft communist dictatorship in the sixties and seventies, whose milder nature led to a milder, non-violent exit from it in 1989.[9] Marked by formal negotiations between the ruling communist party, the opposition, and trade organizations, it was meant to effect a peaceful transition of political power.[10] In contrast, Romania experienced the most repressive version of communism under two leaders—Gheorghe Gheorghiu Dej and Nicolae Ceaușescu—each exercising his own versions of terror and oppression of the population. In 1989, Ceaușescu's dictatorial rule was upended by a bloody anticommunist Revolution that led to the death of more than one thousand victims.[11] Ceaușescu and his wife were captured and executed on December 25th, 1989, after an expedient show trial. Despite the differences in how the transfer of power was accomplished in 1989, neither of the two

---

7   Lavinia Stan, "Romania," *Transitional Justice in Eastern Europe and the Former Soviet Union* (New York: Routledge, 2009), 102–103.
8   Ibid., 103.
9   Cited in Stan, *Transitional Justice in the Former Soviet Union*, 2009, 111.
10 Ibid., 103.
11 See Peter Siani-Davies, *The Romanian Revolution of December 1989* (Ithaca and London: Cornell University Press, 2005).

countries experienced a decommunization of their power structures, one that could have positively affected their transitional justice processes.

In fact, former communists in both countries were heavily involved in processes of transitional justice after 1989. As a result of the negotiated transfer of political power, Hungary adopted a legalistic model of transitional justice. In contrast, because of its violent exit from communism and the persistent presence of the communist elites in the post-1989 government, Romania's reckoning with the past was delayed. Despite these differences, both countries encountered challenges in manufacturing an inclusive collective memory of the past regime. Alongside other forms of memory building after 1989, museological initiatives by private individuals and their associated organizations claimed agency over engraving the memory of past trauma onto the consciences of the Romanian and Hungarian nations; their stated aim was to disseminate historical knowledge about former state terror. Within a complex landscape of governmental and non-governmental practices and concerns, it is important to analyze whether human rights museums participate in, counteract, or find themselves inadvertently caught in the politicization of memory. This analysis explores the extent to which they offer complementary, alternative, or competing versions of national memory compared to those offered by other institutions and social actors.

The types of audiences that human rights museums cultivate and the impacts of their truth-telling upon them are additional aspects that differentiate the museological engagement with the recent past from that of the legal or educational systems, for example. Furthermore, for each of these systems, the status of evidence is a complex terrain. What passes for "evidence" in a prison-turned-museum (artifact/exhibit) or in a literary prison memoir (direct experience, witnessing, etc.) may very well be different from what counts as "evidence" in a court of law (police reports, archival documents, murder weapons, etc.). In terms of the message they transmit, human rights museums and their narratives each grapple in their own way with what kind of truths can be uncovered and made tellable, at what specific points in time, and to what kinds of audiences.[12] Human rights museums build narratives of national history that translate into actual physical itineraries in which the visitors' steps from one room to another are guided according to historical stages of events and poignancy of exhibits. Often, museum guides and handouts indicate where the

---

12   Kay Schaffer and Sidonie Smith, *Human Rights and Narrated Lives: The Ethics of Recognition* (New York: Palgrave Macmillan, 2004).

national autobiographical journey is to begin and end. The museal journey has multiple dimensions: visual, temporal, emotional, political, moral, etc. Ethics and visual aesthetics collaborate to form a specific synesthetic form of historical truth-telling.

The "Black Hole" of History

A significant space that post-communist human rights museums attempt to fill is what has been deemed the "black hole" of history, the supposed absence of data about life under communism. After the fall of the Berlin Wall, the nineties brought about complicated issues of rejection or recovery of recent history in Central and Eastern Europe. The rejection impulses were dubbed "the black hole" of history, with numerous voices declaring that, under communism, history had stopped and had been replaced with nothing but darkness and an absence of history.[13] In the case of Hungary, its new constitution "declares that the Hungarian state was not legally competent for a period of more than forty years—from March 1944 to May 1990, the dates when the Germans invaded in WWII and when the first freely elected government took office, respectively. In effect, this strange declaration excises a half-century from the nation's history."[14] Invariably, the question arises, what is the reason for this excision, black hole, or artificial interruption in the continuity of national history? Hungarian historian István Rév answers, "Hungary, consequently, could not be held responsible either for the Holocaust or for the Gulag, the Germans and the Soviets, respectively, were to blame."[15] Thus, as opposed to the regimes of "organized forgetting," the regimes of organized remembering, despite their most noble claims, may end up deploying sanitized and hyperbolized versions of collective amnesia that have already become part of their respective contemporary national discourses.

Ironically, collective amnesia regarding both recent and distant national histories was exactly what the previous communist regimes in Romania and Hungary had practiced in their propaganda and history text-

---

13 Simina Bădică, "The Black Hole Paradigm. Exhibiting Communism in Post-communist Romania," *The Politics of Memory in Post-Communist Europe*, vol. 1 (Bucharest: Zeta Books, 2010), 81.
14 Jacob Mikanovski, "The Frightening Politics of Hungary's House of Terror," *The Awl*, 30 March 2012, http://www.theawl.com/2012/03/the-frightening-politics-of-hungarys-house-of-terror, accessed 5 May 2020).
15 István Rév, "The Terror of the House," *(Re)visualizing National History: Museums and National Identities in Europe in the New Millennium* (Toronto: University of Toronto Press, 2008), 56.

books. After 1989, what contributes to the formation of black holes of history is the exclusion from national memory of facts or realities that are incompatible with the overly generalized story of victimhood. These include the percentage of the population who supported the communist regimes, the story of social mobility, the spread of literacy and access to education, or even the subsequent life trajectories of prisoners of conscience, some of whom integrated their lives into the larger communist society after release from prison.

The Multilayered Histories of Dark and Red Tourism

Like many other modern sites of remembering, Romania's Sighet Memorial for the Victims of Communism and of the Resistance (the Sighet Memorial Museum henceforth) and Hungary's House of Terror are built on physical sites of abuse, and, therefore, carry utmost symbolic significance. The Sighet Memorial Museum building was erected in 1897 and functioned as a regular prison until World Wars I and II, when detainees of various ethnicities (including Romanian, Hungarian, Polish, Ukrainian, etc.) and political or religious convictions were incarcerated there.[16] From the brochure of the Memorial Museum, we find that in 1948–1950, grade-school students, college students and peasants from the Maramureș anti-communist resistance were jailed in Sighet. Between 1950 and 1955, "the penitentiary became a maximum security one, here being brought, in complete secrecy, two hundred former ministers, parliamentarians, journalists, military figures, archbishops and priests." Among these 200 high-profile political prisoners, 54 died at Sighet and were buried in secret, at still unidentified sites.[17]

The House of Terror in downtown Budapest "had been the 'House of Faith,' the headquarters of the Arrow Cross Party before the World War II,[18] and the Communists, partly for symbolic reasons, decided to move the headquarters of the secret police into the very same building."[19] Later, several waves of violent repression would be perpetrated in the same place. "Immediately after the war, Fascist war criminals were kept and

---

16 Dumitru Lăcătușu, *Dicționarul Penitenciarelor din Romania Comunistă: 1945–1967*, ed. Andrei Muraru (Iași: Polirom 2008), 459–474.
17 Romulus Rusan (ed.), *Memoria Închisorii Sighet* (Bucharest: Fundația Academia Civică, 2003). For the armed resistance in Maramureș see also Cosmin Budeancă, Florentina and Ion Pop (eds.), *Rezistența Anticomunistă: Cercetare Științifică și Valorificare Muzeală* (Cluj-Napoca: Argonaout, 2006).
18 The Arrow Cross Party was the Hungarian national socialist party (*Nyilaskeresztes Párt—Hungarista Mozgalom*) before World War II.
19 Rev, "The Terror of the House," 61.

interrogated in their former House of Faith. Where Jews and Communists had been tortured and killed before 1945, their torturers and interrogators were tortured and interrogated in turn after the defeat of Nazi Germany and its Hungarian ally."[20] These two inter- and post-war periods were followed by the communist state terror in the late 1940s and 1950s, when the Arrow Cross leaders and war criminals were replaced in the cellars by political opponents of the Stalinist regime and "former Communist comrades of the consolidating regime."[21]

Conclusively, the Sighet Memorial Museum and the House of Terror both stand as sites of repression and sites of conscience, and, like the Czech Republic's Terezín Memorial, could accordingly join the International Coalition of Sites of Conscience. Both are also part of the "dark tourism" phenomenon, defined as the form of organized sightseeing that features not only infamous former prisons or places of interrogation and torture, but also "battlefields, assassinations and terrorist attack sites."[22] Since these museums routinely exhibit dark visual narratives of imprisonment, interrogation, disappearance, torture, and assassination, dark tourism has come to be characterized by some as the "commodification of death." However, it must be noted that dark tourism sites are historically and sociologically multi-layered, and various groups and identities derive diverse meanings from their expositions.[23] Where former communist spaces are concerned, this social and historical multi-layering is situated at the intersection of dark tourism and red tourism, two phenomena that fulfill partially overlapping missions.

Though the term 'red tourism' described first the Chinese government's efforts to promote its communist sites in a glorified manner for economic and ideological benefit, post-1989, the term extended to Central and East Europe, where portrayal of the communist past has been decidedly less positive.[24] Communist heritage scholars list routes of red tourism in Poland (Krakow-Nowa Huta), Hungary (Szoborpark, Terror Haza),

---

20   Ibid.
21   Ibid., 62.
22   Jacqueline Z. Wilson, *Prison: Cultural Memory and Dark Tourism* (New York: Peter Lang Publishing, 2008), 9.
23   Ibid., 9.
24   Stanciugelu et al. elaborate: "Without sharing the same characteristics of the Chinese phenomenon also known as "red tourism" (educational role, aimed to stimulate a "nostalgic attitude" in relation to the communist tradition, the defining of a positive-ideological communist tradition, the state involvement, etc.) the Eastern Europe red tourism is directly related to a general attitude of the public space in accordance with the ideological and cultural legacy of communism." Stefan Stanciugelu et al., "The Communist Cultural Heritage in the Social Representations of a

the Czech Republic (the Museum of Communism in Prague), Germany (Berlin Wall, Checkpoint Charlie, the STASI Museum), etc.[25] Incorporative history tends to include the monuments, relics, and paraphernalia characteristic of the now-defunct communist political system under the form of "red tourism" by organizing dedicated touristic itineraries or museums around them. Since both the Sighet Memorial Museum and the House of Terror display rooms and objects of repression and torture, and also communist cultural and propaganda exhibits,[26] they are situated at the intersection of dark and red tourism.

A brief history of the founding of the Sighet Memorial and House of Terror is necessary to understand the roles and missions of these memory-building institutions. In both cases, the museums' founders were inscribed in their countries' post-communist political landscape after 1989. A leader of the *Fidesz* Party (*Fidesz—Magyar Polgári Szövetség*) in Hungary since the early nineties, Viktor Orbán became prime minister of Hungary between 1998–2002 and then again from 2010 on. Orbán's political trajectory went from radical liberal to center-right, turning then to a right-wing orientation. The House of Terror was opened during Orbán's first term in office, on February 24, 2002. Although the museum's website only informs us that the building "was purchased by the Public Foundation for History and Society in Central and Eastern Europe in December 2000," it is known that Viktor Orbán and the Fidesz Party are the museum's founders.[27] Immediately after opening, the building was also the site of a major electoral rally designed to win voters away from rival centrist parties, during which Orbán announced his vision for the museum: its mission was to present the two "bloody periods" of Nazism and Soviet-dominated communist rule together. A group of right-wing advisors, mainly academics, formed around Orbán, offering him ideological support at first and later assuming right-wing political positions during his tenure as prime minister. These intellectuals were preoccupied with the "survival" of communism and the "anti-national" bent of the communist and

---

Post-Communist Generation," *European Journal of Science and Theology*, 9, no 2 (April 2013): 3.
25   Ibid., 1–17.
26   The Sighet Memorial Museum has a room dedicated to the "kitsch communism" of the "golden age" under Nicolae Ceaușescu, and another one dedicated to daily life under the communist rule.
27   Aron Buzogány and Mihai Varga, "Against "Post-communism": The Conservative Dawn in Hungary," in Bluhm, Katharina and Mihai Varga (eds), *New Conservatives in Russia and East Central Europe* (New York: Routledge, 2019), 70–91; Rév, "The Terror of the House," 2008; and Mikanovski, "The Frightening Politics of Hungary's House of Terror," 2012.

liberal policies in the economic and educational sectors.[28] Maria Schmidt is one of these intellectuals, serving as an advisor to Viktor Orbán from 1998–2002, and currently director of the House of Terror. The Museum is in Budapest, at 60 Andrassy ut., in a fashionable part of the capital that attracts tourists. The estimated twenty million dollars of taxpayers' money to establish the House of Terror came from the Hungarian government "in an era when Hungary was suffering financially."[29]

The Sighet Memorial is situated in the small, northernmost town of Sighet on the border with Ukraine, where political prisoners were strategically jailed to be easily transferred to the Soviet Union in the event of a popular uprising against the communist regime. The Memorial's founders are civil society actors. The main founder is Ana Blandiana, a Romanian poet and writer, who, together with a group of notable Romanian intellectuals and academics founded the non-governmental organization The Civic Alliance/*Alianța Civică* in November 1990. Its stated aim was to build a civil society in Romania and some founders left to form an eponymous political party, the Civic Alliance Party/*Partidul Alianța Civică*. They also went on to occupy official positions under the center-right presidency of Emil Constantinescu from 1996–2000.[30] Blandiana began her career in politics very briefly as a member of the transitional National Salvation Front Council in December 1989, then joined the Civic Alliance from 1990 until the present. In the interviews she gives, she insists that she has never accepted a political position and has always remained a civic activist.[31] Daughter of a former political detainee under the communist regime, one of her most important personal and political goals after 1989 was a decided anti-communist stand, as the ex-communists continued to be the dominant force in the government. The museum's guide gives January 1993 as the date when Blandiana submitted the project of the Sighet Memorial Museum to the European Council. She declares that the idea of building such a museum for the victims of the former regime came to her and her husband, Romulus Rusan, after a visit at Auschwitz. At the European Council's suggestion, the Foundation "Civic Academy"/*Fundația Academia Civică* was founded, its main project being The Sighet Memorial of the Victims of Communism and of the Resistance, and

---

28 Buzogány and Varga, "Against "Post-communism": The Conservative Dawn in Hungary."
29 Julia Creet, "The House of Terror and the Holocaust Memorial Centre: Resentment and Melancholia in Post-89 Hungary," *European Cultural Memory Post-89*, 30 (2013): 29–62, 24; and Mikanovski, "The Frightening Politics of Hungary's House of Terror."
30 See Pavel, Dan and Huiu, Iulia, *Nu putem reuși decît împreună: o istorie analitică a convenției democratice* (Bucharest: Polirom, 2003).
31 See Ana Blandiana, *Fals tratat de manipulare* (Bucharest: Humanitas, 2019).

in 1994 the Sighet City Council transferred the former prison building to the Foundation to carry out renovation work.[32] According to Blandiana, the Council offered "moral assistance" only; the funding necessary to restore the former political prison came from donations made by Romanians abroad, residents of Paris, Munich, New York, and Los Angeles. Other funding sources that Blandiana mentions are international grant money and, only later, governmental funding as well.[33] The Memorial has three components: The Memorial Museum—Sighet, The Center of International Studies of Communism (CISC)—Bucharest, and the nearby Pauper's Cemetery, where former high-ranking political detainees (whose bodies were never found) are alleged to have been buried.[34]

Figure 1: The entrance to the Memorial of the Victims of Communism and of the Resistance. Taken by the author, on 23 June 2018, during field research conducted for this article.

---

32 Romulus Rusan, Ana Blandiana and Ioana Boca, *Cum se construiește un miracol* (București: Fundația Academia Civică, 2017).
33 Ibid., Rusan, Bladiana and Boca, 2017.
34 Civic Academy Foundation handout.

A much-debated question is the degree to which memorial museums are to be considered museums of memory or museums of history. Museum literature informs us that museums of memory appeared onto the museal scene after World War Two. Their aim was to counter the established "nineteenth-century nation-state's celebratory—and often forgetful—emphasis on past triumphs, to a reflective effort to come to terms with the negative legacy of the past."[35] Moreover, as a response to the postmodern, postcolonial, and feminist appellation for a better representation of specific social groups' historical and social experience, memory museums "define themselves now not as disciplinary spaces of academic history but as places of memory, exemplifying the postmodern shift from authoritative master discourses to the horizontal, practice-related notions of memory, place, and community."[36]

In short, where museums of history deal mostly with the positive, or golden years of national history, post-World War Two museums of memory address the negative side of national history, particularly the atrocities committed by the nation-state against specific groups. As such, they can hardly place themselves outside of historical narratives; this positioning would amount to a double marginalization, further removing the social suffering of oppressed groups from mainstream history. Though the two main functions of memory museums are to commemorate the victims and educate the public, they are also "a form of historical truth-telling, intended to preserve the past and serve as a record, complete with material and documentary evidence, of what happened."[37] While memorial museums serve healing and restoration purposes and offer symbolic reparations for victims, they also "intellectually educate their audiences about 'history' in order to avoid future human rights abuses."[38]

Both the House of Terror and the Sighet Memorial claim their status as museums of memory. The Sighet Memorial claims to be a victim-centered *lieu de mémoire*. The digital version of the Sighet Memorial leaflet specifies that it is a site of national interest and "one of the first three places of European memory." However, the thematic of all the museum's rooms is historical and many exhibition rooms are labeled according to

---

35 Amy Sodaro, "The House of Terror: "The Only One of Its Kind," *Exhibiting Atrocity: Memorial Museums and the Politics of Past Violence* (Rutgers University Press, 2018), 58–83, 4.
36 J. Andermann and S. Arnold-de Simine, "Introduction: Memory, Community and the New Museum," *Theory, Culture & Society*, 29, no.1, (2012): 3.
37 Sodaro, "The House of Terror: The Only One of Its Kind," 10.
38 Yifat Gutman, Adam D. Brown, and Amy Sodaro, "Introduction: Memory and the Future: Why a Change of Focus is Necessary," *Memory and the Future: Transnational Politics, Ethics and Society* (Springer, 2010), 1–11.

the historical aspect dealt within: "The 1946 Elections"; "The Destruction of the Democratic Parties"; "From Yalta to Moscow"; "The Year 1948—The Sovietization of Romania"; "Communism versus Monarchy"; "A Chronology of the Cold War," etc.

The House of Terror "represents itself as one among the innovative museums of memory that allegedly perform the task of displaying social remembering."[39] Viktor Orbán's declaration at the opening of the House of Terror is both historical and political in nature: "We have locked two terrors in the same building, and they are good company for each other, as neither of them would have been able to survive long without the support of a foreign military force."[40] The conflation of fascism and communism and their ousting from what Fidesz calls "authentic Hungarian history" avoids the problem of stating that, historically, Hungary had its own fascists and communists. Thus,

> [t]his narrative provides absolution for the worst parts of the twentieth century: since both movements were foreign imports, Hungary bears no responsibility for either the Holocaust or the Gulag. At the same time, it promotes a vision of history in which Hungary is a perennial victim, and Fidesz its long-awaited savior.[41]

It can be inferred that the distinction between a museum of memory and a museum of history is quite a blurred, contaminated positioning in the case of both the Hungarian and Romanian museums.

The Evil Aesthetics of Communism

The individual and collective stories retold in these two museums are shaped in a manner reflecting their highly politicized aesthetics. Consequently, visitors leave the museums with an aestheticized version of the dark deeds of the communist regime, its origins, and its unraveling. While much of the characteristic structure and architecture of both museums has been retained during renovation works, an inordinate, eerie beautification marks their respective exhibition spaces. However, in both, only a small number of former cells were left intact or recreated in their original states. Reconstructing the original state of the former carceral space was not the intention of either museum's curators. In the case of Sighet, the guiding leaflet from the Civic Alliance Foundation relates that during the restoration of the building "each cell was transformed into a museum

---

39   Ibid.
40   Mikanovski, "The Frightening Politics of Hungary's House of Terror."
41   Ibid.

room, in which, temporarily first and definitively later, objects, photographs, documents were placed chronologically, creating an atmosphere and documentation of a [typical] museum room."

The Sighet Memorial Museum's main visual effect is that of an all-encompassing whiteness evoking the peculiar atmosphere of an antiquated hospital ward recently repainted. It makes one wonder what has been metaphorically washed out or glossed over. Former Romanian communist political prisons that remain unrestored, such as the one at Râmnicu-Sărat, a city in the Buzău county in the historical region of Muntenia, together with a rich memorialist literature authored by former political detainees remind us that communist prisons were far from white-walled. It is not unreasonable then to question a potential sanitization of a ghastly truth by way of visual sanitization of the former prison's walls. A Civic Academy Foundation handout explains that because the century-old building was in a state of ruin, reconstruction work was extensive, the building's foundation and roof being reworked, while "the interior walls that had been painted over anyway and did not reflect the fifties anymore, were painted white."

Museum literature informs us that art critics trace the aesthetics of uniformly white walls to exhibition designs of the 1920s and 1930s in Germany, though the Museum of Modern Art in New York institutionalized the practice as well.[42] Whether this all-white aesthetic choice at Sighet was one based primarily on practicality, or on more-or-less traditional museological practice of neutrality, or both is unclear.[43] Nonetheless, the whiteness of the vast expanse of the prison's centrally located inner hallway is puzzling. Its impeccability provokes visitor inquiries about the authenticity of the place.[44] This peculiar whiteness contrasts not only with the darkness of the incarceration experience, but also with the gray, drab architecture, and daily life in communist Romania in the second half of the 20th century.

---

42 Katarzyna Murawska-Muthesius and Piotr Piotrowski. *From Museum Critique to the Critical Museum* (New York: Routledge, 2015), 10.
43 Charlotte Klonk, "Myth and Reality of the White Cube," in *From Museum Critique to the Critical Museum*, eds. Murawska-Muthesius, Katarzyna and Piotr Piotrowski (New York: Routledge, 2015), 67–80.
44 During one of my visits to the Sighet Memorial in 2016, I overheard a visitor standing before the white hallway say that ordinary prisons in France looked the same; another visitor, a policeman in his forties, doubted that the prison had been white 'back then.'

Figure 2: White hallways at the Sighet Memorial. Top—Photographer Nenea Hartia, 5 September 2012, released under license CC BY-SA 4.0. Bottom—Photographer Andrei Stroe, 7 August 2010, released under license CC-BY-SA 3.0.

In contrast, the House of Terror's windows are painted gray, while the building's interior is markedly decorated in a disturbingly intense red-and-black chromatic palette, suggestive of a low-budget horror film aesthetic.

Figure 3:   Gray windows at the House of Terror. Photographer Fred Romero, taken 11 August 2017, released under Creative Commons license CC BY 2.0.

The House of Terror impresses visitors with its state-of-the art visuals, technical audio, slow-motion exhibits, and cinematic special effects. If it feels like a haunted movie set, then it is because a movie set designer, Attila Kovács, has built it: the museum "presents history as a nightmare, something that isn't a narrative at all, but a string of ominous sensations. Like a haunted house, it's able to evoke genuine dread while at the same time causing the mind to bubble with unexpected associations."[45]

---

45   Mikanovski, "The Frightening Politics of Hungary's House of Terror."

Figure 4: The House of Terror museum exhibition room. Author N1207 at de.wikipedia, transferred to Wiki Commons; released to public domain under the GNU Free Documentation License.

There is, obviously, nothing wrong with exhibiting the cruelties of torture centers and the unbearable pain inflicted upon the bodies, minds, and souls of political prisoners; it is probably one of the most responsible commitments to the traumatic individual and collective historical truth. Nonetheless, the lack of accompanying cogent and rational explanations about the political and social system that made that suffering possible leaves every (national) abuse story incomplete and open to questioning.

In all likelihood, the founders, curators, directors, and architects of both museums are doubtful that the presentation of things "as they were" is either appropriate for a modern museum visitor's sensibility or, in some instances, sufficiently convincing. Or perhaps they assume that pain and death need to be overly stressed to evoke the magnitude of the violence that occurred within those walls. In that case, the layout of the Sighet Memorial Museum, the interior and exterior walls and windows, and the visual effects in both museums had to be deliberate. A kind of over-remembering takes place, where coercive (or dictatorial) aesthetics become none other than evil aesthetics, implying that not only have unnatural things happened behind closed gates and in underground dungeons, but they were all-encompassing and all-pervasive. The narrative the Hungarian museum presents is a hellish one, "It's a spooky, exhilarating narrative, one in which visitors are stuffed in cattle cars, locked in interrogation cells and sent into torture holes—in this way the House of Terror does for the 20th century what hell houses do for hell." The subliminal appeal of the House of Terror "speaks a language of pleasure and fear."[46]

The inference of this exhibiting technique is that the entire communist order was simply evil. However, for reasons of restoration, the "crime scene" of the later-dubbed criminal system has escaped proper preservation. Exaggerated emotion and an aesthetic disposition to condemn *en masse* what happened under a defunct regime subtly influence the museum visitor to side with the current establishment, namely the powers (political and/or cultural) that helped establish and design the respective memorial museum. Within the same paradigm, a few years later, communism will be indicted as having been a "criminal" and "illegal" regime by the 2006 report of the Presidential Commission for the Study of the Crimes of Communism in Romania.

It has been noted by scholars that dark tourism presupposes an emotional trip for the visitors, with certain high points and a climax, which occur frequently around moments of being physically in the place of torture and execution. At the Sighet Memorial Museum, there are detailed descriptions of horrific torture techniques and two "black" cells where naked and barefoot inmates were isolated to be tortured. At the House of Terror, visitors are held "prisoner" in a painfully slow-moving elevator, in which on a large, in-your-face screen a former guard details the preparations for and the execution of prisoners. The elevator descends exceptionally slowly into the basement, to the (re)created claustrophobic cells in which prisoners were kept and brutal interrogations and assassinations carried out. As expected, the dark tourism visitor feels deep empathy for the victims, while equally experiencing revulsion toward the former communist regime that practiced such large-scale repression. Hereafter, the automatic identification of the museum's founders with being clearly anti-communist and anti-dictatorship (hence on the side of truth and justice) is but a short step. This step further infers that within this shared economy of affect, visitors and founders are, without question, on the same side: not only in shared public opinion, but also on the same political side of engaged individuals for whom civic consciousness and a sentiment of revolt against any form of dictatorship have just been awakened or reinforced. Mission accomplished: museum founders become assimilated in the minds of the visitors as deeply committed champions of human rights.

---

46   Mikanovski, "The Frightening Politics of Hungary's House of Terror."

Over-remembering and Mis-remembering

The act of remembering political violence is neither simple—limited to storage and retrieval of information—nor neutral, as in lacking agency behind it. Moreover, remembering has embedded in it what I term the **R-tropes ensemble**: recollection, reception, responsibility, representation, reverberation, recognition, restoration, redress, restitution, and reconciliation. All these R-tropes have complex historical, legal, and intersubjective conflictual dimensions. To affect one of these tropes is to impact the others as well. To date, no perfect approach has been crafted to deal with remembering violence; it is rather an (in)tensely mediated process between individuals, communities, nations, justice systems, and human rights institutions. In turn, representational museal strategies regarding past violence are inevitably fraught with similar tensions. In what concerns traumatic memory, "the theory goes, the triggering events have taken place in a realm that is so utterly removed from any known set of ethics or values as to remain forever inconceivable in the terms of society outside the realm of the trauma."[47] How to represent the inconceivable is a question that precedes the museal initiatives about the same endeavor. Before post-communist memorial museums ever did concern themselves with representing trauma, prison memoirs grappled with the same dilemma, namely, how to testify to and represent the unrepresentability of previously unheard-of genocidal crimes.[48]

The expressivist ethic of memory tells us that acknowledging human rights abuses and recognizing victims through memory efforts "is morally the correct and necessary response to violence, regardless of the outcome of this remembering."[49] It goes without saying that the moral imperative of remembering places a problematic weight of responsibility on those who engage in it. In the case of memorial museums, this weight often translates into inspired modes of representation, but sometimes also into instances of over-remembering. Over-remembering refers to the gesture of remembering in which the heavy responsibility to represent the suffering in question is, wittingly or unwittingly, over-reached and over-achieved. Also, over-remembering favors certain modes of representation

---

[47] Nicolas Argenti and Katharina Schramm, eds. *Remembering Violence: Anthropological Perspectives on Intergenerational Transmission* (Oxford: Berghahn Books, 2010), 11.

[48] Simona Livescu, "Deviating from the Norm? Two Easts Testify to a Prison Aesthetics of Happiness," in *Human Rights, Suffering, and Aesthetics in Political Prison Literature*, eds. Simona Livescu and Yenna Wu (Lanham, MD: Lexington Books, 2011), 186–7.

[49] Jerry Blustein, cited in Sodaro, "The House of Terror: The Only One of Its Kind," 16.

which become overly-mediated while others remain under-mediated. Over-remembering requires death and suffering to signify beyond, despite, irrevocably, at all costs; as such, museal approaches that elicit emotional responses are cultivated as the most apt representation of collective trauma. The evil coercive aesthetics discussed earlier is just one of these overly mediated modes, with the "banality of evil" that Hannah Arendt warned post-Holocaust audiences about remaining a missing piece of the violent-past puzzle. Memorial museum literature tells us that "it is increasingly being recognised that emotion is the 'elephant' in every room in the museum."[50] But why is emotion capital? Emotion is "so important to community cohesion that we might begin to identify some groups as 'emotional communities.'"[51] In order to build a healthy rapport with its present, a community may feel the need to seek emotional agreement about the shared past.[52]

The next question is, what does emotion do? Emotion mediates the meaning-making process. Suffering cannot and must not be meaningless, lest the sacrifice of the dead, tortured, and abused remain in vain; suffering must carry meaning for emotional communities. Political suffering must signify even more in order to counteract its senselessness, to compensate for the frequent lack of concrete evidence (the absence of bodies, burial grounds, archival records, etc.), and to account for the utter obliteration of those holding opposing views. "When death is violent, both its awesomeness and its meaninglessness increase. And if it is viewed as undeserved, it is asked to signify even more powerfully—or to admit its radical lack of significance."[53] Since the past signification of death and suffering was not and is no longer controllable, present and future significations are possible and necessary to control. Eliciting emotion in museum visitors has the ultimate goal of preventing further atrocities. Paradoxically, the attempt to build emotional communities of the past aims to build more rational communities of the future.

When I visited the Sighet Memorial Museum in August 2014, I heard many visitors' fleeting commentaries about the oppressive building, convinced they had learned enough and had enough of the horrific realities of a terrible era. To be fair, there is no shortage of explicit examples of

---

50 Smith and Campbell, cited in Watson, Sheila, "The Legacy of Communism: Difficult Histories, Emotions and Contested Narratives," *International Journal of Heritage Studies*, 24, no. 7 (2017): 781–794, 2.
51 Light 2015, 149, cited in Watson, "The Legacy of Communism," 2.
52 Fisher and Manstead, cited in Watson, "The Legacy of Communism," 8.
53 Sarah Cole, "Enchantment, Disenchantment, War, Literature," *PMLA*, 124, No. 5 (2009): 1632.

graphic arrest, interrogation, and torture methods specifically designed to inflict enormous pain on both male and female political detainees at Sighet. Their gruesome details shock the visitors, rendering them grave and silent; many choose to leave the museum as soon as they reach their limit of vicarious grief and sadness upon reading of the extreme pain that powerful individuals can inflict on their fellow human beings. I noted that if the goal of the museum was to shock the perceptions (or consciences) of its visitors, then it was duly over-achieved. Conversely, if the purpose of the museum was to inform, through this specific manner of exhibiting the memory of the past, then its strategy yielded an incomplete result; deeply-felt emotions prompted the visitor to leave after a negative gut reaction, only to remain rather deprived of a more complex experience and reasoning about the past. It seemed to me that visitors learned about the existence of torture and pain as something they had never imagined existing, or at least not in that extreme form. For better or for worse, emotion rather than reason seemed to win the day at the Sighet Memorial Museum. I observed similar reactions during my visit to Budapest's House of Terror in September 2014, where visitors reacted by being either eerily silent, or most verbose and disturbed around or inside the reconstructed claustrophobic cells reimagining the underground prison and its tortures.

Theoretical approaches to representations of individual and collective memory of the past range from psychoanalytical to historical, sociological, anthropological, political, etc.[54] The act of misremembering is dealt with differently by each approach. More or less intentionally incomplete, truncated, or missing historical information, the development of false beliefs, and the avoidance of guilt and shame are some of the misremembering strategies deployed by the memorial museums. Within the framework of dark and red tourism, memorial museums shape the awareness of their audiences by presenting a different narrative, a specific type of truth-telling, one in which suffering becomes part of the autobiography of national distress. Autobiographical studies show us that what is missing from any biography, namely the ellipses, shape a biography as much as the information that is being supplied.[55] The interplay between the out-

---

54 See Maurice Halbwachs, *On Collective Memory* (Chicago: University of Chicago Press, 1992, edited and translated by Lewis A. Coser); and Paul Ricoeur, *Memory, History, Forgetting* (Chicago: University of Chicago Press, 2004).
55 Paul John Eakin, "Relational Selves, Relational Lives: The Story of the Story," in *True Relations. Essays on Autobiography and the Postmodern*, eds. G. Thomas Couser and Joseph Fichtelberg (Westport, CT: Greenwood Press, 1998), 63–81.

right telling of memory, the surplus of memory, and the avoidance of untellable memory is what makes memory museums unwitting actors in the conveying of incomplete memorial narratives.

For the Sighet Memorial and the House of Terror, the act of misremembering refers mainly to a selective use or representation of the past. This, in turn, leads to the development of false beliefs about that past and the avoidance of a thorough assignment of guilt. Historical inaccuracies are printed in the House of Terror's information sheets; these white pages (of which two versions are available in each exhibition room, one in Hungarian and one in English), permeated by dramatic language, insist on the complete victimization of a nation. Hungary is portrayed as an innocent and peaceful victim of a double occupation and repression, in addition to having suffered territorial mutilation after World War II:

> As a consequence of the World War and the subsequent revolution, followed by the Bolshevik putsch, Hungary was plunged into a hopeless economic situation. Isolated politically, disarmed, encircled by hostile countries, she became one of Central Europe's weakest, most vulnerable states. Territorial revision by peaceful means and the reinstatement of the historical Hungary became the focus of her policy.

The oppressors, along with their practices and henchmen, are presented as foreign to Hungary, being either German or Soviet. In addition, the historical information is far from clearly presented. A House of Terror handout in English titled "Gulag" begins,

> Everything that happened to the Hungarian prisoners fitted in with the ethnic cleansing (...) The abduction of Hungary's populace took place in two waves. After occupying a larger community, the Soviet forces would put the civilian population to work, but the "malenki robot" (small job) stipulated by the Soviet soldiers turned out to mean years of forced labour for many a luckless person.

At the Sighet Memorial Museum, some handouts also contain dramatic language indicative of instances of misremembering, as the next two examples show:

> The communist system could be maintained only by terror, and its history and dissolution is followed step by step beginning with its inception, then relating the history of the various movements for freedom, and finally describing its fall in 1989.[56] Out of the eight satellite countries and the four states directly incorporated into the USSR, Romania was the only one with a highly respected Monarch.[57]

---

56 Sighet Memorial Museum handout, room 23.
57 Sighet Memorial Museum handout, room 20.

As these examples illustrate, both the Romanian and Hungarian human rights museums promote a myth of national victimization and the alien nature of the communist regime.[58]

Dark tourism visitors come to meet the long-gone prisoners; they see mug shots of former inmates, various personal and official documents, objects and reports from a bygone era, torture cells and instruments, etc. And although each prison museum exhibits cases and cells of several famous political prisoners who died under torture, in the case of both the Sighet Memorial Museum and the House of Terror, the main victims are the Romanian and the Hungarian people, respectively, in their absolute majority, if not entirety. The effort to touch the complex, widespread legacy of communism (and, implicitly, the multifarious nuances of its darkness, grayness, reddishness, blackness, or whiteness displayed in these two museums), and the fascination that this type of social order exercised on the minds and hearts of many people remains always deferred. The explanation for the misremembering that lies hidden under the over-remembering of the recent past may be that the tense dichotomy of a suffering nation under oppression on the one hand, and the same nation dreaming of a better future and social equality on the other is difficult to explore and, most importantly, reconcile.

The Sighet Memorial Museum brochure provides summary information about the formation of the communist political police (*Securitate*) and the existence of the collaborationist phenomenon, i.e. police inspectors, sympathizers, opportunists and informers whose ranks were considerably expanded after 1948 by "a great number of party activists, uneducated, but with a 'healthy social origin.'"[59] No explanation is offered as to the enigmatic creation or continued existence of the considerable number of Romanian people with communist convictions or practices throughout the communist period. Thus, no correct correlation can be made by museum audiences between the harrowing suffering of the victims and their victimizers. Communist repression was enabled by political police agents, torturers, interrogators, prison officials, a legal system ensuring the legality of state-sponsored terrorization of opposing groups, informers, denouncers, communist party sympathizers; in short, a wide range of the population contributing to the maintenance of a "criminal system" and its ideological rationale.

---

58 Monica Ciobanu, "Criminalising the Past and Reconstructing Collective Memory: The Romanian Truth Commission," *Europe-Asia Studies*, 61, vol. 2 (2009): 313–336, and Apor, "An Epistemology of the Spectacle?"
59 Sighet Memorial Museum brochure, *Ghid și activitate 1993–2017*, 17.

While the victim category in a memorial museum is, for sound and obvious moral reasons omnipresent, the category of the enablers of suffering remains rather amorphous, subsumed to a defective criminal ideology. And while an ideology may suppress, repress, and kill a great number of people, it does take a great number of individuals for it to do so, and to also last for decades. The operative word here, or the elephant in the room, that both museums shun is, perhaps, *fratricide*. During the 1989 Revolution in Romania, protesters marching against tanks that were moving against them in downtown Bucharest shouted: "Down with communism!" No one could have shouted the unimaginable: "Down with the half of the country that enabled the suffering of the other half!" If decommunization in Hungary and Romania has failed, it is perhaps because even the best of the memory efforts to unearth and represent past abuse and injustice of an immense scale cannot yet fully or correctly articulate the victim-victimizer rapport. The memorial museums' inferred message is "Here are the victims. Let's all mourn them together and commemorate their suffering every year" to make sure their presence and sacrifice is forever with us. As for victimizers and their supporters, they are relegated to an ideologized, forced-upon part of history brought from the outside, and thus assigned to a different era and place. Victims are here, victimizers are there. Victims occupy the present of memory; victimizers somehow occupy the past of memory.

A blunt visual enumeration of some of the unnamed Hungarian perpetrators of human rights abuse in one of the ominous dark-red hallways at the House of Terror indicates the existence of the collaborationist phenomena, though no explanatory data or analysis are offered beyond the occasional cryptic hint toward a more complicated history. For example, a highly succinct and vague explanation is found in the expensive museum brochure, which defines perpetrators as those "who took an active part in establishing and maintaining the two Hungarian totalitarian terror regimes (Arrow Cross and communist), as well as those who held responsible positions in the executive organs of these two regime [whose] behavior during their earlier or subsequent careers does not absolve them from personal responsibility."[60]

The inner tension among the various social strata, where some were quite ready to accommodate the dictatorial regimes in Romania and Hungary, or the participation of a good percentage of the population in supporting communist ideals and aspirations for decades are missing from both memorial museums. In their current forms, in which both museums

---

60 The House of Terror Museum brochure.

claim to (over) represent more than local and individual histories, a more complex and complete understanding of what made the large-scale suffering and murder possible long-term remains elusive.

Though the implementation of the communist regimes may have come to Romania and Hungary via Soviet tanks and ideology, suffering was made possible not only by repression, but also by the willing participation, compliance, acquiescence, or enthusiasm of sections of Romanian and Hungarian societies. As I previously noted, remembering violence affects the sense of responsibility, by eliciting certain moral responses from audiences. The mis-remembering misses the possibility of eliciting the right questions from the museums' visitors: beyond the forcible, imported communist ideology, and a documented number of murderous, evil characters that enabled the dark legacy of communism, why and how did the communist system last for decades? The answers could be arresting. Lavinia Stan writes "Romania had the largest percentage of party members relative to the total population (3.8 million members in a total population of 23 million) and one of the highest percentages of informers (between 400,000 and a million)."[61] Perhaps each museum visitor would start questioning or even remembering that they might have had family members who were either political victims or perpetrators of abuse, or both. The documented numbers of political prisoners who died in the communist jails and the numbers of the informers, political police officers, spies, denouncers, interrogators, investigators, judges, guards, etc. may even out.

In this economy of trauma, victims and perpetrators were partly engaged in what sociologist Michael Mann terms as classicide, understood as the intentional elimination of a given social group identified by Marxist-Leninist ideology as belonging to a social class opposed to the proletariat class. *The Black Book of Communism* edited by historian Stéphane Courtois offered the term "class genocide." Class genocide or classicide can be ultimately interpreted as *fratricide*. The communist fratricide affected many parts of the national community either directly, or indirectly through family ties. Since neither classicide nor class genocide are legal terms, the only two criminals that were sentenced for their past communist abuses in Romania, labor camp commander Ion Ficior and prison head Alexandru Vișinescu, were charged with "crimes against humanity."[62] Their crimes were perpetrated against members of the same nation

---

61 Stan, "*Transitional Justice in Eastern Europe and the Former Soviet Union*," 147.
62 See Raluca Grosescu, "Judging Communist Crimes in Romania: Transnational and Global Influences," *International Journal of Transitional Justice*, 11, vol. 3 (2017): 505–524.

and community. Mis-representing the fact that the repressive communist regime actively promoted and elevated fratricide as a responsible moral and professional duty of its henchmen misses the possibility of museum audiences learning deeper lessons.

Richard S. Esbenshade's article "Remembering to Forget: Memory, History, National Identity in Postwar East-Central Europe" is particularly helpful in elucidating the holding of false beliefs. It tells us that "the crux of the memory problem in the postwar East-Central European context" was that the communist states "falsified history and manipulated collective memory;" in this context, intellectuals "were still the only imaginable (especially to themselves) resistance to the system, and were thus the saviors of national integrity."[63] Thus, "the celebration of counter-memory or counter-history begs the question of who is doing the remembering and the rewriting of the history? The answer, especially in the East-Central European context, is invariably the intelligentsia."[64] In the case of the House of Terror and the Sighet Memorial Museum, it was the intellectuals gathered around Viktor Orbán and Ana Blandiana who tried to recover and represent the mass victimization that happened under communist rule. However, intellectuals were both privileged and guilty of collaborating with past communist regimes. Acceptance of individual and collective intellectual guilt is not something that intellectuals in either country are willing to dwell upon (collaboration, half-truths, lies, and guilt). In this context, as today's counter memory agents, their dilemma becomes, "there is no pure, pristine memory" beneath the communist state manipulation, "for its subjects are caught up in the process and themselves become guilty of mis-remembering; of manipulation of others' memory; in fact, of all the crimes of the totalitarian state."[65] Other scholars, such as Tony Judt, discuss the problem of mis-memory, asking whether there is not "something to be said, socially-speaking, for taboos," for the "single beautiful lie" that the Communists imposed, to oppose the "many unpleasant truths about that part of the world" (fascism, anti-Semitism, and "hyper-collaborationist regimes").[66]

The "much-agonized contradictions of the intellectuals' role" in the maintenance of a system find their expression in the misremembering of events past.[67] This misremembering is not surprising; its reasoning lies in

---

63 Richard S. Esbenshade, "Remembering to Forget. Memory, History, National Identity in Postwar East-Central Europe," *Representations*, 49 (1995): 76–77.
64 Ibid., 77.
65 Ibid., 78.
66 Tony Judt quoted in Esbenshade, "Remembering to Forget," 85–86.
67 Esbenshade, "Remembering to Forget," 78.

the fact that it is easier "to remind people of being heroes and victims—everyone fought communism—than perpetrators and bystanders."[68] The topic of collaboration is most controversial. As it has been argued for the House of Terror, "any narrative of a 'participatory dictatorship' or a more subtle and ambiguous collaboration based on the desire to build the utopian communist society, are simply missing."[69] The critique of misremembering is that museum visitors may remain with the experience of "how it felt to be a victim under a communist regime" but not necessarily understand what led to large-scale victimhood short and long-term. "The Holocaust Museum Washington is a case in point. As critics pointed out when it first opened, it displays the consequences of evil but fails to help us understand how apparently ordinary people could behave with such cruelty."[70] The most difficult thing that all memory work deals with is "that of defining and locating repression."[71] In Romania's case, the search for answers uncomfortably revealed that the collaboration and cooptation of a wide range of individuals included ordinary people "neighbors, friends and relatives, well-known personalities and current office-holders."[72] Finally, one could see the victimizers occupy not only the space of past memory, but also see some of them well entrenched into the present of memory. But to deal with the present of memory brings back the thorny question of the politicization of memory in the context of post-communist politics in both Romania and Hungary.

The 2006 report of the Presidential Commission for the Study of the Crimes of Communism in Romania remains an incomplete measure of historical and legal justice, a non-legal document, assisting very little in the healing process of a nation. The identity of many of the criminals, murderers, and torturers, let alone their prosecution and indictment are missing in the report. Its public condemnation of the Romanian communist regime as illegitimate and criminal comes to represent only a simulacrum of justice, in that the perpetrators of violence have not been swiftly brought before legal courts. It is an already old *adage* that in Romania, the

---

68 Julia Creet, "The House of Terror and the Holocaust Memorial Centre: Resentment and Melancholia in Post-89 Hungary," *European Cultural Memory Post-89*, 30 (2013): 29–62, 50.
69 Mariya Ivancheva, "Allegories of Transition: Representations of Past and Present Repressive Regimes in Gyorgyi Palfi's Feature Film Taxidermia and the House of Terror Museum in Budapest," *Philosophia*, (2013).
70 Sheila Watson, "The Legacy of Communism: Difficult Histories, Emotions and Contested Narratives," *International Journal of Heritage Studies* 24, no. 7 (2017): 781–794.
71 Ciobanu, "Criminalising the Past," 316.
72 Ibid.

overwhelming majority of human rights violators under the communist regime lived undisturbed for more than three decades after the fall of communism; moreover, they enjoyed large pensions, and many died peacefully in their comfortable homes. Their former victims either died poor and sick under the post-1989 regimes, or, in some cases, remained buried in unmarked common graves, awaiting an always-deferred justice. Because of this lack of justice, the Sighet Museum's founders introduce communism's evil aesthetics by displaying resounding maxims such as "when justice fails to be a form of memory, then memory by itself can be a form of justice."[73] The form of justice that the Sighet Memorial Museum brings is undoubtedly necessary, even if it is only partial in scope. Its incompleteness as a measure of justice is proof that a frank discussion held across political aisles or inclinations about the history of communism in this part of the world has yet to happen. Until this discussion about what made ordinary Romanian or Hungarian citizens collaborate with the communist social order and support it takes place in earnest, the postmemory of both countries will continue to commit to the superficial story of social suffering without a real understanding of its underlying mechanisms and outcomes.

Conclusion

Both museums fulfill, however imperfectly and for more-or-less politically motivated reasons, an important memory role against the forgetting of past crimes. Although, according to critical scholarship on both, the provocative museal style of the House of Terror brought about more political controversy than it did instruction or personal reflection, the museum does fill a gap in the representation of the country's communist past. Since no official agreement exists about how to represent the past, each of these two memorial museums propose their own approaches to how suffering and the ethics of recognition can be read and interpreted by the audiences they envisioned. Between the two, the Sighet Memorial Museum clearly does much better at claiming the legitimacy of representing human rights abuses in its museal practice: it has a solid, three-tiered administrative and governing system, it displays copies of original archival documents, and it enables public access to former political detainees. Its

---

73 In Romanian: "Atunci cand justiția nu reușește să fie o formă de memorie, memoria singură poate fi o formă de justiție" (attributed to Ana Blandiana on the Sighet Memorial Museum's website).

summer school educates the public.⁷⁴ Its visitors' reviews are, in their great majority, positive and highly appreciative. Its funding sources are varied. The House of Terror, on the other hand, enjoys governmental funding, its visitors' reviews are mixed, the historical information offered is somewhat partial and partially offered, the language of the exhibits is solely Hungarian, and the unhelpfulness of staff seems to be a constant source of dissatisfaction for visitors. Both museums receive visits of large organized school groups, being thus involved in the educational process of the younger generations. Their museal strategies cultivate emotional responses to the horrific suffering of the past and neither can be said to offer a thoroughly balanced historical perspective about the victim-victimizer rapport or the national victimhood of the post-World War Two era.

While forms of misremembering and over-remembering abound, those practiced by both museums include the exhibition of a spectral form of history. A sort of hauntology marks the discourse of both the Sighet Memorial and the House of Terror's leaflets and catalogues, in which the specter of the past, as Derrida would put it, is "the tangible intangibility of a proper body without flesh, but still the body of *someone* as some*one other*."⁷⁵ The phantom-like figure of the communist Other, coming from the past with the futile promise of a better social and economic future in one hand and the torture instruments in the other has been properly dislocated to be better misunderstood. In both Romania and Hungary, the lack of a defined process of national reconciliation is marked by the past's haunting of the present.

Perhaps the difficulty in striking the right note in the museal reconstruction of past suffering lies, in part, in the fact that the communist legacy is still an ongoing and much disputed object of debate. Analyzing the political reorganization of memory in Eastern Europe, Paul Williams writes that the "fall of communism has raised important questions about to whom that now largely disowned history belongs, and how it may be reincorporated or rejected by former East bloc nations.⁷⁶ It is well known that "post-communist tourism re-valuing communist heritage has been

---

74 See Monica Ciobanu, "Teaching History and Building a Democratic Future: Lessons from Communist and Post-Communist Romania," *Democracy and Education*, 17, no. 3 (2008): 58–62.
75 Jacques Derrida, *Specters of Marx: The State of the Debt, the Work of the Mourning, and the New International* (New York: Routledge, 1994), 27.
76 Paul Williams, *Memorial Museums: The Global Rush to Commemorate Atrocities* (New York: Berg Oxford International Publishers, 2007), 114.

seen as a form of post-communist countries claiming a form of symbolic capital over the lack of strong economic capital."[77]

At the beginning of this article, I mentioned the Federation of International Human Rights Museums' mission, namely that "museums make a social contribution to the democratization of nations by encouraging free debate and confronting authoritarian versions of the truth." However, as my analysis about these two human rights museums in East and Central Europe revealed, the creation of emotional audiences leads "some liberal democratic societies [to] avoid emotions as dangerous, thus ceding their use to their opponents."[78] Granted, social suffering cannot avoid eliciting incredible emotions in their audiences, regardless of these audiences' political inclinations. Moreover, emotional reactions may have the benefit of expanding continuing debates on painful rights abuse topics. As shown earlier, it also runs the risk of diluting the real causes and consequences of historical and political contexts that generate specific forms of oppression.

---

77 Duncan Light and Craig Young, "Communist Heritage Tourism: Between Economic Development and European Integration," in *Heritage and Media in Europe-Contributing toward Integration and Regional Development* (Weimar, 2006), 249–259.
78 Nussbaum cited in Watson, "The Legacy of Communism," 2.

Law in Action in Romania, 2008–2018: Context, Agency, and Innovation in the Process of Transitional Justice

Dragoş Petrescu

Abstract: *This article tackles a hitherto-unnoticed innovative mechanism of transitional justice. Creatively interpreting the legislation, CNSAS, the institution dealing with the former secret police files, gradually transformed itself from a vetting agency into a fact-finding commission. While the law restricted the meaning of collaboration, CNSAS produced an open-access electronic database including digest versions of the screening process and providing quick access to excerpts from secret police documents. This repository demonstrates the multifaceted nature of collaboration, the wide variety of information gathered and the complicity of individuals originating from all social, cultural, and professional backgrounds. The e-database created by CNSAS offers not a simple list of wrongdoers, but evidence of wrongdoings according to rule of law principles. In brief, this registry of shaming represents a para-legal mechanism of transitional justice, which allows moral judgement, promotes transparency, and legitimizes the mission of CNSAS in fostering democracy by widely illustrating what democracy is not.*

Although Romania caught-up with its post-communist neighbors by the mid-2000s, the country has been a laggard in implementing transitional justice. The Romanian case, however, is not standard in East-Central Europe, but rather atypical due to its significant particularities. Since the Proclamation of Timişoara in March 1990,[1] the general public has focused not on the former nomenklatura as much as on the communist secret police, the Securitate, which is widely believed to have outlived the

---

1 The "Proclamation of Timişoara" practically initiated the debate over lustration in post-communist Romania. It was issued on 11 March 1990 in Timişoara, and its Article 8 requested the banning of former nomenklatura members, party activists, and officers of the former secret police from running in the next three elections. For the complete text, see Annex 2: "Proclamaţia de la Timişoara" in Domniţa Ştefănescu, *Cinci ani din istoria României: O cronologie a evenimentelor decembrie 1989–decembrie 1995* (Bucharest: Editura Maşina de Scris, 1995), 453–54.

regime change of December 1989.[2] While the former Securitate officers and collaborators managed to control key positions in post-communist politics, economy or media, as elsewhere in East-Central Europe, the communist secret police in Romania stirred such a global research interest that it generated a new entry in English dictionaries.[3] Few writings about the communist regime in Romania fail to mention the Securitate, while the archives of this institution have recurrently provoked public controversies. Yet, scholars who have studied topics related to transitional justice have paid more attention to the politics of memory and memorialization, than to the few criminal trials or the delayed and limited administrative justice measures. Consequently, research on public recollections and representations of the recent past has produced solid scholarship which emphasizes the relation between democratization and non-judicial mechanisms of transitional justice, such as remembrance of the communist period.[4] Since 1989, the academic interest has shifted from asserting the uses of remembering the experiences of imprisonment and armed resistance in fostering democratic values,[5] to demonstrating the limits of this strategy in accomplishing historical redress,[6] and to warning against the abuses or misuses of essentializing such a version of the past.[7] Accordingly, research on the memory of Ro-

---

2   Cristina Petrescu, "The Afterlife of the Securitate: On Moral Correctness in Post-communist Romania," in *Remembering Communism: Private and Public Recollections of Lived Experiences in Southeast Europe*, eds. Maria Todorova, Augusta Dimou and Stefan Troebst (Budapest: CEU Press, 2014), 385–416.
3   Dennis Deletant, *Ceaușescu and the Securitate: Coercion and Dissent in Communist Romania, 1965–1989* (London: Routledge, 1995); Idem, "The Securitate Legacy in Romania: Who Is in Control?" *Problems of Post-Communism*, 42, no. 6 (1995): 23–8.
4   Lavinia Stan, *Transitional Justice in Post-Communist Romania: The Politics of Memory* (Cambridge: Cambridge University Press, 2013); Monica Ciobanu, *Repression, Resistance and Collaboration in Stalinist Romania, 1944–1964: Post-Communist Remembering* (London: Routledge, forthcoming 2020).
5   Ruxandra Cesereanu, *Gulagul în conștiința românească: Memorialistica și literatura închisorilor și lagărelor comuniste* (Iași: Polirom, 2005); *Raport Final al Comisiei Prezidențiale pentru Analiza Dictaturii Comuniste în România* (Bucharest: Humanitas, 2007), Romulus Rusan, ed., *Cartea morților* (Bucharest: Fundația Academia Civică, 2013); *Idem, istorie, memorie, memorial sau cum se construiește un miracol* (Bucharest: Fundația Academia Civică, 2017).
6   Cristian Tileagă, "Communism and the Meaning of Social Memory: Towards a Critical-Interpretive Approach," *Integrative Psychological and Behavioral Science*, 46, no. 4 (2012): 475–92; idem, *Representing Communism after the Fall: Discourse, Memory, and Historical Redress* (London: Palgrave Macmillan, 2018).
7   Monica Ciobanu, "Reconstructing the History of Early Communism and Armed Resistance in Romania," *Europe-Asia Studies*, 66, no. 9 (2014): 1452–81; idem, "Pitești: A Project in Reeducation and its Post-1989 Interpretation in Romania," *Nationalities Papers*, 43, no. 4 (2015): 615–33; Cristina Petrescu and Dragoș Petrescu, "The Canon of Remembering Romanian Communism: From Autobiogra-

manian communism has emancipated itself from reiterating the paradigm of criminalizing the communist past for the sake of never forgetting the wrongdoings of the Securitate and the repressive nature of the former dictatorship, perhaps with a few exceptions.[8] More recently, the hitherto marginal recollections of everyday life, mostly expressed by younger generations, disengaged the process of remembering from its assumed mission of supporting democratic consolidation. Contrary to what many feared,[9] this did not result in any nostalgia for the nondemocratic past.

In the meantime, the legal aspects of transitional justice gained momentum, so memory has lost its unique place in the process of dealing with the dictatorial past. Criminal prosecution of past wrongdoings started in the early 1990s with the trials of a few former high-ranking party bureaucrats to extend by the mid-2010s, under transnational influences, to the conviction of two military officials found guilty of perpetrating political crimes in the 1950s.[10] Whereas these legal measures were too limited to have a societal impact, the creation of an institution meant to deal with the secret police files, the National Council for the Study of the Securitate Archives (*Consiliul Național pentru Studierea Arhivelor Securității*—CNSAS), in 1999 and especially the effective opening of these files in 2005 fundamentally changed transitional justice in post-communist Romania. Although the lustration law was declared unconstitutional because it envisaged the removal of former party bureau-

---

phical Recollections to Collective Representations," in *Remembering Communism: Private and Public Recollections of Lived Experiences in Southeast Europe*, eds. Maria Todorova, Augusta Dimou and Stefan Troebst (Budapest: Central European University Press, 2014), 43–70; Mihai Stelian Rusu, "Transitional Politics of Memory: Political Strategies of Managing the Past in Post-communist Romania," *Europe-Asia Studies*, 69, no. 8 (2017): 1257–79.

8   Vladimir Tismăneanu and Marius Stan, *Romania Confronts Its Communist Past: Democracy, Memory, and Moral Justice* (Cambridge: Cambridge University Press, 2018).

9   Diana Georgescu, "Between Trauma and Nostalgia: The Intellectual Ethos and Generational Dynamics of Memory in Postsocialist Romania," *Südosteuropa. Zeitschrift für Politik und Gesellschaft*, 64, no. 3 (2016): 284–306; Simona Mitroiu, "Literary Narratives of the Past: Generations of Memory and Everyday Life Under the Romanian Communist Regime," *Slavonica*, 23, no. 2 (2018): 91–112; Codruța Alina Pohrib, "The Romanian 'Latchkey Generation' Writes Back: Memory Genres of Post-communism on Facebook," *Memory Studies*, 12, no. 2 (2019): 164–83.

10 Raluca Grosescu and Raluca Ursachi, *Justiția penală de tranziție din România postcomunistă* (Iași: Polirom 2009); Raluca Grosescu, "Judging Communist Crimes in Romania: Transnational and Global Influences," *International Journal of Transitional Justice*, 11, no. 3 (2017): 505–24.

crats from public office based on collective guilt,[11] CNSAS has engaged in a unilateral lustration targeting the Securitate based on individual guilt. This process was compatible with rule of law principles.[12] Initially, this confession-based lustration worked only if the CNSAS verdicts formulated after screening the Securitate files contradicted the obligatory yet secret statements of those seeking or holding public offices. Because the administration of these files was regarded as politically manipulated,[13] their content as certainly truncated,[14] and their screening as leading to virtually no significant results, civil society groups made public lists of former Securitate officers by-passing the vetting process and disregarding evidence of guilt.[15] The opening of these archives produced neither significant retribution of wrongdoings nor restoration of rights,[16] but numerous public controversies over the "truth" in, and trustworthiness of, these documents, to say nothing of the legislation regulating the CNSAS mission, in particular the normative definition of collaboration.[17]

---

11 Bogdan Iancu, "Post-Accession Constitutionalism with a Human Face: Judicial Reform and Lustration in Romania," *European Constitutional Law Review*, 6, no. 1 (2010): 28–58; Lavinia Stan, "Witch-Hunt or Moral Rebirth? Romanian Parliamentary Debates on Lustration," *East European Politics and Societies*, 6, no. 2 (2012): 274–95.

12 Dragoş Petrescu, "Dilemmas of Transitional Justice in Post-1989 Romania," in *Lustration and Consolidation of Democracy and the Rule of Law in Central and Eastern Europe*, eds. Vladimira Dvorakova and Andelko Milardovic (Zagreb: Political Science Research Center, 2007), 127–51; Cristina Petrescu and Dragoş Petrescu, "The Piteşti Syndrome: A Romanian Vergangenheitsbewältigung?" in *Postdiktatorische Geschichtskulturen im Süden und Osten Europas: Bestandsaufnahme und Forschungsperspektiven*, ed. Stefan Troebst (Göttingen: Wallstein, 2010), 502–618.

13 Lavinia Stan, "Lustration in Romania: The Story of a Failure," *Studia Politica*, 6, no. 1 (2006): 135–56; idem, *Transitional Justice in Eastern Europe and the Former Soviet Union: Reckoning with the Communist Past* (London: Routledge, 2009).

14 Herta Müller, *Cristina und ihre Attrappe: oder Was (nicht) in den Akten der Securitate steht* (Göttingen: Wallstein, 2009).

15 Lavinia Stan, "Vigilante Justice in Post-communist Europe," *Problems of Communism and Post-Communism*, 44, no. 4 (2011): 319–27.

16 Lavinia Stan, "Reckoning with the Communist Past in Romania: A Scorecard," *Europe-Asia Studies*, 65, no. 1 (2013): 127–46; Monica Ciobanu, "Recent Restorative Justice Measures in Romania (2006–2010)," *Problems of Post-Communism*, 60, no. 5 (2013): 45–57.

17 Gabriel Andreescu, *Cărturari, opozanţi şi documente: manipularea arhivei securităţii* (Iaşi: Polirom, 2013); idem, *Existenţa prin cultură: represiune, colaboraţionism şi rezistenţă intelectuală sub regimul communist* (Iaşi: Polirom, 2015); Dragoş Petrescu, "The Resistance That Wasn't: Romanian Intellectuals, the Securitate, and the 'Resistance through Culture'," in *Die Securitate in Siebenbürgen*, eds. Joachim von Puttkamer, Stefan Sienerth and Ulrich A. Wien (Cologne: Böhlau Verlag, 2014), 11–35; Cristina Petrescu, "Entangled Stories: On the Meaning of Collaboration with the Securitate," in *Secret Agents and the Memory of*

Nonetheless, this story of transitional justice turned gradually from a failure in the regional context into an average example of dealing with the communist past, while research explored the relation between the revelations from these previously secret files and transparency, institutional trust and democratization.[18] Surprisingly, the change of CNSAS legislation in 2008, which restricted the definition of collaboration and delegated the final verdict to administrative courts, actually reinvigorated the activity of this institution, maintaining a strong general interest in the secret police files. This generated new scholarship suggesting that transitional justice does not have a predefined ending.[19]

While the more established transitional justice mechanisms carried out by CNSAS have received substantial attention, the innovations that emerged in this delayed process of reckoning with the communist past passed almost unnoticed. In an attempt to fill this gap, the present paper argues that, under the new legislation of 2008 and in absence of specific norms of application, the main mission of CNSAS transformed itself from a vetting agency into a fact-finding commission. More precisely, the paper illustrates that the context-specific approach to transitional justice carried out by CNSAS between 2008 and 2018 has gradually produced an open-access electronic database including digest versions of the screening process. This repository includes excerpts from documents of the Securitate which illustrate a wide variety of information provided to the secret police by individuals representing both genders, rural and urban areas, diverse professions and levels of education, all counties and ethnic communities in communist Romania. These excerpts

---

Everyday Collaboration in Communist Eastern Europe, eds. Péter Apor, Sándor Horváth and James Mark (London: Anthem Press, 2017), 225–46; Lavinia Stan and Lucian Turcescu, "Collaboration and Resistance: Some Definitional Difficulties," in *Justice, Memory and Redress in Romania: New Insights*, eds. L. Stan and L. Turcescu (Newcastle upon Tyne: Cambridge Scholars Publishers, 2017), 192–213.

18 Cynthia Horne, "Assessing the Impact of Lustration on Trust in Public Institutions and National Government in Central and Eastern Europe," *Comparative Political Studies*, 45, no. 4 (2012): 412–46; idem, "The Impact of Lustration on Democratization in Post-Communist Countries," *International Journal of Transitional Justice*, 8, no. 3(2014): 496–521; idem, *Building Trust and Democracy: Transitional Justice in Post-Communist Countries* (Oxford: Oxford University Press, 2017).

19 Cynthia Horne, "'Silent Lustration': Public Disclosures as Informal Lustration Mechanisms in Bulgaria and Romania," *Problems of Post-Communism*, 62, no. 3: 131–44; idem, "The Timing of Transitional Justice Measures," in *Post-Communist Transitional Justice: Lessons from 25 years of Experience*, eds. Lavinia Stan and Nadya Nedelsky (Cambridge: Cambridge University Press, 2015); idem, "What Is Too Long and When Is Too Late for Transitional Justice? Observations from the Case of Romania," *Journal of Romanian Studies*, forthcoming 2020.

were systematically included in the introductory parts to the certificates issued for individuals who cannot be brought before the administrative court of justice because the evidence from the Securitate archives proves that they offered information to, but did not collaborate with, the secret police in the narrow sense of the law. In short, this database represents a registry of shaming, which not only lists wrongdoers, but gives evidence of their wrongdoings. Their usefulness, however, goes beyond the function of publicly exposing the individual guilt of those who cannot be lawfully declared collaborators and removed from public office. This database, the paper contends, represents a registry illustrating the "banality of evil," which shifted the focus from public personalities to common individuals and provided a sample representative enough for all social categories.[20] Available for free in digital format, the database offers quick access to the most obscure parts of the secret police files and conveys to the general public, in condensed form, excerpts from documents produced for the operational purposes of the Securitate. This registry, the paper argues, represents a para-legal mechanism of transitional justice, which de-politicized CNSAS, legitimized its mission, and facilitated the moral judgement on the act of collaborating with the Securitate. Used for educational purposes, this e-database can teach what democracy is not. In doing so, it fosters a better understanding of democracy in the complex times we live in.

Truth-seeking and Vetting: Law 187/1999 as a Human Rights-centered Initiative

A major step toward a holistic approach to transitional justice in post-1989 Romania was taken in December 1999, when the Romanian Parliament passed Law 187/1999 or the "Law regarding access to the personal file and the disclosure of the Securitate as political police."[21] Constantin Ticu Dumitrescu, the main proponent of the draft law and the head of the Association of Former Political Prisoners in Romania (*Asociația Foștilor Deținuți Politici din România*—AFDPR) was deeply frus-

---

20 After the passing of new legislation in 2008, the CNSAS Board issued on average five certificates of this kind, named certificates with preamble, per meeting. A conservative evaluation puts the number of certificates with preamble issued by CNSAS over the period under scrutiny at over 2,000. Author's calculation; see http://www.cnsas.ro/comunicate.html; accessed on 10 April 2020.
21 *Lege nr. 187 din 7 decembrie 1999 privind accesul la propriul dosar și deconspirarea securității ca poliție politică*, Monitorul Oficial al României (Official Bulletin of Romania, hereafter cited as MO) 603 (9 December 1999): 1–5.

trated by the many hindrances and numerous amendments to the draft law, which eventually changed its substance.[22] As a Senator of the National Peasant Party, Dumitrescu set forth his vision on the basic approaches to the opening of the secret police archives in Romania. Thus, on May 18th, 1999, during the parliamentary debates on the text of the draft law, Dumitrescu stated that the law was meant to enable reparations to the victims of the communist regime and vetting of individuals seeking prominent public office. At the same time, Dumitrescu raised two key issues regarding vetting: (1) first judgement on collaboration/non-collaboration was made by a Board (Collegium) named by the Parliament according to the political representation of the political parties; and (2) vetting was dependent on the transfer of the Securitate files to the new institution meant to administer these files, the National Council for the Study of the Securitate Archives—CNSAS, while the postcommunist secret services were already reluctant to transfer the Securitate files to this not-yet-established institution.[23] Time proved him right. The points raised by Dumitrescu during the debates on the text of the bill in May 1999 would become major hindrances in the process of implementation of transitional justice in Romania.

Law 187/1999 has at its core the concept of political police (*poliție politică*).[24] In this respect, Article 5 of the law addresses three key concepts, as follows: (1) political police; (2) agent of the former Securitate; and (3) collaborator of the former Securitate. Law 187/1999 (Article 5, paragraph 1) sets forth the following definition of political police: "By political police one understands all those activities performed by the Securitate or by other structures or institutions having a repressive character, which envisaged the establishment and perpetuation of the communist totalitarian power, as well as the suppression or limitation of

---

22 AFDPR was established on 2 January 1990, advocated vigorously the rights and dignity of former political convicts and contributed to adoption of legislation in favor of its members. See, for instance, *Decret-Lege din 30 martie 1990 privind acordarea unor drepturi persoanelor persecutate din motive politice de dictatura instaurată cu începere de la 6 martie 1945, precum și celor deportate în străinătate ori constituite în prizonieri*, MO 118 (18 March 1998): 5–7. On 18 May 1999, during the debates on the CNSAS draft law, Dumitrescu stated that AFDPR numbered at that moment 102,800 members.

23 Constantin-Ticu Dumitrescu, *Dezbateri asupra proiectului de Lege privind accesul la propriul dosar și deconspirarea Securității ca poliție politică*, "Ședința Camerei Deputaților din 18 mai 1999," 18 May 1999; http://www.cdep.ro/pls/steno/steno.stenograma?ids=3501&idm=2&sir=&sep=and&idv=532&idl=1&prn=1; accessed on 15 February 2020.

24 For the text of Law 187/1999 see http://www.cnsas.ro/documente/cadru_legal/LEGE%20187_1999.pdf, accessed on April 4, 2020.

fundamental human rights and liberties." As one can easily grasp, such a definition denotes that the said law adopts a human rights-centered approach, very much in line with modern approaches which conceptualize transitional justice as a "response to systematic or widespread violations of human rights."[25] Furthermore, Article 5, paragraph 2 refers to the notion of *agent* (officer) of the Securitate: "Under the present law, an individual is an agent of the Securitate as political police if they were operatives, including operatives under cover, of the Securitate forces during the period 1945–89."

The notion of collaborator of the Securitate is highly relevant from the perspective of public debates at the time when Law 187/1999 was passed. In this respect, paragraphs 3, 4 and 5 of the same Article 5 are concerned with the issue of collaboration with the former Securitate. Paragraph 3 sets forth the following definition of a collaborator: "According to the present law, a collaborator of the Securitate as political police is an individual who: (a) was remunerated or compensated in any other way for their activity in that capacity; (b) possessed a safe house or a secret meeting place; (c) was a Securitate resident according to the present law; (d) any other individual who provided information to the Securitate which affected directly or indirectly fundamental human rights and liberties." Paragraphs 4 and 5 add other important dimensions to the definition of a collaborator by stating that (1) a collaborator is also an individual who "transmitted or facilitated the transmission of information, notes, reports or other documents which denounced activity or attitudes against the totalitarian communist regime and which could affect fundamental human rights and liberties" (paragraph 4); and (2) are assimilated to the notion of collaborator—as defined by paragraph 3—"the individuals empowered to make judicial or political decisions or who, by abuse of political power, made decisions at central or local level regarding the activity of the Securitate or of other repressive bodies of the totalitarian communist regime."

Unfortunately, Law 187/1999 introduces a confusion that has been perpetuated since the passing of the law, despite subsequent changes in the legal framework. This confusion concerns the very notion of collaborator with the former Securitate. Thus, Article 1, paragraph 2 states that an individual put under surveillance by the former Securitate has the right to know the real names of the agents (officers) and collaborators [*sic*] who contributed to the completion of his or her file. At the same

---

25 International Center for Transitional Justice, "What Is Transitional Justice," https://www.ictj.org/sites/default/files/ICTJ-Global-Transitional-Justice-2009-English.pdf, accessed June 29, 2020.

time, Article 5 (paragraphs 3, 4 and 5) sets forth a comprehensive definition of a collaborator of the Securitate. Obviously, the definition provided by Article 5 is the one that matters in the process of transitional justice. Thus, according to Law 187/1999, the CNSAS Board passes an initial verdict regarding collaboration or non-collaboration with the former Securitate. In this respect, Article 16 (paragraphs 1 and 2) states that the losing party has the right to appeal against a verdict of collaboration issued by the CNSAS Board to the civil section of a court of appeal within 30 days. Consequently, an individual may be officially termed collaborator of the former Securitate only after the civil section of a court of appeal passes a final verdict in this respect. In contradistinction, an individual who only contributed with information to the completion of a Securitate file cannot be termed collaborator unless the process mentioned above—a first verdict by the CNSAS Board and a final verdict by the civil section of a court of appeal—has been carried out. From a legal point of view, the term collaborator of the former Securitate can be applied only to an individual who is subject to a sentence (final verdict) by the civil section of a court of appeal. Further discussion is needed with regard to the notion of collaborator introduced by Article 1, paragraph 2. As shown below in the section on the 2008 change of the legal framework, the choice was made due to institutional agency at the level of the CNSAS Board, which introduced in its official documents and press communiques the notion of *source* of the former Securitate beginning in January 2012.

Moreover, Law 187/1999 is concerned with truth-seeking and vetting but it lacks a broader perspective on transitional justice. The focus of the law is not on the reconciliatory aspects of transitional justice, but on collaboration or non-collaboration with the former Securitate. This is understandable considering the context in which the law was passed. Ruti G. Teitel points to the backward-looking aspect of legislation pertaining to transitional justice in the case of post-conflict situations: "Transitional justice tends to be backward-looking, responsive always to the last conflict, and, therefore, not capable of ensuring prospective security."[26] In the case of democratic transitions, the scope of such legislation should also ensure prospective political stability and foster a democratic political culture. To achieve these goals, the process of transitional justice must be accompanied by widespread dissemination of documentary evidence concerning violation of fundamental human rights by the

---

26 Ruti G. Teitel, "Transitional Justice in a New Era," *Fordham International Law Journal*, 26, no. 4 (2002): 905.

communist regime. Law 187/1999 does not fulfill this dimension of transitional justice. Thus, if proof of collaboration with the Securitate is not found, the CNSAS Board issues a decision of non-collaboration which states simply that the respective individual did not collaborate with the former Securitate, but does mention if a file exists or not and if a file exists, what exactly it contains.[27] In case that a final verdict of collaboration was reached, Law 187/1999 requires only the final verdict of collaboration to be published in the Official Bulletin of Romania (*Monitorul Oficial*), that is, the name of the individual concerned and the fact that a final verdict of collaboration was reached in their case.[28]

Law 187/1999 represents nevertheless a breakthrough in terms of transitional justice. For the first time ever after 1989, victims were granted access to their files, vetting of individuals seeking public office was institutionalized, and researchers were finally allowed to work in the archives of the former communist secret police. The context, however, proved to be inimical to transitional justice. The lack of political will to engage in a multilayered process of transitional justice by the powers that be was obvious after the general and presidential elections of 2000. Ion Iliescu and his successor communist party returned to power and this was also felt at the level of CNSAS, the new institution established under Law 187/1999 to administer the Securitate files, which started its activity in March 2000 on a six-year mandate. In terms of fact-finding, vetting and research, CNSAS as a public truth-seeking institution was faced with two major hindrances, one external and one internal to the institution.

The external hindrance consisted in the slow pace of transfer of the Securitate files, which were hosted mainly by the Romanian Intelligence Service (SRI), Foreign Intelligence Service (SIE), Ministry of National Defense (MApN) and Ministry of Justice (MJ), to CNSAS. From March 2000 to December 2005, the Securitate files were transferred to CNSAS slowly and selectively. The small number of files in the custody of CNSAS led to major public distrust in this institution. Victims who placed requests to access their files were almost invariably told that they did not have a Se-

---

27 See, for instance, the following decisions of non-collaboration issued prior to the 2008 change of legal framework: No. 111 of 18 May 2004, No. 172 of 13 July 2004 or No. 821 of 15 March 2007; http://cnsas.ro/documente/mentineri/Abrudan%20Traian.pdf; http://cnsas.ro/documente/mentineri/2017/Abitei%20Ludovic.pdf; http://cnsas.ro/documente/mentineri/Acatrinei%20Stela.pdf; accessed on 19 February 2020.

28 See for instance the verdicts of collaboration published in MO 858 (20 December 2004): 1–2. http://www.cnsas.ro/documente/monitoare/2004/MO%202004.1 2.20_858.pdf, accessed on February 20, 2020.

curitate file, and individuals seeking public office were granted decisions of non-collaboration because no information regarding possible collaboration with the Securitate was found in the available files, while researchers were equally frustrated because of the drastically limited number of files at their disposal in the CNSAS Archive. The transfer of files to the CNSAS Archive effectively started on March 20th, 2001, and until May 31st, 2002, the total number of files transferred was 3,652, comprising 7,020 volumes.[29] In 2003, the number of files transferred to CNSAS was 1,445, comprising 3,171 volumes.[30] By the end of 2004, the total number of files transferred to CNSAS amounted to 9,655 files, comprising 20,575 volumes.[31]

The internal hindrance was equally redoubtable and consisted in the "balance of power" at the level of the CNSAS Board. By 2002, it became clear that the forces less favorable to transitional justice had a majority on the eleven-member board.[32] This led to protracted decisions of collaboration with the Securitate, a process that was anyway slow because of the limited number of files transferred to the CNSAS Archive. When decisions that could affect the image of the ruling communist successor party and its allies were about to be made, the activity of the Board could be easily blocked by simply not ensuring the eight-member quorum (two-thirds of the total) requested under the law to hold an ordinary board meeting. A major crisis at the level of the CNSAS Board occurred in 2004, when the Board issued a decision of non-collaboration in the case of the leader of the Greater Romania Party (*Partidul România Mare*—PRM), Corneliu Vadim Tudor.[33] Combined, these two hindrances

---

29   CNSAS, *Raport referitor la îndeplinirea atribuțiilor ce revin Consiliului Național pentru Studierea Arhivelor Securității, potrivit Legii nr. 187/1999 privind accesul la propriul dosar și deconspirarea securității ca poliție politică 13 martie 2000–31 mai 2002*, 11–2; http://www.cnsas.ro/documente/rapoarte/Raport%202002.pdf, accessed on February 17, 2020.
30   CNSAS, *Raport de activitate pentru anul 2003 referitor la îndeplinirea atribuțiilor ce revin Consiliului Național pentru Studierea Arhivelor Securității, potrivit Legii nr. 187/1999 privind accesul la propriul dosar și deconspirarea securității ca poliție politică*, 16–7; hereafter cited as CNSAS Annual Report; http://www.cnsas.ro/documente/rapoarte/Raport%202003.pdf, accessed on February 17, 2020.
31   CNSAS Annual Report 2004, 24; http://www.cnsas.ro/documente/rapoarte/Raport%202004.pdf, accessed on February 17, 2020.
32   The initial eleven members of the first CNSAS Board were, in alphabetical order: Constantin Buchet, Florian Chirițescu, Ladislau-Antoniu Csendes, Mircea Dinescu, Mihai Gheorghe, Viorel-Mircea Nicolescu, Gheorghe Onișoru, Horia-Roman Patapievici, Andrei-Gabriel Pleșu, Aurel Pricu and Claudiu-Octavian Secașiu.
33   Four of the CNSAS Board members—Dinescu, Patapievici, Pleșu and Secașiu— voted against the decision of non-collaboration. At the time, numerous observers pointed towards an alliance between the Board members nominated by PSD and

created a disastrous public image of CNSAS, along with growing public distrust, especially amongst the urban strata, towards the third Iliescu regime (2000-2004).[34]

The general and presidential elections of November 2004 represented a watershed in terms of transitional justice. Rather unexpectedly, consensus was established at the level of principles regarding access to the Securitate files between civil society organizations, public intellectuals, the government, and the presidential administration. The external hindrance mentioned above was overcome by significantly accelerating the pace of transfer of the Securitate files to CNSAS. As shown above, by the end of 2004 the CNSAS Archive hosted only 9,655 files. After the 2004 shift in power, the Romanian Intelligence Service—SRI proceeded to a massive transfer of files to CNSAS. Thus, during March-December 2005, SRI transferred to CNSAS as many as 1,298,960 files, comprising 1,542,550 volumes.[35] The figures speak for themselves. This massive transfer of files was prompted by a resolution of the Supreme Council of National Defense—CSAT (Resolution No. 13 of 28 February 2005). The transfer of files from SRI to CNSAS was initiated on March 10th, 2005, as a direct consequence of the CSAT Resolution 13/2005.[36] In addition, five resolutions—four by CSAT and one by the government—were passed over the period April-August 2006 to enable the transfer to CNSAS of documents produced by the former Securitate and hosted after 1989 by various institutions or public bodies.[37] The transfer of files to CNSAS

PRM and including the Chairman of the Board, Gheorghe Onișoru, which did not favor transitional justice. See Gabriela Antoniu, "Criza din CNSAS va fi tranșată în Parlament," *Jurnalul național* (18 octombrie 2004); https://www.hotnews.ro/stiri-arhiva-1254204-criza-din-cnsas-transata-parlament.htm, accessed on April 10, 2020.

34 Ion Iliescu and his communist successor party, which changed its name several times, from National Salvation Front—FSN to the present day Social Democratic Party—PSD, stayed in power from 1990 to 1996 and from 2000 to 2004, while Iliescu held three mandates of head of state (1990-92, 1992-96 and 2000-04). For the results of elections held between 1990 and 2004 see National Statistics Institute, *Statistică electorală*; http://www.insse.ro/cms/files/statistici/stat_elec torale.pdf, accessed on February 18, 2020.

35 CNSAS Annual Report 2005, 11-2; http://www.cnsas.ro/documente/rapoarte/Raport%202005.pdf, accessed on February 18, 2020.

36 Ibid., 5 and 10.

37 (1) Hotărârea CSAT nr. 60/17.04.2006 privind predarea la CNSAS a arhivelor fostei Securități; (2) Hotărârea CSAT nr. 61/17.04.2006 privind punerea la dispoziția Comisiei Prezidențiale pentru analiza dictaturii comuniste în România a dosarelor și documentelor fostului Partid Comunist Român; (3) Hotărârea CSAT nr. 117/24.07.2006 privind declasificarea unor categorii de documente create de fosta Securitate și aflate în categoria dosare de siguranță națională aparținând persoanelor care ocupă demnități sau funcții publice; (4) Hotărârea CSAT nr.

continued at a rapid pace throughout 2006, and thus by the end of 2006, the CNSAS Archive contained 1,601,010 files, comprising 1,946,453 volumes.[38]

The internal hindrance mentioned above was overcome through a slight change of legal framework. A Government Emergency Ordinance (No. 149 of November 10th, 2005) extended the application of the law for another six years under a new Board. More importantly, the "balance of power" at the level of the CNSAS Board was changed through a new Government Emergency Ordinance (No. 16 of February 27th, 2006). Emergency Ordinance 16/2006 modified Law 187/1999 with regard to the way the eleven-member Board was named. Initially, all eleven members of the Board were nominated by the political parties according to their representation in Parliament. Emergency Ordinance 16/2006 stated that nine members of the Board were to be named by the political parties according to their representation in Parliament, while the Prime Minister and the President of the country were to name one member each. Considering the shift in power after the 2004 elections from center left to center right, this emergency ordinance envisaged a shift in favor of the forces that favored transitional justice at the level of the new CNSAS Board to be named in March 2006.[39] The shift towards a transitional justice-prone CNSAS Board occurred in March 2006, when a new eleven-member Board took over.

The two hindrances mentioned above once removed, the activity of CNSAS took off. Compared to the previous period of effective activity, that is, 2000–2004, the number of publicly exposed Securitate sources, collaborators and officers grew significantly. Numerous public figures from all fields of activity, ranging from the judiciary to the academia, were disclosed as sources, collaborators, or officers of the former Securitate. In several cases, although the personal files of the individuals under verification were missing, collaboration was proved based on evidence found in the files of the victims, especially copies of informative notes. While the activity of CNSAS gained momentum, the decisions of collabo-

---

130/28.08.2006 privind predarea către CNSAS a dosarelor create de fosta Securitate referitoare la ierarhii și șefii cultelor religioase recunoscute de lege, până la nivel de preot inclusiv, precum și asimilații lor de la parohiile din țară și din străinătate; and Hotărârea Guvernului nr. 731/07.06.2006 privind preluarea în gestiune de către CNSAS a arhivei deținute anterior de fostele organe de securitate, aflată în conservare la Ministerul Apărării Naționale. CNSAS Annual Report 2006, 3–4; http://www.cnsas.ro/documente/rapoarte/Raport%202006.pdf, accessed on February 18, 2020.

38 Ibid., 9.
39 MO 182 (27 February 2006): 1–8 and MO 1008 (14 November 2005): 7–8.

ration issued started to threaten the public image and political careers of a growing number of public figures. Following a decision of collaboration issued in his case, Dan Voiculescu, a prominent politician, media magnate and successful businessman, raised an exception of unconstitutionality against certain provisions of Law 187/1999 before the Constitutional Court of Romania (CCR).[40] CCR admitted the exception of unconstitutionality raised by Voiculescu in January 2008.

Ordinance 24/2008 and Law 293/2008: Depoliticization, Agency and Expertise

In January 2008, the Romanian Constitutional Court (CCR) decided on several grounds that Law 187/1999 was unconstitutional.[41] Decision No. 51 of January 31st, 2008 was severely criticized by civil society organizations and public intellectuals as an attempt by forces inimical to transitional justice to stop a process which had gained momentum tremendously over the previous two years (2006 and 2007). Nevertheless, a thorough reading of the CCR motivation reveals several fallacies of Law 187/1999. Arguably, the major fallacy of Law 187/1999 was that it allowed the CNSAS Board to assume a dual function of prosecutor and judge. As discussed above, the CNSAS Board was empowered to issue decisions regarding collaboration or non-collaboration and thus to formulate a first judgment regarding collaboration or non-collaboration with the Securitate of the individuals subjected to vetting. The decision of the CNSAS Board had to be based on evidence found in the CNSAS Archive, as well as on hearings held with the individuals concerned. In case of a decision of collaboration, the losing party had the right to appeal. The problem, however, was that Law187/1999 stated that the first appeal was examined by the same CNSAS Board which issued the first judgment. Subsequently, individuals concerned had the right to appeal to the civil section of a court of appeal and their appeal had to be examined by a panel of three judges.[42]

---

40 "Excepția de neconstituționalitate a dispozițiilor art. 3^1 alin (9), art. 7 alin. (2), art. 8, art. 9 alin. (1), art. 11, art. 14 alin. (1) și (2), art. 15 alin. (5), art. 16 alin. (1) și (3), art. 22^1 alin. (1) și (2) din Legea nr. 187/1999 ... și a dispozițiilor art. II și ale art. V din Ordonanța de urgență a Guvernului nr. 16/2006 pentru modificarea și completarea Legii nr. 187/1999 ..., ridicată de Dan Voiculescu în Dosarul nr. 8.520/2/2006 al Curții de Apel București—Secția a IV-a civilă."
41 CCR Decision No. 51/2008 regarding the non-constitutionality of Law 187/1999 was published in MO 95 (6 February 2008): 2–8.
42 See Law 187/1999, Articles 13, 14, 15 and 16.

An institutional crisis broke out suddenly. In fact, the very existence of CNSAS as a public body was at stake. Fortunately, the above-mentioned post-2004 political consensus regarding the issue of dealing with the communist past ensured the institutional continuity of CNSAS. The Government issued two successive emergency ordinances: Emergency Ordinance No. 1 of February 6th, 2008, which enabled the continuation of CNSAS activity, and Emergency Ordinance No. 24 of March 5th, 2008, which replaced Law 187/1999 and provided a basic legal framework concerning access to the Securitate files.[43] Finally, Parliament passed Law No. 293 of November 14th, 2008, which modified and completed Emergency Ordinance 24/2008.[44] Taken together, these two legal texts, that is Emergency Ordinance 24/2008 and Law 293/2008 provide the current legal framework governing the functioning of CNSAS. The new legislation adopted in 2008 had three major consequences regarding the process of transitional justice in post-communist Romania, which are best characterized by the following three concepts: (1) depoliticization; (2) agency; and (3) expertise.

Law 187/1999 was based on the concept of "political police," according to which an act of collaboration meant any act of providing information to the Securitate which involved infringement of fundamental rights. Emergency Ordinance 24/2008, modified and completed through Law 293/2008, abandons the concept of "political police" and provides new definitions for the notions of officer and collaborator of the former Securitate. Thus, Article 2, point (a) sets forth the notion of Securitate operative (*lucrător al Securității*) instead of Securitate agent (*agent al Securității*). A Securitate operative is "any individual who, in their capacity of officer or sub-officer of the Securitate or of the Miliția with duties in the area of the Securitate activity, including that of undercover officer, performed during the period 1945–89 activities through which they suppressed or limited fundamental human rights and liberties."

The notion of collaborator of the Securitate was also amended. Article 2, point (b) provides the following definition of a Securitate collaborator: "Collaborator of the Securitate—an individual who provided information, no matter in what form, such as written notes and reports, verbal communication recorded in verbatim reports by Securitate oper-

---

43 Government Ordinance No. 1 of 6 February 2008 was also published in MO 95 (6 February 2008): 9–10. For the Emergency Ordinance No. 24 of 5 March 2008, see MO 182 (10 March 2008): 2–10.
44 *Lege nr. 293 din 14 noiembrie 2008 pentru aprobarea Ordonanței de urgență a Guvernului nr. 24/2008 privind accesul la propriul dosar și deconspirarea Securității*, MO 800 (28 November 2008): 1–4.

atives, through which one denounced activities or attitudes against the totalitarian communist regime *and* which were aimed at limiting fundamental human rights and liberties [emphasis added]." The same Article 2, point (b) states that a collaborator of the Securitate is also an individual "who facilitated the gathering of information from other individuals, by putting their dwelling or other premises they possessed at the disposal of the Securitate, as well as those who, in their capacity of Securitate residents, coordinated the activity of Securitate informers." A parallel reading of Article 1, paragraph 7 and Article 2, point (b), which put forward the definition of collaborator, indicates that the new legislation maintains the ambiguity with regard to the notion of collaborator. This aspect is discussed below when analyzing institutional agency in distinguishing between a source and a collaborator of the Securitate.

The crux of the new legislation consists of three key provisions: (1) it defines collaboration on the basis of the *simultaneity principle*, that is, infringement of fundamental rights *and* denunciation of anti-regime attitudes and activities; (2) it allows for depoliticization of decisions by the CNSAS Board by stating that the CNSAS Board brings cases which fulfill the said principle of simultaneity in front of the Administrative Court of Justice (ACJ); and (3) it enables public exposure of perpetrators through immediate publication on the official website of the final verdicts by the court and of certificates of non-collaboration.

Emergency Ordinance 24/2008 and Law 293/2008 define collaboration with the former Securitate as acts that violated fundamental rights of individuals and "denounced activities or attitudes adverse to the communist state." Such a definition narrows down the number of cases that can be identified as acts of collaboration. According to Article 11, paragraph 1, when relevant information is found in the Securitate files, CNSAS brings the respective case in front of the ACJ. Paragraph 2 of the same Article 11 states that the losing party has the right to appeal the verdict to a higher court (the Supreme Court of Justice). This provision imposes a higher degree of institutional responsibility on the CNSAS Board, which has to ensure that sufficient accurate evidence is found in the CNSAS Archive before bringing a case before the ACJ. The very fact that CNSAS has to build a strong case in front of the ACJ in order to officially establish that an individual was an officer or a collaborator of the former Securitate leaves little room for politicization or administrative manipulation at the level of the CNSAS Board. Under Law 187/1999, the CNSAS Board passed a first judgement and was empowered to examine a first appeal by concerned individuals. A decision of collaboration or non-collaboration issued by the CNSAS Board would thus reach the public and create a certain image regarding collaboration or non-collaboration by the individuals under vetting. As many observers rightly argued, until a final verdict was passed by the civil section of a court of appeal after a long battle, the harm was already done. Under the new legislation introduced in 2008, the role of the CNSAS Legal Department grew significantly and legal expertise became crucial in order to decide if a case was strong enough to be brought in front of the ACJ. In the new situation, the CNSAS Board can only decide to: (1) bring a case in front of the ACJ; (2) issue a certificate of non-collaboration; or (3) delay a case in order to gather further evidence from the CNSAS Archive.

The new legislation introduced in 2008 also allowed for a certain degree of institutional agency regarding the actual application of the legislation. In this respect, two issues are relevant for the present analysis: (1) the distinction between a source and a collaborator of the Securitate; and (2) the information contained by a certificate of non-collaboration with the Securitate.

As already mentioned, one has to distinguish between a source and a collaborator of the former Securitate. In this respect, the new legislation adopted in 2008 did not eliminate some of the confusion that existed in previous legislation. The decision made at the level of CNSAS Board was to use the term source for an individual who only contributed with information to the completion of a given file, under their real or code names. The term source has been used consistently beginning in January 2012.[45] The term collaborator applies to an individual whose case was brought in front of the ACJ, passed through all legal proceedings including the right to appeal, and a final verdict of collaboration was issued by a court of law. This distinction is particularly important for those victims of Securitate who intend to make public the real names of the individuals who informed on them, but whose cases were not brought in front of the ACJ. These victims could face a libel suit if they use publicly the term collaborator.

Article 8 point (b) and Article 9 state that when no pieces of information or documents regarding collaboration with the Securitate are found, the CNSAS Board issues a certificate of non-collaboration. However, there is no indication as to how such a certificate should look like. Furthermore, according to Article 10, paragraph 2, all certificates of non-collaboration with the Securitate issued by CNSAS (the so-called *adever-*

---

[45] The term "source" was used for the first time in the CNSAS press communique of 17 January 2012. See CNSAS, *Comunicat de presă–17.01.2012*; http://www.cnsas.ro/documente/comunicate%20presa/2012/Comunicat%20presa%202012.01.17.pdf, accessed on February 16, 2020.

inţe) are published on the official website of the institution. The parties concerned have the right to appeal against these certificates to the ACJ within 30 days from their publication. Once the activity of CNSAS regained momentum after the January 2008 crisis, it became clear soon that there were two basic situations in which the CNSAS Board had to issue a certificate of non-collaboration with the former Securitate: (1) when no information whatsoever was found in the CNSAS Archive regarding the respective case; and (2) when a file did exist, but the information provided to the Securitate by the respective individual did not fulfill the above-mentioned simultaneity principle, more precisely, when no proof of denunciation of anti-communist activities or attitudes was found. These two situations impose the issuing of two types of certificates of non-collaboration.

The first type might be called simple certificate. This applies to individuals for whom no information whatsoever is found in the Securitate files and thus are "unknown" as far as the CNSAS Archive is concerned.[46] The second type might be called certificate with preamble, which applies to individuals who transmitted pieces of information to the Securitate, but did not denounce activities or attitudes against the communist regime. While the number of cases examined by the CNSAS Board grew significantly, the role of the preamble proved to be increasingly important. Obviously, the cases of individuals "unknown" to the CNSAS Archive do not pose a problem, and a simple certificate is issued. However, when a Securitate file exists, relevant information has to be summarized and made public. The preamble thus mentions the existence of one or all of the following elements: (1) a network file; (2) an agreement of collaboration (*angajament*); and (3) a code name. The preamble also summarizes or provides excerpts from the pieces of information transmitted to the Securitate by the respective individual, and in some cases can exceed ten standard pages.[47]

The information provided in the preamble of certificates of the second type is important for two reasons. First, it enables moral condemnation of the very act of passing pieces of information to the former Securitate. Although such cases cannot be brought in front of the ACJ, the general public can assess the moral implications of informing on some-

---

46 See for instance, the certificates nos.: 1386 of 21 March 2013; 1388 of 21 March 2013; and 1390 of 21 March 2013, posted on the CNSAS website; http://www.cnsas.ro/adeverinte.html, accessed on February 20, 2020.
47 See for instance, certificates nos.: 479 of 21 May 2015; 480/21 May 2015; and 2512/14 July 2015, posted on the CNSAS website; http://www.cnsas.ro/adeverinte.html, accessed on February 20, 2020.

one's fellow citizens. Second, it provides expert information from the files of the Securitate, selected by the CNSAS Legal Department. This information, which is accurate, digitized and open access, constitutes a valuable source of information for researchers and the general public.

The number of cases brought in front of the ACJ grew constantly over time. The CNSAS Board was faced with a difficult dilemma during the period under discussion (2008–2018):[48] to bring a case in front of the ACJ and face the risk of *Persilschein*, that is, the individual in whose case evidence of collaboration was found to be exonerated by the court of law and no information from the respective file(s) to become public, or to issue a certificate of non-collaboration with preamble, in which case relevant information from the file(s) would become public and allow at least moral assessment.

This dilemma became even more difficult after the initiative to implement lustration in post-communist Romania, which provoked heated debates over the period 2005–2010, failed. A bill entitled "Lustration Law regarding temporary limitation of access to public office of persons who held official positions within the power structures and repressive apparatus of the communist regime" was proposed in 2005. The bill was voted by the upper chamber of the Parliament (the Senate) on April 10th, 2006, and was finally adopted by the lower chamber of the Parliament (the Chamber of Deputies) on May 19th, 2010.[49] The law did not go into force. In late May 2010, a number of 87 MPs challenged the constitutionality of the Lustration Law before the Romanian Constitutional Court (CCR), and on June 7th, 2010, the CCR issued Decision No. 820 regarding the unconstitutional character of the Lustration Law.[50] The main features of the process of transitional justice put into motion by the 2008 change of legislation are discussed below.

---

48 In March 2018, a new CNSAS Board was nominated. The activity of this new Board will be addressed in a separate work. See Petru Zoltan and Cătălin Prisacariu, "Diletanții pentru studierea arhivelor Securității," *Newsweek Romania* (11 iunie 2018); https://newsweek.ro/politica/diletantii-pentru-studierea-arhivelor-securitatii, accessed on April 10, 2020.
49 For the text of the Lustration Law, see Parlamentul României: http://www.cdep.ro/proiecte/2006/200/80/2/pr282_06.pdf, accessed on February 20, 2020.
50 The CCR Decision No. 820 of 7 June 2010 was published in MO 420 (23 June 2010); for details, see http://www.cdep.ro/pls/proiecte/upl_pck.proiect?idp=6394, accessed on February 20, 2020.

Fact-finding, Naming and Shaming the Perpetrators: A Comprehensive Digital Open Access Database

Arguably, the most important effect of the 2008 legislative change on opening the secret police files in Romania has been a shift from the backward-looking task of punishing (morally at least) the perpetrators who worked with, or for, Securitate to the forward-looking task of ensuring stability and democratic consolidation. This shift was by no means obvious in 2008.

Over time, however, it became clear that the large corpus of documentary evidence made public under Emergency Ordinance 24/2008 and Law 293/2008 was by no means negligible. Vetting of individuals seeking or holding public office resulted in the ad-hoc creation of a comprehensive digital open access database of certificates of non-collaboration, which contain essential information related to violations of human rights by the Securitate. Under the current legal framework, vetting is performed ex officio or by request. When relevant information is found and the principle of simultaneity discussed above is fulfilled, the respective cases are brought in the front of the ACJ. In all other cases, the CNSAS Board issues certificates of non-collaboration.

For the present discussion, the most interesting case is that of the certificates with preamble. The mechanism of issuing such certificates has been described above, however, one should emphasize once again the role played by the said preamble in disseminating relevant information, including excerpts from the Securitate files, to the widest possible audience. Such information results from an expert fact-finding process which is human rights-centered and comes from reliable and credible sources. Moreover, this documentary evidence is presented in a concise and easily understandable form. It specifies the existence of a network file, an agreement of collaboration (*angajament*) and a code name and summarizes all relevant pieces of information transmitted to the Securitate by the respective individual. Once posted on the CNSAS website, these certificates represent in fact a digital database of concise information on the very act of passing pieces of information to the former Securitate.

The uses of such a database are twofold. First, it allows for moral assessment of informing on fellow citizens and thus contributes to a better understanding of what democracy is not and to the development of a democratic political culture. Second, it helps researchers devise more realistic research agendas on various topics due to the accurate information provided in the preamble, including excerpts from the files, which has a wide social and geographic coverage. In addition, citizens have the right to find out the real names of the individuals (sources) who informed on their fellow citizens during the communist period. Thus, CNSAS communicates the real names of such individuals directly to the victims, who in turn, decide if they want to make these names public. This also contributes to naming and shaming those who passed information to the secret police. Equally important, the number of cases brought in front of the ACJ multiplied, and after a final verdict is reached, the reasoning of the court is published in extenso in the Official Bulletin and is posted on the CNSAS website.[51] This contributes as well to the expansion of the database comprising information resulted from the very process of transitional justice.

Information on Securitate-related cases reaches constantly the general public. Social media, online media portals and news agencies in Romania, such as *Adevărul, Radio Europa Liberă România, Digi24, G4Media.ro, Ziare.com, Evenimentul zilei, Gândul, Hotnews* or *Mediafax*,[52] to name only a few, have constantly kept the general public informed about secret police-related issues, including cases of collaboration with the secret police, abuses committed by the Securitate officers, or violation of fundamental human rights by the communist regime. The local press, both in print and online, also offers coverage of the cases of collaboration with the Securitate, especially by local public figures, ranging from politicians to artists or athletes.

Open access to Securitate documents in electronic form enables the transfer of knowledge to next generations regarding the role of secret police agencies in supporting the communist dictatorship and the dire consequences of non-democratic politics. The Securitate files represent a major source for understanding the essence of non-democratic regimes and the dangers of radical ideologies. In order to reach a wider audience and make these sources available for all those interested in the communist period in Romania (1945–89), CNSAS has engaged in a complex process of publishing on its website a great number of documents that can be downloaded free of charge. This corpus of documents in electronic form constitutes a separate database, which can be divided into

---

51 See for instance *Sentinţa civilă nr. 1479* of 26 May 2015; http://www.cnsas.ro/documente/monitoare/2019/Alexandru%20Stelica.pdf, accessed on February 20, 2020.
52 See www.adevarul.ro; https://romania.europalibera.org/; https://romania.europalibera.org/; www.digi24.ro; (www.g4media.ro; www.ziare.com; www.evz.ro; www.gandul.info; www.hotnews.ro and www.mediafax.ro, accessed on April 10, 2020.

the following categories: (1) secret orders, resolutions, decisions, action plans etc. issued by the Ministry of Internal Affairs over the period 1948–89, as well as other documents, thematically organized (internments in labor camps, the so-called "23 August 1944 Problem," the official Party inquiry of 1968 regarding the abuses of the Securitate during the Stalinist period, etc.); (2) the complete collection of the journal *Securitatea* (1968–89), a journal labelled secret and intended only for the Securitate apparatus, with 88 published issues; (3) propaganda brochures, educational materials for the Securitate apparatus and other similar publications; and (4) relevant official documents of the Romanian Workers Party and Romanian Communist Party covering the period 1945–89.

Considering the current situation in East-Central Europe, with the rise of populism and the illiberal turn in the region, the forward-looking task of transitional justice, that is, to ensure peace, stability and foster democratic consolidation should be stressed once again. Systematic public exposure of the wrongdoing of the former communist secret police through a variety of documents easily accessible in digital form is one of the ways of teaching the next generations that democracy must be preserved and acts of violation of fundamental human rights must be condemned.[53]

Concluding Remarks

In post-1989 Romania, the process of reckoning with the communist past was significantly delayed. At the same time, once initiated through the passing of Law 187/1999, this process gained momentum and has been characterized by some innovations which passed almost unnoticed. The present paper has argued that the new legislation introduced in 2008, which was not accompanied by specific norms of application, enabled a gradual transformation of the main mission of CNSAS from a vetting agency into a fact-finding commission. In other words, the 2008 change of legislation prompted a shift from a backward-looking task to a forward-looking one. Thus, the context-specific approach to transitional justice carried out by CNSAS between 2008 and 2018 has gradually produced an open-access electronic database including digest versions of the screening process. This digital repository includes specific information from the Securitate files, including excerpts from relevant documents, which illustrate a wide variety of acts of informing on other people. This digital repository is characterized by a wide social and geo-

---

53 For more on this, see Dragoș Petrescu, "Romania, Thirty Years After: The Bloody Revolution of 1989 and the Refusal of the Populist Consensus," *Arhivele totalitarismului*, XXVII, no. 3–4 (2019): 229–51.

graphic coverage, since the Securitate targeted both genders, rural and urban areas, diverse professions and levels of education, all counties, and ethnic communities in communist Romania.

The certificates of non-collaboration with preamble are issued for individuals who cannot be brought before the administrative court of justice because they passed information to the secret police, but did not collaborate with it in the narrow sense of the law. In brief, this database represents a digital registry of naming and shaming, which can enable moral assessment of acts of informing on others. This database, the paper contends, represents a registry illustrating the "banality of evil," which switches the focus from public personalities to common individuals and provides a sample representative enough for all social categories. Available for free in digital format, the database offers quick access to the most obscure parts of the secret police files and conveys to the general public, in concise form, excerpts from documents produced for the operational purposes of the Securitate.

This registry represents a para-legal mechanism of transitional justice, which has de-politicized to a large extent the decisions of the CNSAS Board, legitimized its mission, and facilitated moral judgement on the act of collaborating with the Securitate. More importantly, this database should be used for educational purposes. As an e-database, it fits the psychological profile of the new generations who do not have their own memories of the dictatorial past, but are inquisitive and curious to find out more about that past as long as access to specific digital content is fast and easy. In the current context of rise of populism and authoritarian backsliding in East-Central Europe,[54] such digital repositories which illustrate acts of collaboration with communist secret police agencies can help the young generation understand what democracy is not. In doing so, they fulfill the forward-looking task of transitional justice, that is, to foster peace, stability, and a democratic political culture.

---

54 Of the rapidly growing scholarship on authoritarian backsliding in East-Central Europe one can mention: András Bozóki, "Broken Democracy, Predatory State and Nationalist Populism," in *The Hungarian Patient: Social Opposition to an Illiberal Democracy*, eds. Péter Krasztev and Jon Van Til (Budapest: CEU Press, 2015), 3–36; Joanna Fomina and Jacek Kucharczyk, "Populism and Protest in Poland," *Journal of Democracy*, 27, no. 4 (2016), 58–68; Seán Hanley and Milada Anna Vachudova, "Understanding the Illiberal Turn: Democratic Backsliding in the Czech Republic," *East European Politics*, 34, no. 3 (2018): 276–96. See also Cas Mudde, "Orbán's Hungary Is not the Future of Europe: It Represents a Dying Past," *The Guardian* (10 April 2018); https://www.theguardian.com/comment isfree/2018/apr/10/orban-election-hungary-europe-future-past, accessed on April 12, 2020.

Marian Voicu, Matrioşka Mincinoşilor: Fake News, Manipulare, Populism, Bucharest: HUMANITAS, 2018.

Review by Peter Gross, University of Tennessee, USA

The Matryoshka of Liars is an aptly named, timely, and learned explication of the abundant, ubiquitous, persistent, and multi-layered Russian global disinformation war that is an unmistakable threat to the well-being of democracies, their institutions and citizens.

What comes as pleasant surprise and also cause for acclamation, is that in a mere 472 pages Marian Voicu provides readers with a comprehensively overarching coverage and analysis of issues that are daily occupying the attention of scholars and journalists, think tanks and government institutions. He manages to do so quite successfully with a felicitous combination of well-informed journalism and traditional scholarship, resulting in a work that does not skimp on the subject's theoretical contexts nor implications.

Centered mainly but not exclusively on Russian disinformation, the myriad of permutations of what today is called "fake news"—delivered in many guises, beginning with your basic bad and biased journalism, purposeful disinformation and misinformation, false and falsified news —propaganda and their manipulatory effects, the book is organized in 16 chapters. They are assigned to three interrelated thematic parts— "The cold war of disinformation;" "In the labyrinth of lies;" and "Who controls the truth."

Voicu examines the contemporary application of the Russian theory and practice of *Maskirovka*—to confuse, mislead, camouflage intensions, instill fear and doubt—that has its origin in early Soviet doctrine and molds itself according to the notion that "All warfare is deception," as Sun Tzu explained in his *Art of War*. The *matryoshka* Voicu addresses contains the Russian practices of disinformation and, thus, the additional aspects of misinformation, false and falsified news, hoaxes. Propaganda is also a principal focus. Dating back to Grigory Potemkin's time during Catherine the Great's reign and perfected during the Soviet era that followed Lenin's dictates in his 1902 pamphlet, "What is to be done," disinformation and propaganda have perhaps reached their apex of perfection, pervasiveness and potential destructive powers during the Putin era.

Voicu goes well beyond theoretical discussions of the subject matter, weaving into his narrative concrete examples of *Maskirovka* and its delivery systems, i.e. disinformation and propaganda, affecting the European Union (EU), Brexit, France, Germany, Romania, Moldova, Ukraine, the U.S.A, and also Russia itself. Ultimately, he also touches on some of the real and inherent consequences of Russia's information, of its "war to control peoples' minds" (p. 40).

Directed at Eastern Europe's Orthodox Christians who have resolute fidelity to the letter of the Bible, in the hope they will turn against the EU, some example of the bonbons offered up by the Kremlin's sellers of goods include (p. 133),

> European values actually mean homosexuality and pedophilia. Children are forcibly taken from their families and adopted by homosexual couples. Some EU Member States want to legalize pedophilia. Because it opposes these satanic projects, [the] Orthodox [religion] is the main enemy of the West.

The "satanic" EU project is a perfect example of Voicu's additionally important examination of the nature of the language employed in the information war and the "essential link" that is the "presence of a 'distinctive vocabulary'." Thusly, he reminds us that language is a means of control and that it can have calamitous effects on society and its culture, as Czesław Miłosz and Françoise Thom, among others, have told us in their examination of the Soviets' general vocabulary and specific Orwellian newspeak.

From a broader perspective, it is conceivable that the victimizers in this information war are themselves victims, albeit belonging to two distinctive groups. For example, Voicu reminds us when he quotes Yuri Andropov, a Secretary General of the Communist Party of the USSR and KGB chairman, telling Ion Mihai Pacepa, the adjunct director of the communist-era Romanian Securitate, that the use of disinformation is addictive, functioning "like cocaine." (p. 260). Thus, the victimizers are addicts to their own ways of thinking, speaking, writing, and behavior. Furthermore, Russia's disinformation and propaganda aimed at other countries is the same fodder fed to its own citizens, a means of keeping them less than free and living in a still authoritarian society, still willing and unwilling victims.

By the time a reader reaches p. 384 and the subtitle, "The new ritual of communication: emotion, not information"—certainly true of all information with a political and even more so, ideological aim—Voicu has already traversed an enormous amount of thematic territory and impeccably analyzed a theme and its subtopics that will occupy our thoughts, energies, and policies for years to come. And let's not forget that each of the book's three sections and even a number of chapters could potentially be bona fide books in and of themselves.

Voicu, an accomplished journalist and author of several books, demonstrates a thorough understanding of the subject matter, its extant analyses by a wide array of American and European scholars and journalists, think tanks and government institutions engaged in the study of the subject. Which is why it is hoped that this will not be his last foray into the still evolving and always dangerous Russian information warfare, and that which countries like Romania direct at their own citizens.

Matei Călinescu, Ion Vianu, *Scrisori din exil: corespondenţă inedită*, Cuvânt înainte de Ion Vianu, Notă asupra ediţiei de Adriana Călinescu, Bucharest: HUMANITAS, 2019, 528 p.

Review by Iuliu Raţiu, Babeş-Bolyai University, Romania

Part of a projected two-volume series, the correspondence collected in this book starts with a postcard from Ion Vianu dated June 19th, 1977, and ends with a letter from Matei Călinescu dated June 24th, 1992. Călinescu left Romania first, in 1973 as a Fulbright Scholar. For the next four years, until Vianu joined him in the West, the two friends kept in touch sporadically, mainly because they did not want the *Securitate* to intercept their letters. Once both of them started living on the same side of the Iron Curtain, one in the US and the other in Switzerland, their correspondence intensified. And what a treat that is!

In his postcard, the only one sent from Bucharest, a month or so before leaving communist Romania for good, Vianu references but does not name the March 4th, 1977 earthquake. For him, there is a *before* and *after* in which Bucharest became not only subjectively, but also objectively ghost-like and haunted—*un Bucureşti care a devenit nu numai subiectiv, dar şi obiectiv fantomatic*. The devastations caused by the earthquake only accentuate the terrible conditions in which the Vianu family and many others led their lives in Romania during Nicolae Ceauşescu's dictatorship. It was as if those who left the country and those who remained behind were ghosts to each other.

Fast forward to 1992 and to the last letter of the book. Here Călinescu writes about sending to his publisher the revised proofs of *Rereading*, which he considered his best and most personal criticism book; about continuing work on the memoir both of the them were writing together; and, about Louis Althusser's autobiography, which invited reflections on some heavy topics, such as folly, the feeling of unreality, and the notion of the ghost (being someone else's ghost)—*nebunia, sentimentul irealităţii, noţiunea de fantomă (a fi fantoma altcuiva)*. After almost twenty years of exile, the alienating effects of being apart seem to be sublimated as long as there is the possibility of revisiting both the past and the home country. The transition from letter writing to memoir, from reading each other's letters to writing together about their own intertwined pasts, constitutes the shift from conjuring someone else's ghost from afar to coming to terms with one's own ghost from long ago.

The fact that the book opens and ends with *spectral* references is a brilliant editorial gimmick. The earthquake Vianu alludes to in his postcard is a not-so-veiled symbol for the world-shattering experience of exile, hinting both at the destruction of life in one place and its reconstruction in another. Leaving behind a dead or dying realm in exchange for renewal and reinvention someplace else could be a remorseful act. The tension between the promise of a second chance in exile and the lives of quiet desperation friends and family led in communist Romania is a constant haunting presence in all their letters. And yet, even though *specters* bracket this volume, the book is about much more than that.

At one point in their correspondence, Călinescu tells Vianu that for him writing letters is an alternative to keeping a journal. While diarists keep track of changes in their lives and in the world, correspondents address those changes with their interlocutors in mind. The soliloquy of one's journal is therefore replaced by the dialogic nature of letter writing. Thus, one entrusts another with making sense of their life written down. The letters they exchanged during the 15 years between Vianu's postcard and Călinescu's letter encapsulate personal histories centered around themes such as life in exile, family, friendship, professional advancement, and the creative process. In addition to shedding light on the life narratives of the two authors, this correspondence is a must-read for all those interested in better understanding Romania and the Romanian diaspora against the backdrop of events leading to the fall of communism in Central and Eastern Europe.

Looking over somebody else's shoulder as he or she writes a note addressed to someone else, and then waiting (or rushing) to write a response together makes you wonder how your own self and your own life might have fared under similar circumstances to those laid bare in front of your eyes. Finding meaning in my life as I read Călinescu and Vianu's letters about finding meanings in their lives was a humbling experience. I was born the summer Vianu went into exile and I finished elementary school the summer Călinescu sent the last letter collected in this volume. I met my wife a year after college at a Călinescu lecture at my home university in Cluj-Napoca. Finally, my son started walking around the time I bought this book in December 2019 and murmured one of his first words, *cartea*—the book, when I finished reading it in March 2020, during the first days of the Covid-19 lockdown. Now I can hardly wait for the second installment of their correspondence, from 1992 to 2009, with the hope that by vicariously living through their lives our current pandemic will make more sense in retrospect.

EAST EUROPEAN STUDIES: JOURNALS AND BOOK SERIES

Soviet and Post-Soviet Politics and Society

Editor: Andreas Umland

Founded in 2004 and refereed since 2007, SPPS makes available, to the academic community and general public, affordable English-, German- and Russian-language scholarly studies of various empirical aspects of the recent history and current affairs of the former Soviet bloc from the late Tsarist period to today. It publishes approximately 15–20 volumes per year, and focuses on issues in transitions to and from democracy such as economic crisis, identity formation, civil society development, and constitutional reform in CEE and the NIS. SPPS also aims to highlight so far understudied themes in East European studies such as right-wing radicalism, religious life, higher education, or human rights protection.

Journal of Soviet and Post-Soviet Politics and Society

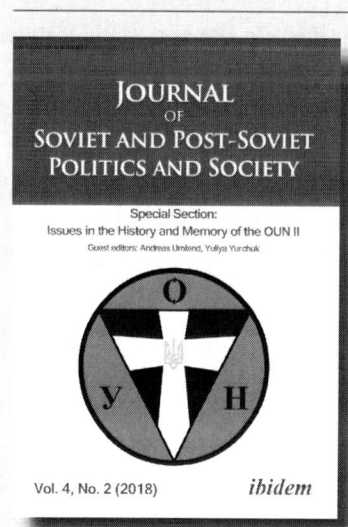

Editors: Andreas Umland, Julie Fedor, Andrey Makarychev, George Soroka, Tomasz Stępniewski

The Journal of Soviet and Post-Soviet Politics and Society is a new bi-annual journal that was launched in April 2015 as a companion journal to the Soviet and Post-Soviet Politics and Society book series (founded 2004 and edited by Andreas Umland, Dr. phil., PhD). Like the book series, the journal will provide an interdisciplinary forum for new original research on the Soviet and post-Soviet world. The journal aims to become known for publishing creative, intelligent, and lively writing tackling and illuminating significant issues and capable of engaging wider educated audiences beyond the academy.

UKRAINIAN VOICES

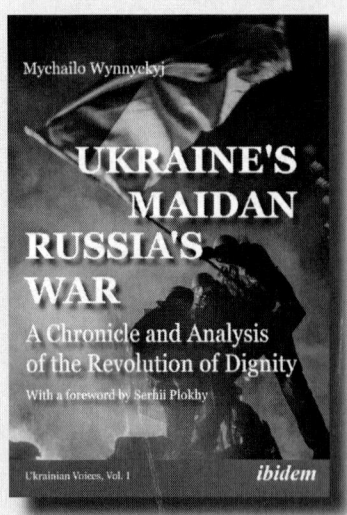

Editors: Andreas Umland

The book series "Ukrainian Voices" publishes English- and German-language monographs, edited volumes, document collections and anthologies of articles authored and composed by Ukrainian politicians, intellectuals, activists, officials, researchers, entrepreneurs, artists, and diplomats. The series' aim is to introduce Western and other audiences to Ukrainian explorations and interpretations of historic and current domestic as well as international affairs. The purpose of these books is to make non-Ukrainian readers familiar with how some prominent Ukrainians approach, research and assess their country's development and position in the world. The series was founded in 2019, and the volumes are collected by Andreas Umland, Dr. phil. (FU Berlin), Ph. D. (Cambridge), Senior Research Fellow at the Institute for Euro-Atlantic Cooperation in Kyiv.

FORUM FÜR OSTEUROPÄISCHE IDEEN- UND ZEITGESCHICHTE

Editors: Leonid Luks, Gunter Dehnert, Nikolaus Lobkowicz, Alexei Rybakow, Andreas Umland

FORUM features interdisciplinary discussions by political scientists—literary, legal, and economic scholars—and philosophers on the history of ideas, and it reviews books on Central and Eastern European history. Through the translation and publication of documents and contributions from Russian, Polish, and Czech researchers, the journal offers Western readers critical insight into scientific discourses across Eastern Europe.

ibidem Press | Leuschnerstr. 40 | 30457 Hannover | Germany
Phone: +49 (0) 511 2 62 22 00 | Fax: +49 (0) 511 2 62 22 00 | sales@ibidem.eu